THE
TIME
AND
PLACE
THAT
GAVE ME
LIFE

ACCLAIM FOR
THE TIME AND PLACE THAT GAVE ME LIFE

An arresting, beautiful, often searing study of humanity during the racially turbulent 1940s, '50s and '60s. Peers inside the straight lines of a history book to where the lives were actually lived and the pain and joy and anger felt. I was seriously moved by [this] book.

> ~ **Ted Green**, documentary filmmaker

This is more than a memoir. Janet Cheatham Bell has seasoned her personal story with some little-known history of African Americans in Indiana.

> ~ **Julian Bond** (1940-2015) former Professor,
> University of Virginia; Board Chairman, NAACP

The Time and Place That gave Me Life should be intentionally placed in public libraries and school media centers, private, public and charter, throughout the state of Indiana. It is a must read because it's about US! It magnificently describes how racism (the glue that holds all the other isms in place) impacts, influences and shapes not only the author's internal and external experiences, but that of others as well. I applaud and am so proud of Janet Cheatham Bell whom I have known and admired for many years.

> ~ **Patricia Payne**, Director Office for Racial Equity,
> Indianapolis Public Schools

Here is the best form of social history: This memoir focuses on an ordinary individual but also illuminates the experiences of many over time.

~ **Nancy Gabin**, author
*Feminism in the Labor Movement and
the United Auto Workers, 1933-1975*

Janet Cheatham bell has crafted a compelling memoir about growing up in Indiana.

~ **Monroe Little** in *Indiana Magazine of History,*
December 2008

The Time and Place That Gave Me Life sounds a familiar horn, one that echoes tremendous struggles that blacks in America have endured. Yet it is a refreshing voice speaking to blacks' belief in family, faith, community, and education. A memoir that renders a great service. Bell helps us hope in the ideals of freedom, democracy, progress, self-preservation, and determination.

~ **Valerie Grim**, Chair, African American and
African Diaspora Studies, Indiana University

THE TIME AND PLACE THAT GAVE ME LIFE

Janet Cheatham Bell

SABAYT
PUBLICATIONS

Originally published by Indiana University Press

SABAYT PUBLICATIONS
ISBN 978-0-9616649-0-9

Bulk rates available.
To contact the author or to purchase copies, please go to
www.janetcheathambell.com

Book design by Merridee LaMantia
Cover design by Sharon Sklar

Belmantia Publishing Services
BelmantiaPublishing@gmail.com

৪৩ ❖ ৫৪

It is impossible to pretend that you are not heir to, and therefore, however inadequately or unwillingly, responsible to and for, the time and place that give you life—without becoming, at very best, a dangerously disoriented human being.

James Baldwin from *The Evidence of Things Not Seen*

Race has no genetic basis. Not one characteristic, trait or even gene distinguishes all the members of one so-called race from all the members of another so-called race. … Race is a powerful social idea that gives people different access to opportunities and resources.

Race: The Power of an Illusion,
PBS Documentary from California Newsreel

৪৩ ❖ ৫৪

৪০❖ଓଃ

For my granddaughters, Sami and Juno because someday
you may want to know more about your ancestors.

৪০❖ଓଃ

Contents

Chapter 1

Rigged Outcome: The Overture

Race is a clue; a sign the outcome is being rigged.

~ John Edgar Wideman in *Fatheralong*

"Don't ever say that you want to be white. Be proud that you're Negro!" My mother sounded angry as she jerked me down off the couch. I was about three years old, and to amuse myself I had stood on the couch to look out the window. I saw a woman all dressed up in a suit, high heels, gloves, hat, and fur stole. I liked the way she looked and perhaps the way she carried herself, so I said, "I want to be like that lady when I grow up."
But that lady was white.

At age three I had no idea what being white or Negro meant, but Mama's reaction and her tone made the words ominous. I knew I had said something bad. That was my introduction to the idea of *race,* and the memory of that incident has remained with me for more than sixty years, having been reinforced by countless other *race* bulletins.

Here I am circa 1940, about the time I first heard about race. From the way I'm holding the doll it must be a prop.

I received confusing messages about whites while I was growing up. I knew from my parents and other authorities that whites had all the power. I also learned that they refused to share power with us because they didn't like us and thought we were inferior. And we despised them in return. (Until I was in my thirties I thought white lies were the really bad ones.) Although whites were the enemy, we were working hard to be like them and hoping to gain their approval and acceptance. In the environment in which I grew up whites were not only idealized, they also had concrete advantages that were unavailable to us. I thought they were omnipotent. (There were no Jerry Springer or Dr. Phil shows where I could see that they didn't have it all together.) While I was internalizing an image of whites as impregnable, whites were being indoctrinated that we were lazy, dumb, dangerous, and consequently in need of being corralled. The restrictions on us made many things difficult—finding a decent, affordable home—and other things impossible—working in a downtown office.

As I got older I found out that the color proscriptions did not apply to everybody with dark skin; only to Negroes born in the United States. If somebody looked like us, but spoke with an accent, or wore a turban, he was much less circumscribed. I remember laughing with other Negroes about a black man who regularly put on a turban and affected an accent so that he could dine in a fine restaurant where Negroes were not allowed. (Ironically, here at the beginning of the twenty-first century, there have been occasions when those who traditionally wear turbans no doubt would have preferred to be mistaken for African Americans.) The reverse of this conundrum is that if a person looked white but was known to have some African ancestry, she was as limited as we were. My guess is tens of thousands of these light-skinned African Americans have clandestinely helped themselves to the advantages of being white. Often, their families of origin are the only people privy to the secret, while others pass merely for practical and economic reasons—to enjoy a forbidden luxury or to obtain a better job. For much of his life people were unaware that "one of literary America's foremost gatekeepers," Anatole Broyard, had African ancestry. Broyard was a daily book reviewer for the *New York Times* from 1971 to 1984, but even his own children did not know he had a touch of the tar brush.

Something else also puzzled me: in the books we had at home, I read about people of African descent like Frederick Douglass, who went from being born into slavery to U. S. Minister to Haiti; like Mary McLeod Bethune, born to parents who had been enslaved, who took $1.65 and founded a college; and like Richard Wright, the son of migrant Mississippi workers, who wrote a novel that became a main selection of the Book-of-the-Month Club. I also learned that Gordon Parks, a black man, was a photographer for *Life,* a big white magazine that was sometimes among the reading material Daddy brought home for us. These people and many others, *in spite of rampant racism,* had somehow broken through the barriers to participate in activities that had been reserved for whites only. I wanted to know *why.* How could some blacks (actually we were Negroes then) get past *racism* to achieve greatness when most of us weren't able to? More important, I wanted to know if I, too, could outwit *racism.*

I am a black (colored, Negro, African American) woman, born in 1937 and reared in Indianapolis, Indiana, United States of America. And I am not being flip about the changes in what we black Americans are called. Black and African American are names we chose for ourselves, so I prefer those terms. Colored and Negro were labels imposed on us that we tolerated for a very long time. Richard Wright explained it this way, "The word 'Negro'…is not really a name at all nor a description, but a psychological island whose objective form is the most unanimous fiat in all American history; … a fiat which artificially and arbitrarily defines, regulates, and limits in scope of meaning the vital contours of our lives." My birth date is included here because I am one of those women who will tell anything, but also because when you're discussing *racism* in the United States, the era is significant. When he came to live in this country, Albert Einstein, the renowned German scientist, was appalled by the treatment of Negroes. In 1940 he said, "As for the Negroes, the country has still a heavy debt to discharge for all the troubles and disabilities it has laid on the Negro's shoulders, for all that his fellow-citizens have done, and to some extent, are still doing to him."

When I was a child, the *racism* permeating America affected how we lived, who our friends were, and determined how and where we worked and were educated. I used much of my energy thinking about and coping with *racism* and *racists.* My parents provided my siblings and me a loving and secure home, but *racism* was a lurking bogeyman that spawned regular reminders that we didn't measure up to whites. At this point, however, I've concluded that *racism* and *racists* are largely irrelevant for my life. This should not be interpreted as meaning that *racism* was never relevant, or that it has been eradicated. Anybody who is hoping for the end of *racism* to start enjoying and appreciating life has a long and probably fruitless wait. In fact, I confidently predict that no amount of marches, litigation, or legislation will ever make *racism* totally disappear. America has never acknowledged the actual history of this country, and for this reason I don't believe the nation will ever be able to accept a people once considered "real estate" as equal citizens. *Racism* is irrelevant to me because I've decided that I will no longer be bound by it. I reached this decision while rearing my son, Kamau. I didn't want him to grow up feeling that whites were all-powerful and that he was at their mercy. I presented whites to him not as omnipotent but as humans whose life experiences differed from ours in some ways. I indicated that his skin color had no bearing on his aspirations. Although Kamau has had his share of encounters with *racism*, those events have not diminished his sense that he deserves the best the world has to offer. With satisfaction, I have watched him make decisions without *racial* considerations, and select friends for their attributes, not their color. From him I learned that this approach could work for me as well. My father always said, "You will learn as much from your children as you teach them." Of course, rearing my child this way was made considerably easier by the fact that he was born in the 1970s, not the 1930s.

While I was growing up, the public spaces in Indianapolis were as rigidly segregated by *race* as any place in the South. The only thing missing were the signs White and Colored. My childhood experiences made indelible imprints to be sure, but I have been discriminated against because of my *race* all over the United States. I took a job in Saginaw, Michigan, and was refused housing near where I worked. I rented an apartment in Palo Alto, California, without knowing there were no other blacks in the complex. I found out months later, when an older couple from Mississippi took over the management. They determined to get rid of me and harassed me constantly; for example, every morning they told me they had poured acid into the pool to "clean" it so I could no longer take my morning exercise.

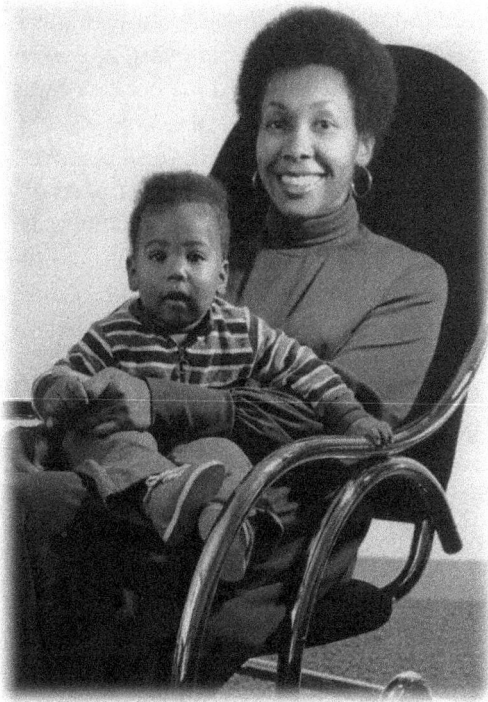

This is the little guy who changed my perspective on the world. Kamau is six months old here, and I'm 36. East Palo Alto, California, 1973. Photo by Walter A. Bell.

Also in California, as a doctoral student in English, I wanted to do a comparative study of the literature of African writers from the Caribbean, the United States, and continental Africa. My committee chairman at Stanford would not approve it because, he said, it was not "academically valid."

Back in Indiana after ten years away, I was the first black hired as a consultant in the curriculum division of the state department of education. These were coveted positions because they paid well, and each consultant was essentially autonomous. One of the other consultants, a white male several years younger than I, could hardly believe that I had been hired and said to me, "The only reason you got this job is because you're black."

"Well," I responded, "they really lucked out because I am also good." Obviously, he believed that his gender and skin color trumped the fact that I was better educated and more experienced than he. This was in 1974, but in a 2005 issue of *Time,* an article on minority women in the workplace revealed that little has changed.

I moved to the East Coast to accept a position as a textbook editor in a Boston suburb. I got a surprise my first day at work. An older white man, who was introduced as my department manager when I was hired, had been demoted. The man selected to replace him told me his predecessor had refused to have me on his editorial team. I assumed it was because I was black. But to be fair, after living in Boston for a while, I came to believe he could have rejected me because I was not a fifth-generation New Englander with a Harvard degree.

These samplings of my experiences with *racism* have all occurred in the democracy that boasts of serving as a model for other parts of the world. What makes *racism* especially galling in the United States is that we do have a Declaration of Independence, a Constitution, and Bill of Rights that, in a variety of ways, say all people are equal. Of course, the founding fathers were referring only to white men with property, but over the years these venerated documents have been amended to cover everybody except the GLBT (gay, lesbian, bisexual, transgender) community. I don't believe anybody should be excluded, but then I'm usually out-of-step with conventional wisdom in this country.

Despite irrefutable biological evidence that there is only the *human race*, it matters so little to Americans that we rarely bother to mention it. What is apparently an essential human need is finding some "other" to blame for, or divert attention from, our own shortcomings. And politicians maintain their power by shamelessly manipulating the electorate to reinforce this human weakness to scapegoat. From this country's inception and in an unbroken line since then, so-called *racial* characteristics have been used to oppress, divide, and manipulate. In the Boston Massacre of 1770, the first person killed was Crispus Attucks, the son of an African man and American Indian woman. However, in the engraving Paul Revere created to stir indignation among the colonists over the "massacre," all five of the people killed were depicted as white. I suppose Revere didn't believe the colonists would become agitated over the death of a man who did not look like them.

That initial inclination began a tradition of *race* contrivance that continues to the present day. In his anguish about the devastation of Hurricane Katrina, Wynton Marsalis spoke elegantly and passionately about the ways in which politicians and American mythology polarize us along class, and particularly color, lines.

Harsh evidence of this polarization, and the demand for fall guys, is that in the United States we actually spend millions of tax dollars to incarcerate, rather than thousands to educate, African Americans. Between 1980 and 2000 there was a fivefold increase in the number of black men in jail or prison. African Americans are incarcerated at a rate six times that of Americans of European descent. I suppose locking black men up rather than educating them "proves" our inferiority. It reminds me of a poem Langston Hughes wrote in 1922, but that is still quite timely. In the poem Hughes referred to Justice as a "blind goddess" whose blindfold is a "bandage" hiding "festering sores" that may once have been eyes.

African Americans are particularly susceptible to putting the blame for our difficulties on whites, because so often whites have been responsible. Some of the more egregious forms of institutional *racism* have been removed, but the caste system that operated for four hundred years was corrosive and it left pollutants. When apartheid was ended in South Africa, their leaders were wise enough to pass a law that set up a Truth and Reconciliation Commission. They believed it was a "necessary exercise to enable South Africans to come to terms with their past on a morally accepted basis and to advance the cause of reconciliation." South Africa's commission conducted a public investigation to establish "as complete a picture as possible of the nature, causes, and extent of gross violations of human rights."

Whenever the United States has undertaken an official scrutiny of its *racist* practices, it fails on the follow-through. The country's Reconstruction after the Civil War, fraught with controversy from the start, was doomed by the Compromise of 1877 that gave Rutherford B. Hayes the presidency. Nearly a hundred years later, in 1967, President Lyndon Baines Johnson appointed a National Advisory Commission on Civil Disorders, the Kerner Commission, to find out why urban blacks were exploding in anger and destroying property. The president asked the commission to analyze the "specific triggers" for the eruptions and to suggest remedies. The report famously warned that this country was "moving toward two societies, one black, one white—separate and unequal." The commission's recommendations for federal action to correct the situation were never implemented. Thirty years later in 1997, President William Jefferson Clinton launched an initiative to open a national dialogue on multi-racial issues saying, "Ready or not, the nation is headed for the day when no race will be in the majority.... The fundamental issue is, we know what we're going to look like—the demographers can tell us that—but they can't tell us what we're going to be like. That's a decision we have to make." John Hope Franklin chaired Clinton's nine-member advisory board to his Initiative on Race. Dr. Franklin's book *From Slavery to Freedom: A History of Negro Americans*, first published in 1947, had changed the dynamic of American history. Franklin said they "were embarking, with the full support of the executive office, on a sincere effort to confront and further erase the color line in America." The Initiative was undermined almost immediately by a variety of attacks, including willful misinterpretation of its task by major media. However, it mostly suffered from being ignored because the media preferred to focus on the investigation into Clinton's sexual peccadilloes. Franklin concluded that the "unfortunate short-sightedness on the part of the national press too often forestalls rather than furthers the needed national conversation [on race]."

In 2003 Ruth Simmons, the first African American to head an Ivy League university, appointed a Steering Committee on Slavery and Justice at Brown University. Dr. Simmons' goal is "to help the nation and the Brown community think deeply, seriously, and rigorously" about the debate over slavery and reparations. With national government efforts having been short-circuited, I hope efforts similar to Brown's will go on around the country until we build a ground-swell as eager to face the damage caused by hundreds of years of apartheid here as we are to fight "oppressors" around the world. When prominent blacks have spoken out against this country's oppression, they have had their livelihoods ripped away—Paul Robeson, Muhammad Ali—or been killed—Malcolm X, Martin Luther King Jr. Ali and King may be celebrated icons now, but when King was alive and preaching, and Ali was in his ass-kicking prime, they were both pariahs. Robeson and Malcolm have been added to the Black Heritage series of postage stamps, but I wonder how much, if any, information about them can be found in school textbooks. We pretend that everything is fine because the For Whites Only signs have been removed, and King's birthday is now a national holiday. But people and institutions go on practicing *racism,* sometimes simply because they don't know any better, but primarily because it is one of the country's most cherished traditions.

I received my first lessons on *race* while growing up in Indiana. Few places in the United States of America roll out the welcome mat for people of African descent, but Indiana has been less congenial than many. A National Association for the Advancement of Colored People (NAACP) official noted this in 1935: "Violation of the unalienable rights of colored people to life, liberty and the pursuit of happiness is more flagrant and vicious in Indianapolis and Indiana than in any Northern or Western city and state." Throughout its history, this state has consistently and officially discouraged black settlers. Even before it became a state, the territorial legislature petitioned Congress in 1813 to bar Africans from settling in the area. When Congress ignored the petition, the legislature passed a law prohibiting "Negroes, mulattoes and slaves" from immigrating into the territory. The governor's veto prevented the law from going into effect. Most of my formal education took place in Indiana, but this information was not included in any textbook. The one oblique reference to blacks in Indiana was about the Continental Congress and the Ordinance of 1787. This ordinance, passed to govern the Northwest Territory—Wisconsin, Michigan, Illinois, Indiana, and Ohio—our textbooks proudly proclaimed, prohibited slavery and involuntary servitude. There was no mention that Indiana ignored the ordinance and allowed both slavery and involuntary servitude to flourish, sometimes in the guise of indentured servants. Even Indiana governors William Henry Harrison and Thomas Posey held African people captive as part of their personal property.

When we studied Indiana history we didn't learn that the Indiana Colonization Society was established in 1829 to persuade blacks to emigrate to Liberia. In 1848 the Indiana General Assembly expressed its approval of the society's work by passing a joint resolution praising their efforts. Nor were we taught that after 1831, people of African descent who wanted to settle in Indiana had to register with county authorities and post a bond. Nor that when the state constitution was written in 1851, it explicitly stated, "No Negro or mulatto shall have the right of suffrage." Quakers and a few other courageous whites refused to go along with this brutalization of other humans. In 1824 and 1825, in two separate trials, four white men were sentenced to death for murdering two Indian families, including women and children. In the first trial, Judge William W. Wick pointedly asked, "By what authority do we hauntingly boast of being white? What principle of philosophy or of religion established the doctrine that a white skin is preferable in Nature or in the sight of God to a red or a black one? Who has ordained that men of the white skin shall be at liberty to shoot and hunt down men of the red skin, or exercise rule and dominion over those of the black?" Unfortunately, people like Judge Wick have not been heralded in Indiana history. Purveyors of hate like the Ku Klux Klan have received more attention because their attitude has largely prevailed. When that terrorist organization was revived in the 1920s, the national headquarters was in Indianapolis. In 1930 the Klan lynched two black teenagers in Marion, Indiana, and a third, James Herbert Cameron, narrowly missed being strung up. In 1988 Cameron, who moved out of the state, founded America's Black Holocaust Museum in Milwaukee. The Klan is splintered and much weaker now, but a group still operates in Indiana. Since I'm not recruiting for them, I won't say where.

I am amazed that with all these official barriers—and who knows what kind of horrors were happening unofficially—that a number of Negroes actually settled here. Early on, most Negroes went to Randolph County on the Ohio border, where Quakers welcomed them. There was also a community of free Negroes at Lost Creek in Vigo County near Terre Haute. They came to the area in covered wagons from North Carolina around 1830. After the Civil War large numbers of Negroes left the South and some of them came to Indiana, believing that their reception here would be more cordial than in the states they were fleeing. Indiana's efforts to keep blacks out, however, seem to have been effective. The black population in Indiana is 8.4 percent, lower than the national average of 12.3 percent, and lower than all but one of the four surrounding states. Illinois's black population is 15.1 percent, Michigan's 14.2 percent, and Ohio's 11.5 percent. Only Kentucky, on Indiana's southern border, one of the states Negroes fled, has a lower percentage of blacks, 7.3 percent.

With this kind of animus against Negroes, Indiana has been a difficult place for a proud, ambitious black person to flourish. It was clear to me very early that I was expected to be compliant and grateful, no matter what was asked of me or done to me. I have always questioned—in my mind and often openly—the prevailing expectations of blacks, in particular the deference many whites feel entitled to in their interactions with us. As a result, friends, employers, co-workers, and some family members have described me as angry and confrontational. I cannot disagree with that portrayal because I have usually preferred defiance to compliance, particularly when I sensed that I was being challenged because of my *race* or my gender.

As far back as I can remember I've wanted to leave home. I just didn't know how, or where I would go. When I graduated from college, I told the placement office I would take any job so long as it was not in Indiana. For twenty-five years I lived in three major cities: Boston, Chicago, and San Francisco. I love the feeling of being in the center of things that comes from residing in world-class cities. My son's childhood was invigorated by regular visits to Boston's aquarium and children's museum, and acting classes at the Boston Children's Theatre. In Chicago we could walk to the Museum of Science and Industry, and the Field Museum of Natural History was a short ride away. Just as important, he had a happier mother who enjoyed Boston's intellectual community and abundant bookstores, and the proliferation of great blues, jazz, and gospel music in Chicago. While the people reared in San Francisco and Chicago are friendly and welcoming, I noticed they have a swagger indicating they have an edge over those of us from places like Indiana. Most Hoosiers seemingly have no desire to preen, but despite my roots, I wanted that swagger, or at least enough moxie so that I could hold my own anywhere. I suspect it's that collective lack of confidence that has driven some Hoosiers, much like Southerners, to be cruel to those they want to believe are beneath them. It's a macro version of the schoolyard bully who beats up the smart kid on the playground in a vain effort to destroy his dominance in the classroom. I prefer to live among people who are propelled more by their hopes than by their fears.

Because, as a member of America's most despised group, I have been rejected and prohibited from doing what others take for granted, I spent a good part of my life blaming *all* white people for the blatant inequities I encountered. I was fettered to these negative experiences, and unwilling to risk bridging the *racial* divide. The mystery writer Walter Mosley put it this way, "There is the rattle of chains behind the music of our laughing. Chains we wear for no crime; chains we've worn for so long that they've melded with our bones. We all have the chains but nobody can see them—not even most of us." To be free of these psychic chains, I had to grow up, step outside my comfort zone, and engage in some self-examination. I let go of my preconceived notions—my prejudices—and began to observe whites as distinct individuals. That allowed me to see that whites are not all-powerful. In fact, most of them are as fearful and loving, weak and sturdy as I. They may receive more benefits from this society's systems, but they are often as overwhelmed as blacks and lead similar quietly desperate lives. I now consider whites innocent of *racism,* unless they incriminate themselves. Revising my thinking has to some extent been made possible by a few whites who, throughout my life, braved the *racial* chasm and reached out to me.

Since the first Africans were brought here in 1619, we have sought to thrive while living among a people who, in the words of James Baldwin, have "had the deepest necessity to despise" us. In this book I refer to this persistent battle against *racism* as the Struggle to Uplift the *Race*, or the Struggle. I italicize *race* and its derivatives to call attention to the absurdity of the concept and the fact that the meaning of the word has been, and is, so fluid in America. At one point *race* people were those who, like my parents, worked to improve conditions for people of African descent. The founders of the NAACP, both black and white, were considered *race* people. The musical recordings of Bessie Smith, Ma Rainey, and other Negro artists were called *race* records. Here in the twenty-first century *race* continues to play a titillating and vacillating role in American society. You never know where or how it may be used. Prize-winning author John Edgar Wideman describes *race* this way, "It is impossible to pin down a definition… because race is a wild card, it means whatever Humpty Dumpty says it means. …The meaning of race is open-ended, situational, functional, predictable to some extent, but a flexible repertoire of possibilities that follow from the ingenuity of the operator privileged to monopolize the controls. On the other hand, race signifies something quite precise about power, how one group seizes and sustains an unbeatable edge over others."

Even the U. S. Census's definitions of *race* have been transient. Until 1920 the census counted people of "unmixed" African descent as "Negro" or "black." Those perceived to be "mixed" were designated "mulatto." After 1920 and for the next eighty years, anyone admitting to any trace of African ancestry was considered a Negro, physical appearance notwithstanding. For the 2000 census, after a lengthy debate over how to identify people of mixed *race*, respondents were given the option of selecting one or all three *racial* categories—black, white, American Indian. The 2000 census lists eleven Asian *racial* categories, basically corresponding to country of origin; whereas people who identify as Hispanic/Latino could check their country of origin *plus* one or all three *racial* designations. If this seems confusing, it's because it makes no sense.

Not surprisingly, the net result of the changes in the 2000 census has been to lower the count for African Americans. Several television news pundits saw this as a problem for African Americans, apparently believing there was some benefit to being the largest minority ethnic group. Or perhaps they saw this change as a further diminution of the clout blacks supposedly attained as a result of the Civil Rights Movement, and the aborted affirmative action programs.

Affirmative action was conceived as a step toward compensating African Americans for hundreds of years of negative action—twelve generations of people of African descent being held captive as nonhuman beasts of burden. (Except that when the U. S. Constitution was written, Article 1, Section 2, Clause 3 defined us as three-fifths human for the benefit of Southern white politicians.) After being robbed of our ability to participate in the American Dream for twelve generations, we were released from captivity without *any* compensation for three hundred years of unpaid labor; free to fend for ourselves among a people who largely treated us as objects of disgust. I have no idea how many generations it will take for Americans—black, white, and other—to recover from this horrific debasement of us all. But I know it will take much longer than it should if we keep refusing to face it. Although affirmative action was a move in the right direction, many institutions and workplaces preferred to diversify with people from other marginalized groups, such as white women, Chinese Americans, and immigrants from India. The faces of these people were not guilt-inducing reminders of America's shameful, but unapologetic, history in the commerce of African people. There was also the belief that members of these other groups would be more competent than those regarded as the shiftless offspring of slaves, sharecroppers, and servants. In spite of these sentiments, I and several hundred other African Americans did manage to obtain positions previously denied us. Although American mythology says otherwise, we were usually better qualified than whites hired at the same level. Our abilities and intelligence are often underestimated; something I find annoying, sometimes amusing, and occasionally advantageous. Not much affirmation occurred for African Americans before politicians either created, or capitulated to what was called a white backlash.

Despite my desire to be away from here, I keep returning to Indiana. According to theologian Howard Thurman, "A woman must be at home somewhere before she can feel at home everywhere." I have felt less at home in my birthplace than anywhere else I've lived, and I want to understand why. I came back home in late 1973 when my dad died, stayed for five years, but couldn't wait to leave. Thirty years later I find myself back home again in Indiana. This time I'm writing the story of my Indiana years in the hope that I can better understand my birthplace. I agree with South Africans that truth is the road to reconciliation. Perhaps if I learn and tell the truth about the *racist* traditions here, it will help me establish some affinity with the place of my birth. I also believe there is wisdom in Alice Walker's statement that "healing begins where the wound was made." As well I want to explore my memories, because I know, as Baldwin so eloquently put it, "What memory repudiates controls the human being. What one does not remember dictates who one loves or fails to love…. What one does not remember is the serpent in the garden of one's dreams." Have my memories served me well? Or are my feelings about Indiana simply unresolved pain?

I do take pleasure in Indiana's hot summers that last longer than the winters. Winters in Boston and Chicago seemed interminable, and San Francisco's year-round sixty degrees feels great in December, but I find it annoying in July. I also enjoy Indiana's changing seasons—the golden-red colors of fall and the multihued blooms of spring. The wild growth of grass, myrtle, weeds, trees, and bushes just outside my sliding glass door are a welcome contrast to concrete interrupted occasionally by flower gardens. Being able to step outdoors without taking the stairs or waiting for an elevator is also a treat. When it's not too humid, I open the doors and windows and take deep breaths, especially just after the lawn has been mowed. I love the fresh clean smell of newly cut grass—a smell that doesn't make it to the thirty-seventh floor. The lush green outside my door is also the source of relentless spiders, threading connections that you don't know about until they're in your face. A variety of bugs find their way inside, especially after a heavy rain. One night I found a six-inch worm slithering across my carpet. At first, I thought it was a snake. I have no idea how it got in, the doors were closed and locked, but there it was, moving quickly for a worm, undoubtedly as distressed at being there as I was in finding it.

Although *racism* is alive, well, and here to stay, like Bethune, Douglass, and countless others, I've decided that *racism* may be an obstacle, but it will not be a deterrent. What I've learned over these sixty-plus years is that *everybody has problems.* Of course, not everybody suffers from *racism,* including not even all African Americans, but nobody gets through life without critical challenges of one kind or another. Our particular irritations are not so important as whether or not we learn and grow from them. And that's precisely what *racism* has done for me: fertilized my growth.

This story of my battle against *racism* and the outcome rigged for me begins in Indianapolis, a city that has also been referred to as India-no-place and Naptown. One writer said, "Naptown appeared to sleep through much of the century, retaining anachronistic practices and traditions that were out of step with its regional neighbors." However, no matter how often I, or others, disparage this apotheosis of the nation's heartland, it is the place that gave me life.

Chapter 2

My Gifts

> You don't choose your family. They are God's gift to you,
> as you are to them.
>
> ~ Desmond Tutu

From the start, I did things my own way. Mama swears she carried me for ten months and you could never get her to say otherwise. My mother had some large babies. The size of each of her twins, my younger siblings, would have sufficed for most single births. They weighed in at five and a half and seven and a half pounds, a thirteen-pound total. My older brother, James, was a hefty ten pounds. And I was the biggest, outweighing James by half a pound. And *big* was my mother's adjective of choice to describe me. As we all were, I was born at home, at 4:30 a.m. the day after Mothers' Day, May 10, 1937. We were living in one side of a rented double house at 1208 Harlan Street, about four miles southeast of downtown Indianapolis. Homer L. Wales was the attending physician. Like a number of Negro professionals, Dr. Wales's office was in the Walker Building, then the manufacturing site and headquarters of Madam C. J. Walker's hair care products. Mama's younger sister, Lula Lacey, was there helping out on my birth day. Aunt Lula lived a few doors away with her husband Roosevelt Lacey and his two children from a previous marriage. Three months later on August 20, she gave birth to a son, Ronald, my first playmate. I was my parents' second child and first daughter. On school records my name is Janet Mae; however, the first time I obtained a copy of my birth certificate, I saw that Dr. Wales wrote my name as Jennett May. I prefer that spelling of the middle name, but decided to keep Mama's form of the first name.

The month I was born the local white newspapers were twittering over England's royal family. George V's coronation was approaching,

In December 1937 at seven months old, I was driving four-month-old Ronald around in my new Christmas scooter/walker. Within a few months, he took over. Taken in front of our house on Harlan Street. In the background you can see five-year-old James on his tricycle talking to Margaret Blaine, whose family lived in the other side of the double house.

and his brother was about to marry the American woman for whom he had abdicated the throne—"Jewels, Ermine and Rich Velvet Add to Coronation Splendor," "Hairdresser Visits Duke and Fiancée." My family and other Negroes were not so interested in the British soap opera; they were following a more malignant story in the Negro weekly paper. The *Indianapolis Recorder* was reporting on the sixth anniversary of the arrest of the Scottsboro boys. The case, which was publicized internationally as a symbol of America's *racial* injustice, began when two white women in Alabama said they were raped by nine young Negroes. Although the accusations were false, and one of the women recanted, the young men were incarcerated in Alabama for a combined total of over a hundred years.

A few months after I was born, my mother decided to write about her life. Thank God she did because I learned so much about her that she never told us. As we were cleaning out the house after Mama died, my siblings and I found her notebooks and diaries—between layers of unused bedclothes in a box, in the corner of a dresser drawer, in the back of the linen closet. In one of the notebooks she refers to the birth of her first two children.

I had began to think that we weren't going to have any children but five years and six months after we'd been married a son [James Henry] was born on Dec 11, 1932 weighed ten lbs at birth. He has grown fast, and at this writing is about five years old, very ambitious, apt to learn, and inquisitive. Love the outer doors and likes to go at anytime, has way like his father and also resembles him in looks....
Four years and five months after, a little girl was born. I had always wanted a girl, everyone says she resembles me in looks. At this writing she is almost eight months old.

I know that my brother James was a baby at one point, but he looked like this when I met him. This was taken a month before I was born in April 1937 when he was four years and four months old. Harris Brothers Studio.

My earliest memory is of being put down for a nap with my cousin, Ronald. He got out of bed, woke me up, and pulled out my toys. He wanted to play instead of napping. I was sleepy and didn't want to play, but he kept pulling at me, so I got up. My mother heard us, came upstairs, spanked us and put us back in bed. I remember how disappointed she was in me. I was really angry with Ronald for getting me in trouble. This happened before I turned three, because when I was two years and seven months old, we moved to a single story house. Before we moved, my parents were shocked by the birth of the twins. Reginald and Rosie Ann were born June 13, 1939, thirty-four days after my second birthday. Mama said they had prepared for only one baby and had to hustle up a second crib and additional baby clothes. With four crumb-snatchers my parents needed a larger house.

I almost feel that I remember an incident at my grandparent's house because I heard the story so many times. When Mama was about to give birth, I was taken to my grandparents to stay for a few days. My first night there, expecting that I would be a little fearful away from home, Uncle Oliver left the light on in the bedroom after he tucked me in. As he left the room, I called, "Turn out the light." Grandma told this story for years. Apparently, my lack of fear was surprising and endeared me to her.

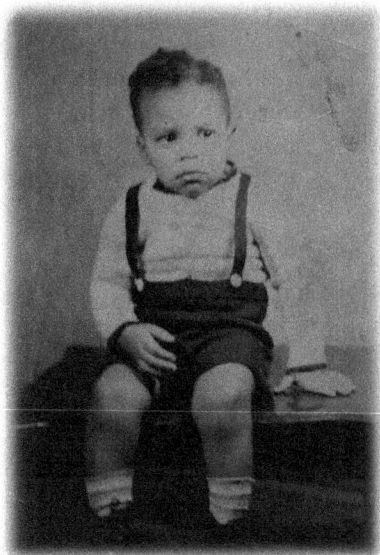

Ronald Lee Lacey, my cousin and first playmate, circa 1938, possibly around the time he suggested we skip napping to play. Courtesy B. Denise Owens.

I do remember the day we moved. The open truck was overflowing with our household goods. It must have been a mild winter day because seven-year-old James was sitting on top of the pile of furniture. To my eyes, it looked as if my brother were on top of the world. I started climbing up to share his perch, but Aunt Lula grabbed me and put me in the truck cabin. Daddy was behind the steering wheel ready to drive off; Mama sat next to him with a bundled–up baby in each arm. I was jammed between Mama and the door. *I SHOULD BE SITTING IN THE MIDDLE LIKE USUAL. IF AUNT LULA HADN'T PUT ME IN THE TRUCK, WOULD I HAVE BEEN LEFT BEHIND? DID THOSE BABIES MAKE MAMA FORGET ABOUT ME?* I was squeezed in so tight that I thought the door would fly open and I'd go tumbling into the street. My feelings of detachment from my family may have begun accumulating that day. Two blocks away we stopped at 1138 South Randolph Street, our new home. It was December 1939.

My next memory is Mama sitting in a rocking chair in the parlor of the house on Randolph, which served as a nursery for the three younger children. I tried to climb into her lap, but she wouldn't let me. She had Rosie in one arm and Reggie in the other. There was no

The usurpers who took all Mama's lap space. Reggie (left) and Rosie in 1939. Now I can admit they are adorable. Rosie sucked her thumb until she was about ten years old.

room for me. The only other memory I have of my first few years was the one of standing on the couch looking out the window.

Like many African Americans, my roots go south before they turn east to Africa.

My mother, who was born and reared in rural Tennessee, described her childhood in the earliest of her journals.

> *Having been restless in mind for months I've decided to write my life story for my children to read. Today, Nov. 15, 1937 I'm beginning it.*
>
> *I was born [October 26, 1906] in a loghouse on a farm at Woodlawn, Tennessee in Montgomery County on the Dover Road (Austin Peay Highway now) ten miles from the County Seat Clarksville, Tennessee.*
>
> *My mother was a quiet religious light brown skin woman, tall and slender and had large eyes. My father always said she was "better looking than either of us." My father was a tall dark man, also religious. He always talked of the Lord and bowed in prayer twice a day. My mother only lived a short while but she bowed on her knees three times a day in prayer.*
>
> *I have two sisters Virgin Mary [my aunt added "ia" to her first name to make it Virginia] oldest and Lula Elvester*

The grandparents I never knew: James Halyard and Webbie Johnson Halyard, my mother's parents, circa 1900. Courtesy B. Denise Owens.

the younger of us. My name Annie Rivers. My mother's maiden name Webbie Johnson and father James Halyard. I don't remember either of my grandparents, although I was named for my paternal grand-mother, Ann Halyard.

Mama says she doesn't remember her grandparents, but later she mentions that her grandfather came to live with them. According to the Johnson family Bible, Mama's maternal grandfather John Wesley Johnson, who had been a teacher, died in 1899, before she was born. Mama's family was living on land inherited from him. There was no information in the Bible, and none of Mama's relatives knew anything about James Halyard's parents or where he was from, so it wasn't his father. I recall that Mama talked about her Uncle William, an older man who came to live with them. Her younger cousin Alma Johnson Civils can't recall Uncle William living with the Halyards, but she does remember William Smith, their grandmother's brother, quite well. Perhaps Mama thought of him as a grandfather because they had no living grandparents.

My first grief was when my mother died; I was only six years and six months old, although I didn't realize what all she meant to me, I did know that something very sad had happened. She died suddenly April 15, 1913. [My mater-nal grandmother was only twenty-nine when she died of

Annie Rivers, Lula Elvester (standing), and Virginia Mary Halyard, my mother and her two sisters, circa 1922.

"female trouble."] *My oldest sister and I were at school and father out on the farm working. A cousin of my father's was there and Lula. It was a shock to us; my father was years getting over it.*

I believe that being reared without a mother was the defining characteristic of Mama's life. It strained her ability to be affectionate and emotionally vulnerable. She was at her best with children, especially those who were neglected, but she seemed baffled by adults, including her own grown children. We had special services on Mother's Day at our church, and I remember feeling bad for Mama. Everybody wore a flower on that day—red if your mother was alive, and white if your mother was deceased. Mama was the only one in our house who had to wear a white flower.

Our father reared us from that time until we were all grown, without the aid of any woman. He was very strict in his disciplining. No boys were allowed to come around our house until we were at a "courting age," fifteen years old. [We had] no games like most other children played such as checkers, cards, and dominos. We liked to play baseball outdoors but weren't allowed to play on Sundays. We didn't have very many toys as we were told at an early age what

Santa Claus was, and at Xmas, aside from fruits, nuts, and candies, we got something to wear, not toys. We didn't ever have a party after my mother died. I can remember she had one for my oldest sister's ninth birthday in August before she died in April, but we didn't ever have any more until we were grown. My father didn't allow any dancing so I've never learned to dance.

The following passage caught my heart because I knew how much Mama loved to read. And I could see that my own enchantment with books, words, reading, and writing was inherited from her.

Didn't have any daily paper to read. I was so fond of reading I would borrow my uncle's papers and read them. I read the Bible, and after my grandfather came to live with us, he bought a "Bible Story Book." I would sit up late at night and read it to he and my father until my eyes filled with water as the lights were dim; a kerosene lamp was the only light.

A year after she completed elementary school Mama got a job with a white family where she "milked six cows twice a day, helped with cooking, cleaning and whatever there was to do around the farm home." Her salary was three dollars a week, later raised to four. From her earnings she saved the twenty-five dollar tuition and money for other expenses she needed to enroll in a six weeks teacher-training course offered at the Negro state college, Tennessee Agricultural & Industrial in Nashville.

I went to A&I State College during the summer of 1925. I liked the school and enjoyed being there although I was lonesome for home as that was the first time of being away from home. It was real fun. I saw my first real dancing and first tennis games and first moving pictures while there. We were taken to [a] circus when we were small, but had never been in a picture show. In the fall of that year I was chosen for one of the County School Teachers. I liked it, but I wanted to go to school some more. My school was ten miles

from my home near Cumberland City—"Evergreen School."
I only taught one year.

> *After school closed in April 1926, I decided I'd like to come to Indianapolis, In. to try and get work and go to school some more. My classmates* [she crossed out "girl chums"] *had both married, but I was anxious to go to school if I could.*

Mama was forced to leave home to obtain additional education because the nearby high school was for whites only. Her brief training at A & I qualified her to teach only in Tennessee's rural Negro schools and she wanted to be a fully certified teacher. In Indianapolis Mama was essentially on her own and overwhelmed by the large city. She moved in with her only relative in the city, a distant cousin who was married and had "a house full of children." The house was small and Mama had no privacy. Consequently, she took a job as a maid where she stayed on the place, but on her day off she had no place to go, except back to her cousin's. She often said she got married to make a home for herself. In those days, and up to about the 1960s, it was unheard of for single women to live on their own. Aunt Lula said she married at age seventeen in order to get away from home, and my Cousin Nannie Brewer told me the same thing about her first marriage. At one point, Mama provided a self-assessment in her notebooks.

> *I was never anxious to marry although I had several proposals from the time I was sixteen until I married. I've only got a common school education. I liked school…. I was always called an old-fashioned girl; some said I was selfish. I didn't care about going anywhere very often. In my heart I've never meant to be conceited or selfish, but very few (if any) people understand me. Things that most everybody desire to do in the way of recreation don't amuse me, such as dances, card clubs, drinks, smoking, infidelity and other things such as neighborhood gossip. I'd much rather be at home reading a book than do any of those things, even today. I don't visit often, unless it's sickness or something that I can help someone.*

I felt overwhelmed by my mother; she towered over me, had fixed convictions, and didn't welcome challenges. Mama was five feet nine inches tall, buxom, with clear, smooth skin the color of biscuits removed from the oven at the right moment. Her eyes were deep brown and she straightened her short black hair. She didn't discuss her weight, but for all of my childhood, she was two hundred pounds or more. That was fine with Daddy. His maxim when it came to women was, "Nobody wants a bone but a dog."

Mama hummed and sang gospel hymns as she went about her endless household chores. Her voice was not strong, but she made up in feeling what she lacked in power. Mama's singing was full of sadness, longing, and determination. Her favorite song "His Eye Is On the Sparrow" typified her melancholy.

> Why should I feel discouraged,
> Why should the shadows come
> Why should my heart be lonely
> And long for heaven and home
> When Jesus is my portion?
> My constant Friend is He:
> His eye is on the sparrow,
> And I know He watches me.

Mama also liked "Precious Lord, take my hand" and "Come what may, from day to day, my heavenly Father watches over me." I hoped the songs consoled her because she seemed deeply unhappy. I was driven to try to make her happy, but I never succeeded, or stopped trying. Not only did Mama sing around the house, but she cajoled Daddy into buying a used upright piano, an extravagance for them. Nobody knew how to play it, but Mama would see to it that I learned.

Before she had children my mother, who liked having her own money, earned it in a number of ways. She took in boarders, worked in a restaurant, and was a stock "girl" at H. P. Wasson's department store in downtown Indianapolis. After James was born she stopped taking outside jobs. Mama disdained working mothers saying that any woman with children who worked outside the home had three jobs—

My great-uncle Steven Penner, Grandpa's half-brother; James S. Cheatham, grandpa; Lillian Cheatham, grandma; and great-uncle Tommy Cheatham, grandpa's brother. This photo was taken behind Uncle Steven's house on his small farm in Lovetown, sometime in the 1950s when they were in their mid-sixties and seventies.

her paid employment, caring for her home, and rearing her children. She often said, "A man is not going to make a horse and a mule out of me." Daddy didn't even consider doing household chores, and he bragged that he had never changed a diaper. I silently vowed not to get stuck like Mama. Daddy's life seemed more interesting to me.

My father, Smith Henry Cheatham, was born May 25, 1903 in rural Trigg County, Kentucky and reared in Bumpus Mills, Tennessee. His parents, James and Lillian Cheatham were the only grandparents I knew; both of Mama's parents died before any of us were born. In addition to my father's unique name, my grandparents came up with unusual names for several of their ten children—Zeffie, Ovella, Rozell. And their first child was given a name that is currently popular—Christy. Often semi-literate folk took children's names from the Bible, but these names are not Biblical, and I have no idea where they originated.

I asked Grandpa about his family and he told me his dad was a Cherokee named Kit who was enslaved on the Cheatham plantation in North Carolina. (When I worked in the Genealogy Division of the Indiana State Library, I found a landowning Cheatham in North Carolina who listed the first names of the people he held in slavery. One of them was named Kit.) After slavery was abolished, Kit migrated to Kentucky. There, my great-grandfather, a widower with two sons, married Mrs. Pinner (also spelled Penner), a widow of African descent who also had two sons. Together they had two more sons, Thomas and my grandfather James Solomon born in 1879. Grandpa was a pale tan with straight white hair and prominent cheekbones. He and Uncle Tommy looked alike to me, so I thought I had two grandpas. Grandma, however, looked more like my idea of an Indian than they did. Grandma was the color of dark chocolate, often wore her hair in braids, and had a profile that I thought was an exact replica of the one on Indian-head nickels. All I learned about Grandma was that her maiden name was Coleman; she wasn't as talkative as Grandpa.

Daddy was proud that he had Grandma's "Indian nose." His skin was dark like her's as well, except that he had a splash of milk in his chocolate. My father was taller than everyone else in his family, and his favorite brother, my Uncle Rozell, teased him, sometimes calling him "Big Boy." I could tell that the appellation stirred sour memories for Daddy. Perhaps that's what Southern whites had called him. Daddy was six-feet

Smith Cheatham, around age 20. He is so sharp that I'm guessing Daddy purchased a new suit for the occasion, possibly in 1923, a few months after he arrived in his new home. Harris Brothers Studio in Indianapolis took most of the family's formal portraits. Harris Brothers Studio

tall and lean with broad shoulders and heavily muscled arms and back. Men spend hours in the gym to get muscles like he had; his however, came from a life of heavy, hard work. James, Lillian, and their ten children sharecropped a tobacco farm in western Tennessee. Smith was their second child and first surviving son. His birth was bracketed by the loss of two sons in infancy. As soon as Smith was big enough to do a day's work, he was taken out of school—at the end of fourth grade.

I'd always wondered why Daddy claimed to hate farming, yet he planted vegetable gardens every chance he got. He always had something growing along the fence in our backyard and he had a larger plot on the grounds of the plant where he was employed. During World War II, he regularly took the family to work a Victory Garden. I was eight when the war ended, so all I remember is that the garden was away from our house. Daddy tended his gardens with loving care and seemed pleased and proud when he showed us the green onions, cabbages, lettuce, tomatoes, corn, string beans, and Kentucky wonders that his gardens produced.

Daddy and Mama took their first airplane trip to visit me in Menlo Park in the San Francisco Bay area in 1971. During that visit Daddy told me a story that explained his bitterness about farming. Whenever I left the house, Daddy was eager to join me. He had never expected to see California and wanted to experience as much of it as he could. In the car we could talk at length without Mama's commentary and interpretation. Daddy and I were riding on the Junipero Serra Freeway, when I asked him why he left home to come to Indianapolis. Daddy said that Ovella, his younger sister and the seventh child, remained in school long enough to get past simple addition and subtraction. After the white landowner gave Grandpa a tally of the harvest indicating, as usual, that the family was in debt to him, Ovella checked the figures. She discovered that, in fact, the Cheathams had made money. Surprisingly, when Grandpa pointed this out, the owner paid up. By not objecting, he no doubt hoped to keep Grandpa from spreading the word to other sharecroppers that they were being cheated.

"Every harvesting season after that," Daddy said, "we made money. Pretty soon we had enough to buy our own farm. I started looking around and found a good piece of bottom land."

Smith showed his find to Grandpa who agreed to purchase the land. However, when Grandpa talked to the white boss, he was upset at the prospect of losing a large, hardworking family. Unfortunately, Grandpa was more reluctant to rile the boss than he was weary of sharecropping. When the boss offered him two handsome horses if they stayed, Grandpa accepted the bribe. Then he killed any hope Smith might have of persuading him to change his mind. Grandpa used the family savings to buy a fancy buggy for the horses to pull. He gloried in the envy generated by the new rig. Other Negroes largely traveled by wagon and mules, or on foot. Smith was totally disgusted and left home immediately. It was 1922 and he was nineteen years old.

When Daddy told me this story, he was sixty-eight years old, but I could hear his sorrow and anger as he recounted this painful break with his family. When he left Tennessee, he first went to St. Louis where he had relatives, but he didn't stay there long. He moved on to Indianapolis where his older sister, Christy Mayweather lived with her husband Bracie and their son James Horace. Daddy told us he obtained his first job in Indianapolis by repeatedly stopping at a construction site and asking for work. One day after the site supervisor told him yet again that he was not hiring, Daddy didn't walk away. He stayed to watch what the workers were doing. He saw that he could outwork any two of them. When he spotted an unused wheelbarrow, Daddy picked it up. Then he filled it with sand and hauled it to where the concrete was being mixed. He continued doing this while the astonished boss watched. Daddy delivered more sand in less time than the supervisor had ever seen, and kept at it until the boss changed his mind. He was hired that day. Daddy delighted in showing us the buildings he had helped construct.

Negroes have perpetually looked for refuge outside the South beginning with those who escaped slavery. After World War I, however, the continuing stream of northward bound Negroes became a flood that included my parents. Between 1920 and 1930 the population of Indianapolis's Marion County increased by nearly eighteen percent from 348,061 to 422,666. In the same decade Montgomery County, Tennessee, Mama's birthplace, lost four percent of its population, and Trigg County, Kentucky where Daddy was born experienced a fourteen percent reduction.

Southern whites were not happy about losing a source of cheap labor, but they were unwilling to treat Negroes fairly to keep them from leaving. Northern whites, on the other hand, feared competition in the labor market. The same year that my father left Bumpus Mills, the White Supremacy League, also called the White Protective Association, was organized in Indianapolis. The whites in the association wanted to circumscribe Negroes by demanding separate schools, and by barring Negroes from theaters, hotels, and certain residential areas. David Curtis (D. C.) Stephenson, a Texan lately of Evansville, Indiana was also actively recruiting whites into the Ku Klux Klan. By 1924 more than ten percent of the state's population had joined the Klan—nearly half a million people. Klan membership exceeded the number of Negroes living in the state, but of course the Klan had Catholics, Jews, and foreigners to terrorize as well.

This was the Indiana that greeted Smith Henry Cheatham and Annie Rivers Halyard when they came north seeking opportunity— education for Mama, non-farm work for Daddy. They also expected some respite from the oppressive *racism* of the southern states they were leaving. They didn't know that Indiana had a furtive slaveholding history and a tradition of intolerance. The state's narrowness and fears were enshrined in the constitution in 1851. Article XIII declared "No negro or mulatto shall come into, or settle in the State, after the adoption of this Constitution." Several Indiana towns boasted signs at their borders reading, "Nigger, Don't Let The Sun Set On You Here." Despite this environment, my parents *believed* they had more latitude in Indiana and took risks they may not have considered in the former openly slaveholding states they left behind.

Smith never owned a car before he came to Indianapolis, but he soon fell in love with automobiles. When he arrived in Indianapolis the city was at the height of its luxury car manufacturing industry and perhaps that's what captured his attention. However it started, cars mesmerized Daddy. He couldn't afford the locally produced Stutzes and Duesenbergs, so he bought a Model T Ford. Although the Model T's retained the same style, every year Daddy traded his current car in for a new one. When the Model A came out in 1928, he bought one of those. Smith must have been excited when he heard about the first Negro car race. According to Mama, before they married, Daddy was a good-time guy who caroused around with his friends. I have no doubt Smith and his buddies were among the twelve thousand fervent Negroes in attendance at the Gold and Glory Sweepstakes in August 1924. At the time, Indianapolis was the car-racing capital of the country, but Negroes were not allowed to compete. Some white drivers asked for Negro participation, but the American Automobile Association that governed car races, absolutely refused to allow Negro drivers or mechanics to be involved.

Not to be outdone, a group of black businessmen found two white businessmen to help them organize a competition for Negro drivers. Emulating what Negroes had done a few years earlier in baseball, these men created a car racing circuit that attracted drivers from around the nation, and culminated in the Gold and Glory Sweepstakes. These popular competitions continued for twelve years until 1936 when the economic fall-out from the Depression wiped them out. All but two of the twelve Gold and Glory races were held on a dusty one-mile dirt track at the Indiana State Fairgrounds in Indianapolis. Smith Cheatham would have been in the stands for every race because he was ardent about fast cars.

Mama said she met Daddy in Indianapolis, but as children they had lived about thirty miles from one another. Bumpus Mills, where Daddy grew up, is in Stewart County, which is adjacent to Montgomery County, Mama's birthplace. They never talked about how they met, although, romantic that I was, I surely asked Mama. She said I asked more questions than her other three children put together. She must have diverted my attention because I don't recall ever hearing a word about it, and I couldn't find anybody who knew that story. Whenever they met, not much time elapsed before they made a permanent commitment. Mama came to Indianapolis in April 1926, and in June 1927, they were married. I do remember Mama telling me they were married by a Justice of the Peace. She also said their only gift was a homemade quilt. When they married he was twenty-four and she twenty-one. At the time, "the Klan dream of complete political power [had come] to fruition, not in the South, but in Indiana." The governor was Ed Jackson, "who did not deny that he was a member of the Klan."

Each of my parents had a formal portrait made in which they look quite young. (Unfortunately, most of our family pictures are not dated.) They had another formal portrait together that Mama told me

Smith Cheatham and Annie Halyard in 1927 just before they married. I don't know what happened to that spiffy-looking suit Daddy wore in his earlier portrait. Perhaps Mama insisted that a dark suit was more appropriate and he pulled out his ill-fitting suit from down home.
Patton Studio

was done just before they married. I can see from these photos that, just as Mama claimed, she was slender before her children were born. Alone, Daddy looks like he's just waiting to jump up and party, but with Mama he looks stern and uncomfortable. If the attraction of opposites makes a good match, then my parents' contrasting personalities made for a classic marriage. Mama, as she indicated in her journal, preferred solitude to socializing. Daddy, on the other hand, loved people and never met a stranger. He would talk to anybody about anything at anytime, regardless of the person's color or status. Anyone who listened heard his stories many times over; he'd keep talking even if you said, "I remember you telling me that." Daddy's stories about his exploits were for me an essential balance to Mama's running commentary about his shortcomings. My parents apparently accepted one another's differences and respected each other's traditionally defined roles because "Daddy made the living, and Mama made the living worthwhile."

Chapter 3

Daring to Hope

Through the centuries of despair and dislocation, we
had been creative, because we faced down death by
daring to hope.

~ Maya Angelou in
Wouldn't Take Nothing for My Journey Now

One story Daddy repeated opened with the line, "I made twenty-
five dollars a week all through the Depression." The fact that Daddy
could provide for us while other Negro men were standing in bread
lines, or making thirty dollars a month at the government's Civilian
Conservation Corps in Corydon, Indiana, was one of many reasons
I considered him invincible. And, it's a good thing Daddy was financially stable during the Great Depression because four of his five
children were born between 1932 and 1939. Daddy talked his way
into the job that made for this steady income. He was in Habig's,
a neighborhood grocery store at the corner of Harlan and Orange
streets, where he did much of our shopping. As usual Daddy found
somebody to talk to, this particular day it was the man behind the
meat counter. When Habig's order from Stumpf Brothers Meat Packers arrived, Daddy included the deliveryman in the conversation.
Making the delivery was Earl Stumpf, one of the brothers who owned
the business.

Frank and Earl Stumpf had been in the meat business on South
Meridian Street for several years, and by 1929 were calling themselves
Stumpf Brothers Meat Packers. Daddy learned that the Stumpfs' family business was growing rapidly and they needed help. It was 1933
and steady work was hard to come by. Not only that, but James was
nearly a year old, and Mama wasn't earning money anymore. Daddy
was not about to let this opportunity slip away; he convinced Earl he

was the man for the job. The Stumpfs hired him and Daddy worked there until 1966 when the business closed.

In the mornings while Mama prepared our breakfast, I remember seeing a lone bowl with a spoon sitting in the sink. I knew it was Daddy's because he ate his cereal and ice cream from serving, rather than soup bowls, underscoring for me his larger-than-life presence. Like clockwork, six days a week before dawn, Daddy rose in a dark house and quietly ate a bowl of Wheaties covered with cream and sugar with a banana sliced on top. Then he slipped out the back door and walked the few yards to the garage where he kept his carefully polished car. As gently as possible, he raised the garage door, backed his car out, pulled the door back down and drove off to work. By the time we got up, Daddy's workday was half over. That solitary bowl in the sink was a reminder that Daddy ate breakfast alone, and that made me sad.

My brothers went to work with Daddy on several occasions and I recall going once myself. My memories of that visit are rather hazy except for the smothering stench of puddled blood and decomposing flesh in the place where the hogs were killed. That was when I learned that all pigs are not smooth and pink like Porky and Petunia. The pigs at Stumpf's were black, white, brown, or dappled, and covered with stiff hair. My older brother James has a better memory of Daddy's work and he described it for me. He said that Daddy chained the leg of a hog to a belt with its head hanging over a pit. The belt turned and as each hog passed, Daddy stabbed it in the neck and the hog bled into the pit.

Once when Reggie, my younger brother, visited Stumpf's he told Daddy, "I'm going to come work with you when I grow up."

Daddy's response was fierce and emphatic. "You don't want to work here. You'll be able to do a lot better than this!"

James said Daddy was the only black person working at Stumpf's, but Daddy didn't mind. He was comfortable with the immigrant family who owned and worked the business. Daddy paid attention when they spoke in their native German and learned several words and phrases that he taught us. We learned to say Good Morning, Thank You, and You're Welcome in German. Daddy took pride in everything he did, was always prompt, and did his work thoroughly and with great care. However, he was not about to have the smell of the slaughterhouse in his car or his house; I never saw his bloodstained coveralls at home. Daddy washed himself and his work clothes at the plant.

When the United States entered World War II Daddy wasn't drafted; he was thirty-eight years old with four children. He often said, "I was too young for the first war and too old for the second one." As the number of able-bodied men on the home front dwindled, Daddy had more than one opportunity to get a better-paying job. The Stumpfs did not want to lose him, but they couldn't compete with the salaries being offered elsewhere. James told me that Daddy proposed a solution to their mutual dilemma that allowed him to make additional money while remaining at Stumpf's.

Stumpf Brothers had been discarding the hog guts, considering them garbage. Daddy asked Stumpf's to let him have the guts. He also requested permission to use their equipment to clean the partially digested food and mounds of fat off the hog intestines. Daddy could sell the intestines as Kentucky oysters or chitlins, thereby increasing his income. If Stumpf Brothers agreed to this, he'd stay. The Stumpfs had nothing to lose. They could keep their best worker without increasing his salary, and he would unload some of their garbage. They struck a deal. Daddy shared the chitlin work and profits with his father and brother—Grandpa and Uncle Rozell. (By 1938 Daddy's family had stopped sharecropping, left Tennessee, and followed him and Aunt Christy to Indianapolis.) Aside from the time the Cheathams put in to make the guts fit to eat, there was little operating cost for this family business within a family business. Stumpf's even provided reusable tin pails with the company logo in which ten pounds of chitlins were packed for sale.

Many Negro families would not consider a Thanksgiving or Christmas dinner without chitlins, but if they couldn't buy from the Cheathams, they had to settle for the fatty, frozen supermarket version. Daddy always had more customers than chitlins because people liked how clean and fresh they were. Twice a week, hours after the hogs were slaughtered, chitlins, at a price of $1.75 for a ten-pound bucket, were delivered to customers' doors. After a while, sales increased to a point where Daddy sold most of his chitlins to neighborhood grocers. He made home deliveries only to a few special people, like older folk who would have found it difficult to carry the chitlins home from the grocery. I became accustomed to seeing buckets of chitlins lined up on our back porch and in the trunk of Daddy's car during the season—November to March. Daddy's chitlin money eased the strain of providing for a family of six on a butcher's salary. The additional income also allowed him to indulge us at Christmas and take the family on vacations. There were no chitlins in our house though. Mama thought they were nasty and said she wouldn't cook or eat them. After cleaning hundreds of pounds, Daddy didn't want any chitlins on his plate anyway.

In 1939 when my parents decided to buy a house, they faced a formidable challenge. A survey that year reported that, "limited housing opportunities was one of the most significant problems [Negroes had in Indianapolis]. Regardless of their neighborhood or economic status, [Negroes] looking for housing faced overcrowding, dilapidation, health hazards and over pricing." The Klan's grip on Indiana politics had loosened somewhat, and the ordinance passed by the Indianapolis City Council in 1926 to guarantee that neighborhoods would be segregated by *race* had been struck down in court. However, real estate agents maintained *racial* boundaries by not showing houses in white areas to Negroes. Most Negroes "lived on the east side, or in the Bottoms west of downtown. In 1945 the Bottoms were called the worst Negro slum in America." Negroes with higher incomes had better housing north of the Bottoms.

Given these circumstances, it is astounding that my parents found a house meeting their requirements that they could afford. Mama and Daddy meant to have a decent home, but the affluent Negro section was beyond their means. They also preferred to remain on the south side, close to family members, their neighbors of the last twelve years, and Daddy's job. The house they bought was just two blocks from where they were living. Knowing the way my father operated, he probably found the house, then talked the white realtor into selling it to him. The home they purchased was in a neighborhood made up of modest, single-story, mostly Victorian-era frame houses occupied by their working-class owners. It cost thirteen hundred dollars and had a thirteen-dollar-a-month mortgage. The house was on a pleasant street where most of the homes and yards were well kept. There was only one other Negro family on the block, and very few Negroes living anywhere on Indianapolis' south side. That was fine with Mama. She often said, "I don't know why, but our people act

Rosie and Reggie in 1946 when they were seven. I found this photo in Rosie's scrapbook. Her caption, "Just came from school program. James Graduation," enabled me to date it accurately. This is also the best snapshot I found of the house on Randolph where we lived for twenty years. You can see one of our dwarf catalpa trees in the yard. At this point we still had a wooden porch and brick walk, both of which were later replaced with concrete.

a whole lot better when there are some white folks around." I hated hearing her say that and, when I was older, tried to convince her otherwise, but she never relented.

The other Negro family on Randolph Street, Mr. and Mrs. Roberts and their grown daughter, Selma, lived next door to us on the north. On the other side was Miss Myers, a gangly and slightly bent older woman who never smiled. Low hedges enclosed both their yards, but our lawn, with a five-foot-high tree shaped like an umbrella on either side of the entry walkway, was open to the sidewalk. I don't think either of our neighbors was thrilled about the arrival of a family with small children. And at various times we children managed to offend both of them. Once I was riding my tricycle on the sidewalk and ran the wheel off the edge. I fell from the tricycle into the flowers Mrs. Roberts had planted between the sidewalk and the curb. From her porch she yelled at me to stay off her flowers. Miss Myers had a big mulberry tree in her backyard, several branches of which hung over the fence into our yard. Miss Myers told us not to touch her tree, but the dark ripened berries were sweet and tasty. We picked and ate all we wanted while we played out back in the summer. Miss Myers's lack of forbearance simply made the berries more delicious.

Within a year after we moved in, the McClure family, our friends from Harlan Street bought a house down the block. A few years later Aunt Lula, Ronald, and Uncle Leonard bought the house on the other side of the Robertses. The house between Aunt Lula and the Mc-Clures was rented by a series of Negro families—the Morgans, the Glaspies, and our cousins, the Ransoms. That made a total of five Negro families on the block for much of my childhood. Realtors hadn't yet invented blockbusting so there was no wholesale exodus of whites when the Negro families moved in. Or, perhaps it was as Daddy said, "These white folks too poor to move anywhere." We lived on Randolph for twenty years, and when we moved into our new home, there were still only seven Negro families on the block.

Most of our neighbors were amiable and there was some chatting in the yards and on the street, but no in-house visiting, an unspoken rule that I broke. When I rode my tricycle on the sidewalk, I wasn't allowed to go far from home. Fortunately, just two doors away was the most attractive house on our street. I was enthralled by it, perhaps because it was different from all the other houses; it was the only brick house on the block. I usually stopped in front and gazed at it, wondering at the mysteries inside. The Hermans, a childless, gray-haired white couple, lived there. I sometimes saw Mr. Herman cutting their front lawn. One day, Mrs. Herman was sitting on the steps of her small porch and spoke to me. We started talking and after that I visited with her regularly. These visits continued after I outgrew my tricycle, and eventually she invited me inside. I had to check with Mama first, but she needed reassurances from Mrs. Herman that I was welcome before she let me go inside. Mrs. Herman's house seemed to gleam, reminding me of the pristine homes in the *Better Homes and Gardens* magazine that Mama subscribed to. Stiffly starched white doilies curled around the table lamps and were evenly spaced above each seat and on the arms of her sofa. Doilies were also displayed on the backs and arms of each chair. Our house was filled with the clutter of six people living in close quarters, but the Herman's house looked as though nothing was ever used or disturbed. I liked the quiet serenity. Mama would not allow me to visit as often as I wanted saying, "You don't want to wear out your welcome." Apparently, Mrs. Herman enjoyed my company when I did stop by. She gave me candy and sometimes treated me to cookies and chocolate milk at her dining room table. I looked forward to my occasional visits because it was something I did all by myself, and, best of all, in their house I was the center of attention. In a way the visits fulfilled my fantasy about packing up my tricycle and riding off to some magical place where I could do whatever I wanted.

Otherwise, the only neighbors we visited were family members and the McClures, who lived five houses away on the same side of the street. The McClure's two daughters and two sons were older; their youngest child was a boy the same age as James. The twins and I most often played with each other because there were no Negro children on the street our age. James, four and half years my elder, hung out with Raymond McClure and other Negro boys their age who lived on Harlan Street. Some of the white children yelled "nigger," "jungle bunny," "chocolate drop" at us, usually from a distance. I don't recall anybody ever getting in our faces with those names. Mama told us to ignore them, but when she wasn't around we shouted "cracker," "peckerwood," "poor white trash" back at them. One evening a neighbor I'll refer to as Jones stepped out on his porch and yelled threats at us as we responded to his daughter's name-calling. I was probably eight years old at the time, and Rosie and Reggie were six. We were scared and ran home to tell Daddy. Daddy immediately jumped up to go see Jones. Mama pleaded with him not to, but Daddy didn't break his stride. He went to his car first and got the axe handle he kept between the driver's seat and the door. Reggie, Rosie, and I were right behind Daddy, but Mama called us back and told us to stay in the house. While she stood on the front porch anxiously watching Daddy go up the street, we slipped out the back door. The three of us ran down the alley as fast as we could; we didn't want to miss seeing our big, strong Daddy beat up Jones. Few of the houses had fenced yards, but we knew some neighbors wouldn't be receptive to having us cut through their property to get to the street, so we waited until we got to the McClures. We ran through their backyard, but went no further than the front lawn where we could see, but also be out of Mama's sight line. The McClures lived across the street and a few houses away from the Joneses. We could see everything, but we couldn't hear what was being said. We saw Daddy standing on Jones's porch, probably inviting him outside. To our disappointment Jones never came out of his house. All we saw was Daddy talking to the screen door and belligerently shaking his axe handle.

After a few minutes, Daddy left their porch. When we saw him leave, we went down to the sidewalk to wait for him, and for the first time he saw us. He walked over to where we were and said, "Let's go home." On the short walk home, Daddy put his arm around my shoulder and told us, "You won't have to worry about him anymore. I straightened him out. "

Mama was so upset with Daddy that she ignored our disobedience. "What is wrong with you? You could have been killed! What kind of example is that to set for your children?"

"That Georgia cracker better learn he can't get away with that stuff up here." Daddy went back to his chair and continued reading the evening newspaper.

Jones never said another word to us. So far as we were concerned that proved Daddy had done the right thing. Mama was also correct about Daddy setting an example. We admired Daddy for standing up for himself, and we imitated him. We weren't belligerent, but the four of us did not back down from anybody, especially whites.

The aging house on Randolph Street had a warped wooden front porch that we replaced with concrete. The concrete porch was much better for playing jacks—no chance of splinters—and pick-up-sticks. I considered myself a whiz at jacks and loved to play, but often had no one to play with. Rosie didn't want to get beaten again, and Reggie wouldn't play at all, considering it a girl's game. We also had a back porch that was enclosed, but unheated. My parents had tan imitation brick siding installed on the drafty house. There was no garage, but Daddy shortly built one of concrete blocks with the help of Mr. Wilkey, a neighbor from Harlan Street, who was a skilled carpenter and bricklayer. In addition to housing Daddy's car, the dry, two-car garage was used for storage, clearing space on the back porch for Mama's new wringer washing machine. Garages on our street were located behind the houses on the alley. The alley was a lively place. Sometimes we played back there with the white kids who lived in the house behind ours. On garbage day, we set out our trash for collection and although we liked to watch the pick-up, we ran deep into the backyard to avoid being close to the fetid smell. More interesting were the ragman and the junk man who plied the alley looking for salvageable material, and the vendors with their rhythmic chants. "Waaaatermelons! Waaaatermelons! Come get your sweet, ripe, watermelons!" The most alluring character coming through the alley, however, was a distant cousin, Zack Pinner. Cousin Zack looked dirty and ragged when he was out collecting junk, but the horse that pulled his wagon is what fascinated us! A real live horse was so unusual that when we heard the bells jingling on his wagon, we ran out to gape.

The milkman and the iceman, our most regular vendors, drove down the street in front of the house. The milkman put three or four quart bottles of whole milk, and a quart of clabbered milk, or buttermilk, into the insulated metal box that sat on the porch beside the front door. Nobody drank buttermilk except Mama, and she also put it into the batter for cornbread and biscuits. The whole milk had thick pale yellow cream on top, some of which we poured on our cereal before we shook up the bottle. On rare occasions Mama treated us to a bottle of chocolate milk, but usually we added Nestlé's cocoa powder to white milk. We made hot cocoa with water, and I was about fifteen the first time I had it with milk. I nearly gagged it seemed so thick. Empty bottles were rinsed and left beside the box for the milkman to pick up. For the iceman we had a square card with a number on each of its sides—25, 50, 75, 100. We put the card in the window facing the street. The number showing at the top of the card let the iceman know how many pounds of ice we needed that day. When he saw the card, he'd stop, open up his truck and use his large black tongs to grip a block of ice, hoist it onto the quilted pad on his shoulder and bring it around the side of the house, through the back porch, into the kitchen. We opened the door at the bottom of the insulated icebox and he set the ice inside.

We had a nice lawn in front and back. Daddy cut our grass and trimmed the edges just as carefully as he did the yards he was paid to maintain. (In the chitlin off-season Daddy supplemented his Stumpf's salary with four or five lawn-care clients.) Mama contributed to the beauty of the yard by lovingly planting and tending an array of bushes and flowers ranging from blazing yellow forsythias and fragrant lilacs in the spring to red velvet coxcombs and plump orange marigolds in the fall. In the summer our yard was a palette of color. The sweet peas were a delicate pink blossom on a vine climbing a trellis between the two front windows. Flanking the trellis were purple and yellow irises, snapdragons in an array of colors, the marigolds, and red four o'clocks that I periodically checked to see if they ever opened *before* four o'clock. They didn't. In the small shady space between the front porch and the walkway to the backyard she planted tiny white lilies-of-the-valley. My parents were proud of their meticulous front lawn and we rarely played there. Mama said we would have grass, not dust, in our yard. In the backyard wild morning glory vines, the coxcombs, and Mama's prized rosebushes lined the fence on one side. Along the fence on the other side were Daddy's vegetables—vines of bright red tomatoes tied to sticks, delicate pale green leaf lettuce, and darker green bulging heads of cabbage. The space beside the back steps was filled with red, white, pink and purple petunias.

Inside, our new home not only had more rooms, but we had central heat, a bathroom with a tub and, when we lit the tank in the basement, hot running water. Sometimes the bathroom pipes froze in the winter, and Daddy removed the floorboards, and using a torch made of rolled up newspapers, thawed them out. None of us liked going down to the gloomy, cobwebby cellar to light the gas heater, but that was the price we had to pay for the wonder of a bathtub of hot water. The basement was dank in the summer and torrid in winter after Daddy built an enormous fire in the coal-burning furnace. Our other house had been warmed by a wood-burning potbellied stove. It had a toilet, but no bathtub; we bathed in a round galvanized tin tub after heating water on the kitchen stove.

The largest rooms in the house were the parlor, living room, and dining room. There were two other smaller rooms, one an extension of the living room, and the other off the dining room. Behind the dining room was a kitchen spacious enough for a table and six chairs. The door to the bathroom opened off the kitchen. Daddy said the bathroom and back porch had been added to the house after the initial construction. As we children got older, the front parlor that had been a nursery for the three younger children became my parents' bedroom. At that point, the parlor door that opened onto the front porch was permanently closed. The door opening into the living room became the sole front entrance. My brothers slept in the room off the dining room. It was just wide enough for a double bed and a chest of drawers with no more than a couple of feet between the two pieces of furniture. For two or three years, until Reggie outgrew his crib, James had his own room, a luxury I didn't enjoy for many years to come. James and Reggie hated having to sleep together. James, who often exaggerated, claimed that he woke up one morning to find Reggie's big toe in his mouth. But they were stuck with each other until James joined the army when he was seventeen and Reggie was ten. The boys hung their clothes in a wooden chifforobe in the dining room just outside their bedroom door. They may have been forced to sleep together, but at least they had a *door*!

Rosie and I were given the narrow room off the living room. Mama put up a rod and hung thick drapes at the wide entrance, but the curtains served only as a room divider; we never felt that our room was private. It was large enough to hold only twin beds and a double dresser. Rosie's bed fit snugly between the north and south walls. Two feet away, my bed was perpendicular to hers in the corner against the other end of the south wall, next to the closet. More than half of my bed was separated from the living room by a mere curtain. The dresser was on the wall across from my bed; I could touch it by reaching a bit. Our room did have a couple of advantages: we had the only closet in the house, save the one in the bathroom, and our bedroom window looked straight into the Robertses' house, no more than ten feet away. Long before we ever heard of television, we entertained ourselves watching the Robertses go about their evening routine. We were never invited inside the Robertses', so we two nosy little girls felt we were pulling one over on them: we could see inside their house and they didn't even know it. When the windows were open, we could even hear what they were saying. On a few occasions Selma undressed for bed with the shade open, and we saw a naked adult body! We knew that was against the rules, so enjoyed it all the more. We never got caught watching the Robertses; my parents undoubtedly thought we were sleeping.

Rosie and I hated that we did not have a bedroom door. So far as we were concerned, those curtains didn't sufficiently close off our room. We were constantly pinning the center of the drapes together and trying to tape or tack the sides to the woodwork. Finally, my parents switched rooms with us. At the time I thought our complaints had gotten through to them, but with the hindsight of age and experience, I am now certain they were having a marital crisis. Not only did Rosie and I get their room, but their double bed as well.

Be careful what you wish for. Now we had a larger room with a door, but Rosie and I had to sleep together and she snored like a tired old man. She often woke me up with her snorts and loud gurgling noises. When I was pulled out of my slumber, I'd roll her onto her side and get some sleep until she started again. In addition, if our bed was not made we both got in trouble, but Rosie rarely made the bed when it was her turn. I became adept at smoothing out my side of the bed, placing my pajamas under the pillow, carefully covering the pillow with the bedspread, and tucking the spread beneath the pillow exactly the way Mama liked it. I also hung up my clothes, put my clean clothes away and my dirty clothes in the hamper. The other side of the bed was left rumpled and Rosie's clothes, clean or dirty, would be on the floor, the chair, or wherever she dropped them. Sometimes I had to kick her clothing away from my side of the room.

Maybe the bedroom switch had something to do with Mama's taking night classes at Crispus Attucks, the Negro high school. One thing was certain, Daddy didn't approve of her going to school. Nobody in our family expected to go to college, but I knew learning and reading were important. My parents subscribed to, read, and discussed several magazines, in particular, the Johnson Publications' *Negro Digest* and *Ebony*, and the NAACP's *Crisis*. We also had four different newspapers delivered—the daily Indianapolis *Star* and *News*, the weekly *Indianapolis Recorder*, and the *Pittsburgh Courier*. At one time the *Courier* was the country's most widely circulated black newspaper and one of the first black papers to publish both national and local editions. The paper counseled readers on financial matters, encouraged political participation, and also urged Negroes to support organizations like the Urban League and the NAACP. We had books around as well. For a while, the Prospect branch of the library was half a block from our house at the corner of Randolph and Prospect streets. James regularly came home with library books. I was four years old and unable to read, but I could see how people reacted to books, so I knew they were exciting. I wanted a library book and asked James to bring me one. He did. I either learned to read it, or memorized the words after they were read to me. I was so happy to have a book of my own that I still remember it. The simple story was about a farmer collecting eggs laid by his hens. From then on James brought me a book every time he went to the library. By the time we three younger children were in school, the Prospect Branch had been moved to a larger brick building about a mile away. We regularly walked to the library to borrow books, and every summer joined their reading club. The Summer Reading Club was a competition to see who could read the most books. We gave oral reports to the librarians about each book we read. Reggie read stacks of thin books and usually won the competition. Although I would have enjoyed winning, I wasn't willing to bypass thicker, chapter books in order to do so.

All four of us were avid readers, but I was obsessed with books and words. I craved the solitude that would allow me to indulge my preoccupation. To obtain time to read, I locked myself in the bathroom or "borrowed" Daddy's flashlight and read under the covers after I went to bed. I never saw print without stopping to read it. The family teased that I would read *anything* after Mama caught me reading the words on a box of pepper. That incident became shorthand for my obsession. Whenever I couldn't be found, family members concluded that I was "somewhere reading off the pepperbox." My best friend Laura Noel loved books as much as I did. We were in the same grade and both read and discussed the Maud Hart Lovelace's Betsy, Tacey and Tib series about the life and adventures of three good friends our age. We also enjoyed Laura Ingalls Wilder's *Little House on the Prairie* books that decades later became a television series. *Little Women* was another favorite that we read over and over again. Finding out about the lives of other girls who lived in different places and different times fed my longing for an exciting life. I still remember how much I admired the spirited Jo, the sister who was a writer in *Little Women*. During my infatuation with that book, I began calling my mother Marmee. I called Daddy Popsy, a name I picked up from a comic book. Rosie, of course, imitated me. Laura and I also had a secret; we wrote stories that we shared only with each other.

Perhaps because she lacked reading material in her childhood, my mother never restricted our reading. We read anything we could get our hands on, including comic books and romance magazines. By the time I was nine or ten, I had read every book in the children's section of the Prospect branch. I wanted to read other books, but the librarian said she needed parental permission before I could borrow books outside the children's area. Without hesitation Mama wrote a note to the librarian permitting me to take out any book I wanted. I never saw books about Negroes at the library, but Daddy found some and brought them home.

Despite his limited schooling, Daddy could read, write, and do complicated math in his head much faster than any of us could work it out on paper. He liked to be on top of things and routinely asked us for help with unfamiliar words he heard or read in newspapers. He also wanted us to tell him what we learned in school. So far as I know, the only book Daddy ever read was the Bible, but he took pride in buying books about Negroes for us, and he knew Mama would be pleased. I think he bought them at the meetings he attended or possibly from the trunk of somebody's car. I know they weren't sold in Indianapolis bookstores until many years later. He brought home a copy of Richard Wright's *Black Boy* that I read when I was eight years old. When I read it again as an adult, I realized how much of that book had gone over my head. During the 1960s I discovered that many of my peers were seeing books by and about blacks for the first time, but as a child in the 1940s I read a number of *race* books by Negro authors. I particularly enjoyed the biographies of George Washington Carver and Frederick Douglass written by the black Indiana-born author, Shirley Graham (DuBois). I felt gratified every time I read about one of my people who managed to accomplish great things despite *racism* and having started with very little, some even born into slavery.

I was introduced to a group of outstanding Negroes like Mary Mc Leod Bethune, W.E.B. DuBois, and Langston Hughes in *Thirteen Against the Odds* by Edwin Embree. It was in Embree's book, published in 1944 that I first saw George Washington Carver referred to as a wizard. A local newspaper, a book written about him, and John Hope Franklin also called Carver the Wizard of Tuskegee. Negroes called Carver a wizard because of his work at Tuskegee Institute with peanuts and sweet potatoes. He discovered three hundred different products that could be made from peanuts, and one hundred eighteen from sweet potatoes. His efforts made it possible for Southern farmers to end their dependence on cotton as a cash crop. I have been surprised in recent years to read books that referred to Booker T. Washington, Tuskegee's founder and first president, as the Wizard of Tuskegee. I believe this misnomer began when, nearly forty years after Embree's book, Louis Harlan dubbed Booker T. the Wizard of Tuskegee. In explaining his selection of the term, Harlan cites Luther Burbank, "the plant wizard," and Thomas Edison, the Wizard of Menlo Park. Perhaps Harlan didn't know that Negroes had designated Carver the Wizard of Tuskegee decades earlier. In any case, subsequent to Harlan's book, more than one writer has appropriated that term for Booker T.

Mama never stopped wanting more education. She started taking night classes before she had children, but after James was born, she stopped. When James got big enough to look after us, probably around 1944 when he was twelve, she started her classes again. In addition to her yearning for a high school diploma, Mama said she just needed to get out of the house. Daddy did not approve of Mama going off on her own doing something without him, and we found that out one evening. Daddy came home and we told him Mama had just left for school. He ran back out to his car and drove to the bus stop less than a block away, where Mama was waiting. Daddy offered her a ride to school, but instead he turned the car around and brought her back home. We were sitting on the living room floor playing a game, probably pick-up-sticks. Suddenly, Mama came in the door with a fierce look on her face. We were so startled that we didn't say anything, nor did she. It was almost like she didn't see us. Mama strode straight through the house and out the back door. I jumped up to follow her and see where she was going. I watched as she walked quickly through the backyard, up the alley, and presumably, back to the bus stop. I was seven and not allowed beyond the backyard. Daddy didn't come inside after he dropped her off, so he didn't know that Mama left again. I guess he thought when he told her to stay home, she would.

Mama talked to me about it later, "Your daddy is just old-fashioned. He thinks I should be right here in this house if I'm not with him. Going to school is the one thing I do for myself and I am not going to stop until I finish."

I also heard Daddy complaining to her about it.

The Attucks High Night School Class of 1953 at their graduation ceremony in the school auditorium. Mama is fifth from the left. The man to her left is Russell A. Lane, long-time principal of Attucks. On the other side of Lane is Mrs. Foley, a new friend Mama made in school. The auditorium stage was also the school gymnasium.

"What good is it gonna do for you to go to high school? You should be here with these children."

Education was valued in our family, so I was surprised Daddy didn't want Mama going to school. I know Daddy took a singular pride in providing for his family, so he may have feared that, with more education, Mama might command an income that rivaled or surpassed his. For all of his charm, Daddy was not immune to male chauvinism. Despite his efforts to sabotage her, Mama continued taking classes. We liked that Mama had homework like we did. Years later, Reggie found several of Mama's report cards. All of her grades were As and Bs, except in algebra and chemistry, where she made Cs. At the end of her first grading period in 1951, I had signed my name in the space provided for the parent's signature. I was fourteen at the time. Rosie, who insisted on copying *everything* I did, signed at the end of the second marking period. In 1953, after years of starting and stopping, and taking no more than three, but usually two, classes at a time, Mama graduated from high school. It had been twenty-seven years since she had come to Indianapolis for more education. We all dressed up and went to the ceremonies. Mama was so proud and we children shared her joy. But Daddy didn't see what difference it would make.

Chapter 4

Priceless, but Not Material

The legacies that parents and church and teachers left
to my generation of black children were priceless, but
not material. ...[My elders] had grit. They valued family
life, family rituals and tried to be and to expose us to
good role models.

~ Marian Wright Edelman
in *The Measure of Our Success*

As a child, I took my parents for granted, assuming that all families were like ours. I discovered that, in fact, Mama and Daddy did
things that other kids' parents didn't do. Smith and Annie Cheatham
were especially remarkable when you consider that they were from
isolated communities in the rural South, and that neither of them was
educated beyond eighth grade. My parents added mother wit, common sense, and a willingness to work hard to their experiences and
created a space for us that was more stimulating and nourishing than
that of their own childhoods. In addition, Mama and Daddy felt duty-
bound to do whatever they could to improve the general condition of
Negroes, and were committed to the Struggle to Uplift the *Race*. Their
primary obligation, however, was to their children, and we knew it.

Mama had vivid memories of the times while she was growing
up when their evening meal was pot likker and cornbread, and she
was determined that her children would be better fed than that. Every
morning she cooked breakfast, usually bacon or sausage, eggs, and
toast made from Wonder or some other light bread. All bread that
wasn't homemade—like biscuits or cornbread—Daddy aptly called
light. If somebody was in a rush—often me—breakfast would be
Wheaties with cream, sugar, and fresh peaches or bananas. On Sun-

day breakfast was a special occasion because we all sat down together to chicken battered in seasoned flour and fried in bacon drippings, steaming rice smothered in butter, sugar, and cream, and hot buttered biscuits served with Mama's homemade fruit preserves. Chicken was a treat because most often we had the pork Daddy brought home from his job. Occasionally we had neck bones and pigtails, but ordinarily we ate high on the hog—ham, pork chops, and roasts. We looked forward to the chicken, hamburgers, and salmon croquettes Mama served on the weekends. As young children, we loved Sundays because, except for holidays, it was the only day the whole family spent together.

After breakfast Daddy drove us to Sunday school. We had to leave early because he was the superintendent, Mama taught a class, and I played the piano for the opening songs. Mama and Daddy believed it was never too early for children to learn public poise. All four of us had been memorizing and reciting poems for Christmas and Easter programs since we were old enough to speak. James found himself grateful for that training when he was asked to give the opening prayer at his first YMCA staff meeting. He was fourteen years old and the only child in the room, but he handled the assignment with aplomb. Mama longed to play the piano herself and when I was eight, she insisted that I take lessons. My piano lessons were like punishment for something I hadn't done. I practiced only when I was forced, and my teacher was usually disappointed in my progress. I begged to be released from the daily round of practice and the torturous weekly sessions with my instructor, but Mama would not be deterred. We had a piano, and somebody needed to learn to play it. As the elder daughter I was that somebody.

By the time I was ten, my parents decided that I played well enough to accompany the congregation during the two opening songs at Sunday school. I had heard skillful piano players and recognized how pitiful my attempts were by comparison. Our hymnbook was *Gospel Pearls*, first published in 1921 by the National Baptist Convention, the largest organization of Negro Christians in the country. We had a copy of *Gospel Pearls* at home and I practiced the songs that were easiest to play. Daddy's favorite was "In the Garden."

I come to the garden alone,

While the dew is still on the roses,

And the voice I hear,

Falling on my ear,

The Son of God discloses.

And He walks with me, and He talks with me,

And he tells me I am His own;

And the joy we share as we tarry there,

None other has ever known.

He asked me to be sure to learn it, and, fortunately it was simple enough that I could. I played "In the Garden" often, plus the few other songs I could make it through. On occasion a member of the congregation, possibly tired of my limited repertoire, would raise a hymn that wasn't even in the book, so I sat there with my hands in my lap. The leader would begin by rapidly singing, "I heard the voice of Jesus say." The congregation would repeat the line, but much more slowly. "IIIIIIII heeeeard the-uh voooice offff Jeeeeesus sayay." Before they let go of the last note, the leader quickly sang the second line, "Come unto me and rest." The same pattern was repeated for the entire song. If somebody started a *Gospel Pearls* song, Daddy would find the page number and give it to me, to little avail. With my heart pounding and embarrassment flooding my body, I would bang whatever notes my fingers landed on in a vain attempt to decipher the unfamiliar song. Daddy and Mama insisted that I was providing a service because nobody else was available to play the piano during Sunday school. There was nothing I could say that would change their minds, so I suffered mostly in silence, plunking away every Sunday, swallowing my public humiliation with as much grace as I could muster.

About two years into this weekly mortification, I was unexpectedly rescued. As always Rosie wanted to do whatever I was doing, and she asked for piano lessons. Mama put her off. "You're not old enough yet. Besides I don't have the money to give both of you lessons." To Rosie "no" always meant, keep asking until you get the answer you want. She continued to pester Mama until she was allowed to take lessons. After a couple of months, Rosie was playing as well, or better, than I was after four years of instruction. I saw a way out of my weekly suffering and eagerly suggested that Rosie take over playing piano for Sunday school, but Mama and Daddy wouldn't have it. Rosie was only ten, and I believe they felt it would be improper for her to supplant me, who was two years older. After another six months, Rosie was so much better than I that it seemed ridiculous for me to keep being humiliated. I invited Rosie to join me on the piano bench one Sunday morning. After we sat down, I told her to go ahead and play. She was thrilled. Not only could she play songs she'd never seen before, but Rosie could play anything she heard. When people started singing, she could accompany them without any music at all! Everybody raved about how well Rosie played, especially for a child her age, not yet eleven. The contrast between her ability and mine was so stark that Mama and Daddy probably would have been drummed out of church if they had insisted I continue playing, which thankfully they didn't. Whew! Sweet relief. After that Rosie played for Sunday school, for the Junior Choir, and eventually, got a prestigious position at Mount Paran Baptist Church. Mount Paran was a large black church on the west side whose choir was acclaimed throughout the city.

There was just more thing. "Mama," I said, "I don't want to take anymore piano lessons. I'll never play like Rosie."

"What kind of attitude is that? You could play a lot better if you put your mind to it, and practiced."

"I play the cello at school, and I like that better than playing the piano. And you could save the money you spend giving me piano lessons." Since Mama's desire for someone to play the family piano was now satisfied, and I had not completely abandoned the refining influence of music, she let me off the hook.

When I was eleven years old there was a revival at church. Week-long revivals were held periodically to revive the church's spiritual focus, and in particular, to save lost souls. A dynamic preacher from another church, or perhaps from out of town, offered fire-and-brimstone sermons every night and encouraged the congregation to shout their joy and loudly amen their approval. Mama came home from the revival on a Tuesday night and accosted me.

"Rozzie joined church tonight." Rosalind "Rozzie" Trabue was in the same grade as I, but she was a year older because I started school when I was five. "You need to start thinking about your soul's salvation. Tomorrow night you're going to revival with us." I think Mama was distressed that Dorothy Mae's daughter had found the Lord before her own daughter had. After all, the Trabues were not the pillars of the church that the Cheathams were. I knew what I had to do, not only to please Mama, but also because I knew she woukd keep nagging me until she got what she wanted. The following night Rosie, Reggie, and I joined Mama and Daddy at the revival service. When the minister asked all sinners to come up front to the mourner's bench, I went. When he opened the doors of the church and asked who wanted to join, I stood and stepped forward. When he asked why I wanted to join, instead of admitting that I was trying to satisfy my mother, I repeated what I had heard others say, "I want to be saved." My decision for Christ elicited several loud amen's from the church sisters and deacons, then I heard Mama's joyous shout of approbation. Ironically, Jesus saved all three of us the same week: Reggie and Rosie joined church the very next night. Mama's first-born, James, had been a member for several years, having joined when he was about six years old. He said Reverend Poole called the sinners up front and opened the doors of the church right after Sunday school services. James knew what to say when he joined because he had seen and heard many other converts. Mama could relax now; her whole family was saved. Our church did not have the indoor plumbing required to fill a pool, so our baptism took place at Mount Pilgrim Baptist, another small black church a couple of miles away.

Baptism is a sacrament, so our congregation sang a number of solemn hymns while we new converts went to the back of the church to change our clothes. We dressed all in white, then were lined up according to height, basically resulting in younger children in front with adults at the end of the line. As the ritual began, the congregation repeatedly droned the song, "Take me to the water, take me to the water, take me to the water to be baptized." We were in a strange, dimly lit church—the lights may have been turned off in favor of lighted candles to create a properly sober atmosphere—but it was surreal to me. Adding to the unreality, all sound was muffled because the girls were wearing snug white swim caps with straps running under our chins that fastened below the ears. The caps were supposed to keep our hair from going back when we were dipped in the water. Rosie was in line immediately in front of me, but I felt alone and disconnected in the eerie scene. And, although I was rarely apprehensive, I was rigid with fear. Rosie, who shrieked in fear whenever she saw the tiniest crawling bug, was quietly sobbing. Reverend Charles Poole, our pastor, was a tall man, but the baptismal water was up to his waist. The deacon helping people down into the pool was wearing rubber hip boots. That water was deep! I watched as the smaller children descended the stairs and were handed off to the pastor. A couple of them looked as though they would be covered as soon as they stepped in the water because it was up to their chins. Each convert stood next to the pastor with his or her hands folded over the heart. The pastor put his right arm around the convert's shoulder or back, and his left hand over the convert's clasped hands. Then he said the person's name, and the words, "I baptize you in the name of the father, the son, and," he plunged the person's whole body backward into the water, "the holy ghost." It looked mighty scary to me. I didn't like the idea of getting my clothes wet or having my head under water. Reverend Poole was old. Maybe he could hold onto the smaller children, but what if he couldn't handle somebody as heavy as I was? Would I drown? I desperately wanted to escape, but obediently remained in line. As my turn got closer, my body quaked and my teeth chattered. Just as the deacon reached for Rosie, she darted behind me, "Janet, you go first." I wanted to snatch her back in front of me, but I knew Rosie was subject to have a tantrum right there, and get us both in serious trouble. I trembled my way down the steps, feeling the cold water soak into my clothes nearly up to my shoulders. Reverend Poole held out his hand and I went over to him. When he put his arm around my shoulder, I closed my eyes, clasped my hands in the proper position, and listened for the fateful phrase, "the son and..." Suddenly, Reverend Poole pushed me under and quickly lifted me back up. It was over. I waded through the chest-high water to the other side of the pool towards the extended hand of a church sister standing at the top of four steps. I didn't feel saved, but warm tears of relief welled up in my eyes because the frightening ordeal was over and Reverend Poole had not let go of me while I was underwater.

Aside from the music, church didn't appeal to me. I attended because I had no choice, but I rebelled in the small ways available to

Daddy was proud of his large Sunday school, here gathered on the front steps of the church in 1953. The first little girl you see standing on the ground is my cousin Margo Ransom whose presence helped me date the picture.

me. Like every other child and many of the adults in the church, I got new spring clothes for Easter, and new winter clothes at Christmas. Church was always crowded on Easter and the first Sunday after Christmas because everybody came out to show off their brand-new duds. Beginning when I was ten or so, I stopped wearing my new clothes on those two Sundays. I'd wait a couple of weeks, or perhaps a month, so I would be the only one in a new outfit. As we got older and partied late on Saturday nights, Daddy had trouble getting us out of bed on Sunday mornings. I have never wanted to do anything before 9 a.m., so getting me up was especially difficult. Daddy would wet my washcloth in cold water and drop it on my face to wake me up. He had a rule that no matter how old we were or how late we stayed out the night before, so long as we lived in his house we would go to Sunday school. "What will I look like telling other folks to bring their children to Sunday school if my own children don't go?" Daddy reinforced this rule with one of his many axioms, "You can't lead where you don't go, and you can't teach what you don't know."

To grow his Sunday school, Daddy began offering free trips to anybody who attended every Sunday and contributed to the collection. On these daylong bus trips we visited zoos (Indianapolis didn't have one at the time) and other places of interest in cities like Cincinnati, St. Louis, Detroit, and Chicago. Not only did attendance increase, but so did the treasury, outstripping the income from Sunday morning services. Later, after I had left home, Daddy began organizing overnight trips to places like Niagara Falls, Washington, D. C., and New York City. These trips allowed a lot of people who had never been beyond downtown Indianapolis, to see other parts of the country.

Our church, New Garfield Baptist, was a small frame structure with hard wooden pews that seated possibly two hundred people. It was located at the corner of Minnesota and Golay streets in a Negro neighborhood called Lovetown. Lovetown reminded me of Tennessee, where our relatives lived out in the country, because it resembled rural living more than our neighborhood less than two miles away. Lovetown was one of Indianapolis's several substandard Negro neighborhoods—within city limits, but without city infrastructure. The houses on Randolph Street where we lived were no more than ten feet apart. The street was paved, and we had sidewalks, sewers, and curbs. Lovetown had open fields, sparse housing, and the only paved street at the time was Minnesota. The other roads in the area soiled your Sunday shoes with either dust or mud. The toilets, including the one for church, were outhouses. We did everything possible to avoid the gag-inducing smell of the outhouse. My brothers could easily dart off into nearby bushes if they had to urinate, but Rosie and I were forced to use the outhouse if we couldn't hold on until we got home. We felt sorry for our friends and relatives who lived in Lovetown. Mama and Daddy however, decided to offer something more than pity.

Daddy knew that nothing would change in Lovetown unless the people living there insisted on it. To work on bringing city water to the area and getting sidewalks, in 1950 he and Mama organized the residents into the Southeast Civic League and Daddy was elected president. Together with Alene and Charles Crenshaw and other Lovetown families, my parents put in years of work and finally succeeded around 1954 in getting basic city amenities for the church and the surrounding neighborhood. After that achievement, the League acquired land next door to the church to build a community center for young people. Daddy plied his considerable talking skills to raise funds and to get needed materials donated for the building. Then he managed to convince the Indianapolis Parks Department to staff and operate the building.

Aside from Lovetown, Daddy was looked up to by many of the Negroes living in southeast Indianapolis. Not only was he a force in the church—Sunday school superintendent, chairman of the deacon board, and on the board of trustees—but he had chitlin customers in the area. He seemed to know everybody, and people came to him with their problems. If he couldn't resolve the situation himself, he would put them in touch with somebody who could. Daddy was also a Notary Public, which gave him a kind of official standing. Some folk even referred to him as "mayor of the southside," and he relished that. In 1954, the year I graduated high school, Daddy made the front page of the *Indianapolis Recorder* as Father of the Year. The *Recorder* cited his success in rearing four children, and his "loving and abiding interest in all children of the community." The article named Daddy's many activities, including his stint as general chairman of the Senate Avenue Y's recent membership drive.

In seeing to it that her children did not have the joyless child-hood she had experienced, Mama regularly made us great desserts. One of her quick treats was baking a cake in a flat pan and making a delicious sauce to pour over it. I have no idea what was in the sauce, but it was sweet and kind of lemony. I loved it. In the summers we often had homemade ice cream—usually on weekends or holidays. We knew we were going to have ice cream when we saw Daddy getting a big block of ice out of the car trunk. We would immediately run to the back porch and get one of Mama's galvanized tin washtubs and set it in the backyard. By the time Daddy came around the side of the house with the ice, the tub was waiting for him. Daddy placed the ice in the tub, then went to get his sharply pointed ice pick, because it was kept out of our reach. I liked watching Daddy repeatedly stabbing the block of ice to break it into pieces small enough to fit around the cylinder in the ice cream bucket. After Mama cooled the mixture of milk, cream, eggs, sugar, and vanilla flavor, she poured it into the gray metal cylinder. Daddy twisted the top on tight, then fit the handle on the dark green wooden bucket. The pieces of ice were placed around the cylinder along with some rock salt. Daddy said the salt made the ice cream freeze faster. Then the four children, sometimes joined by Raymond McClure or our cousin Ronald, took turns turning the handle that moved the dasher so that the mixture froze smoothly. You could tell when the ice cream was nearly ready because the handle was harder to turn. In our eagerness for the cold sweet taste of the ice cream and tiring of turning the handle, we often announced that it was ready before it reached the consistency Mama desired. We called her out to the backyard and watched while she checked it. Usually we had to keep churning. When the ice cream was finally ready, Mama removed the dasher to a plate where Reggie, Rosie, and I ate whatever ice cream was clinging to it. James disdained such childish behavior. Mama's homemade ice cream was so much better than what we bought at the store.

Mama's presence was to be expected. She was always there. But when Daddy was around, it was an occasion. With his jobs and volunteer work, he wasn't often there. Daddy took obvious pleasure in us, and his praise made me feel that I exceeded his expectations. That was a welcome respite from Mama harping on my shortcomings. Plus, Daddy was entertaining. In addition to stories about his experiences, he told jokes and had a saying for every occasion, like: "You have to stand for somethin' or you'll fall for anything." Some of his sayings were funny, "Don't worry 'bout the mule goin' blind, just sit in the slough and keep 'em alive." I think that meant you should do your own job and not concern yourself with what others were, or were not, doing. For every holiday Daddy did something special; he even bought red heart-shaped boxes of chocolates for Valentine's Day—a small one for us to share and a larger one for Mama. Mama would come up with ideas and plans for community activities for children, and Daddy would do the legwork required to pull them off. On Halloween we dressed in homemade costumes and went to a Sunday school party Daddy and the Sunday school teachers organized in the church basement. At the party, we played pin-the-tail-on-the-donkey and other games, bobbed for apples, and received little bags of candy. I don't know if going door-to-door saying, "trick or treat" was popular then; if so, we didn't do it. For sure, my parents would not have allowed us to eat anything given to us by unknown neighbors.

"You a story." We weren't allowed to call anybody a liar, so I said "story," the word Mama approved of. It was Christmas afternoon and James's claim horrified me. Like most children, we considered Christmas the best holiday, but when I was eight and James thirteen, he ruined it for me.

"For real. There is no Santa Claus." He emphasized each word. "Mama and Daddy bought all these toys."

"I don't believe you!" This couldn't be true.

"I helped 'em put the toys together. Come on. I'll show you the boxes they came in." I followed James to the basement and he showed me the discarded boxes in which our toys had been packed. *Santa Claus wasn't real?* Unbelievable! I was crushed. I didn't have the words for it then, but I could barely take in the idea that Mama and Daddy had lied to us. Why would they do that? I wanted to run tell Rosie and Reggie, probably so I'd have somebody to help share the burden. But James said I couldn't tell anybody. It was our secret. I felt some pride that my adored older brother and I shared a secret, but I was deeply hurt. Honesty was important in our family, and this didn't make sense. I kept the secret for a short time, but it was probably a matter of weeks before I told Reggie and Rosie. Learning at age eight that my parents had duped me for no good reason was so traumatic that when my own child was growing up I would not allow him to believe in Santa Claus. We celebrated the holiday, had a tree-trimming ritual, and I read him "The Night Before Christmas," but I also made damn sure he knew exactly who provided his gifts.

I wasn't about to confront my parents about their duplicity, so I didn't say anything to them. After a while I saw an advantage to knowing that Mama and Daddy, not Santa, picked out my toys. "Mama, I wish Santa Claus would bring me books; I don't want any more dolls." In the 1940s it was the custom to buy girls miniature household items—ironing boards, brooms, sewing machines, stoves, and every kind of doll, from virtual babies that could be "fed" to elegantly dressed stand-alone dolls. Every year Rosie and I each got identical new dolls. I would play with the toys while they were new but shortly lost interest. One year we got brown dolls. I was happy to see a doll that looked more like me, but it still didn't hold my attention for long. As a small child, I enjoyed cutting out and dressing paper dolls, all of whom, of course, were white. By the time Negro paper dolls came out in the 1950s, I was too old to be interested. Pretending to cook, sew, and change diapers was not really my thing. Once James had revealed the actual source of the toys, I decided to put an end to the Christmas dolls. Mama took the hint and from then on, along with new clothes and games, I started receiving books. My favorite, one that I read several times, was *Nancy Blake: Copywriter*. Nancy was a young aspiring writer who eventually got a job writing copy for an advertising agency. I secretly longed to have a career as a writer and that book encouraged me.

The most exciting Christmas gift we received was a film projector. We could barely believe the luxury of being able to see movies at home. We tacked a white sheet to the dining room wall, set the projector on the table and watched children's movies; the ones I remember best were the *Our Gang Comedy* series. I must have been around six years old at the time, so it was the early 1940s. Daddy was always attracted to technological innovations, and didn't hesitate to purchase items he believed would be useful or fun. So far as I know, we were the first black family on our block to get an electric refrigerator and a wringer washing machine. He also bought an electric carving knife for Mama. "I'm not using that thing. Somebody might get hurt." She wouldn't touch it and told us not to either. The knife remained in its box on a high shelf except when Daddy used it on Thanksgiving and Christmas turkeys.

We had big feasts on Thanksgiving and Christmas and ate in the dining room using our good dishes. The table was set in the morning, long before dinner was served, usually around two o'clock. My sister and I enjoyed making the table beautiful—spreading a white tablecloth that we had pressed the creases out of, using cloth rather than paper napkins, placing the silverware Daddy gave Mama for their twenty-fifth anniversary beside the plate in its proper places—forks on the left, knives and spoons on the right. Someday I'll find out how this protocol started and why we think it's so important. In our house, it was important only on holidays, or when we had company. The rest of the time we were quite casual, although we always sat down and ate together at a table, but it was usually in the kitchen not the dining room.

The smell of nutmeg, cinnamon, vanilla, and baking cakes permeated the house as Mama began preparing food days in advance. By the time Rosie and I were ten or so, we helped bake two- and three-layer cakes and learned to make and apply the icing. I made so many cakes I still remember the basic recipe. The day before the meal was served, we assisted in the preparation of the stuffing for the huge turkey Daddy bought. Then you could smell onions and celery being sautéed in butter, and the turkey neck and innards being cooked in preparation for pouring the broth over the broken pieces of stale bread and crumbled cornbread. When Mama poured on the hot liquid, you could smell the sage, rosemary, and thyme she'd added to the stuffing mix. Rosie and I mixed it all together.

The morning of the meal, Mama rose early to put the turkey on and that savory aroma awakened us. She also made gravy, adding the cut-up giblets, and cooked greens and green beans, mashed potatoes, fried corn, candied yams, and macaroni and cheese. For dessert we had yellow cake with chocolate icing, Daddy's favorite coconut cake, sweet potato pie, and fried pies—dough wrapped around a filling of sweetened dried fruit: peaches, apricots, or apples. Although we cooked with lard that Daddy brought home from work in ten-pound buckets, Mama maintained her childhood habit of limiting the shortening in her dough. It was never flaky enough to suit me. Sometimes, I would station myself nearby and insist that she use more lard. She was pleased with the results when she did, but left alone she continued to skimp.

I enjoyed the Christmas holidays tremendously. Not because we used our fancy dishes, but because I liked the lights, decorations, festiveness, and the steady flow of company. Everybody was in a good mood, smiling, laughing, being convivial. Friends and relatives stopped by for half an hour or half a day, including sometimes one or two guests for dinner. They were usually men who were alone—Uncle Oliver between wives; Cousin Lucian, who was divorced and lived in a rooming house; and, after his mother Aunt Christy died, Horace Mayweather, before he married and had his own family. We'd receive visits from kinfolk we rarely saw, like Mama's Uncle Shannon. Mama's mother was from a family like ours with two male and two female children. Both of the females died before age thirty, but their brothers, Maynard and Shannon, lived to be old men. Uncle Shannon was the proverbial rolling stone; wherever he laid his head was his home. We reveled in his occasional visits because he laughed a lot and told funny stories. Uncle Maynard was married with ten children. While

Mama and her sisters were growing up, Uncle Maynard and his family lived on the adjoining farm.

There was always plenty of food for our guests from Christmas Eve through New Year's Day. As visitors entered the house they greeted us with "Christmas Gift, Christmas Gift." We gifted them with a plate of food or a piece of cake or pie with a small glass of wine, or both; whatever they preferred. For some relatives, our cousin Horace in particular, there would also be a present under the tree. So far as I know, Christmas was the only time we had alcohol in our house. Daddy always brought home a bottle of Mogen David that we sipped with the cake. Even the children were allowed small amounts; the wine was as sweet as syrup.

On January 1, along with many other Negroes, my parents attended Emancipation Day services. These services were often held at Phillips Temple C.M.E. church on West Street, or one of the other large black churches. In 1946, there were five preachers on the program, and Reverend J. T. Highbaugh, the pastor of Good Samaritan Baptist Church, gave the main speech. Reverend Highbaugh was one of my parents' favorite preachers, and that day he talked about vigilance being the price of freedom, and said that freedom originates within the individual. In addition to spirituals and gospel songs by the Mount Paran Baptist Church choir, the congregation always sang the inspiring words of "Lift Every Voice and Sing," the Negro national anthem.

Emancipation Day commemorates the abolition of slavery in the rebellious Southern states. President Lincoln's proclamation said in part, "On the 1st day of January, A.D. 1863, all persons held as slaves within any State or designated part of a State the people whereof shall then be in rebellion against the United States shall be then, thenceforward, and forever free." This proclamation made Lincoln a hero to people of African descent even though those enslaved in the states *not* in rebellion—Indiana, for example—remained in bondage. In 1922, in an ironic reminder that they were still not free, Negroes were forced to stand behind a rope separating them from whites at the dedication of the Lincoln Memorial in Washington, D. C.

Our summer trips were possibly more precious to me than the Christmas holidays, and the preparations were equally extensive.

Reggie, Mama, and Rosie on a picnic table during a stop on one of our road trips, circa 1944.

Daddy had the motor and tires of his well-worn car thoroughly checked to preclude any breakdowns. With six people to provide for, Daddy was no longer able to purchase a new car every year. We had a beige two-door 1939 Chevrolet until he purchased a new black four-door Studebaker in 1950. Mama often stayed up all night before we left on a trip. Not only did she get our clothes ready and supervise the packing, she also baked a ham, made potato salad, fried chicken, baked beans, cooked ribs in barbecue sauce, and prepared Kool-Aid or lemonade, and a jug of water. We carefully covered the food and packed it in coolers and a large picnic basket. Sometimes Daddy filled a five-gallon Stumpf's can with iced bottles of pop. To avoid any *racial* incidents, and to save money, we didn't purchase anything along the road except gasoline. When we needed to relieve ourselves, we did so in bushes along the road using toilet paper we brought along. My parents knew we would either be refused access to gas station restrooms, or be directed to nasty facilities reserved for Negroes.

We stopped regularly because either driving made Daddy sleepy, or he was simply exhausted from the schedule he kept. Mama didn't drive and she watched him carefully, talking to him to make sure he stayed awake.

"Smith, are you awake?"

"Yeah, I'm awake."

"I saw you nodding off."

"I'm fine."

"No, you're not. I can see your eyes closing. Pull over at the next roadside table."

Two or three hours into a long trip, we stopped at a roadside picnic table and had lunch. Mama wiped the table off and spread a tablecloth. After we ate we helped put things away then stretched our legs by running and playing. Daddy unfolded the army cot he kept in the trunk and took a nap for about thirty minutes. Following this routine, a five-hour drive could take us eight hours. I remember that it took twelve hours for us to drive the four hundred miles to Chattanooga, Tennessee, but we didn't mind. It was like an extended picnic for us. We played games or read in the car, took naps, and ate and romped during our stops. I don't know how my mother held up, though. Not only did she work hard before we left, but she was the one person in the car who didn't get to nap during the trip. Yet, she continued to plan these excursions for us.

Every year on the third Sunday of July we drove "down home" to Woodlawn, Tennessee, for the rally, or homecoming, at Mama's childhood church. Traditionally, Negroes who had fled North for an easier life made annual pilgrimages to reconnect with family and old friends at official reunions. The date of these gatherings varied by locale. For years people talked about the bad accident Daddy, Mama, and Aunt Lula had on the way to one of these rallies. It happened before any of us were born. Everybody said when Daddy was young he drove as fast as he could. Both Mama and Aunt Lula were injured. After the accident they refused to ride with him for years. He'd drive to Tennessee and Mama and Aunt Lula would take the train. By the time we were all going down home, Mama was riding with Daddy again, and regularly telling him to slow down.

We stayed with Mama's sister, Aunt Virginia, and her husband, Daniel, whom we called Uncle Dawya. Their two children, Ophelia and Daniel, were already off on their own. Aunt Virginia and Uncle Dawya lived on a large farm and raised hogs, chickens, and lots of vegetables. Their cash crop was tobacco and, like many self-employed Negro landowners who remained in the South, they had less debt and more cash than their salaried Northern relatives. However, the amenities—electricity and indoor plumbing—that we took for granted in the city, had not yet been brought to their rural area. When we children first started going down home, we liked to watch Aunt Virginia add wood to the fire in the cook stove, and enjoyed pumping water in the front yard. The nighttime slop jars and outhouse were less appealing, but unavoidable. As we got older we became persnickety. Rosie and I in particular complained about the outhouse. As Daddy drove the family around to greet old friends, we started making fun of the country folk. Mama and Daddy scolded us for that, although we weren't foolish enough to say anything outside the car.

Reggie told me when he was about ten years old he and Daddy went for a drive while we were visiting in Tennessee. Daddy took Reggie to Bumpus Mills to show him the house where he had grown up. Reggie estimates that they drove probably twenty-five miles from Aunt Virginia's home in Woodlawn. They turned onto a dirt road and went as far as they could, then got out of the car and walked about half a mile to reach the abandoned house, surrounded by tall weeds. Reggie said the house was small—four rooms plus a kitchen—with old newspapers covering the walls. The front door was missing and Daddy pointed out that the out buildings—barn, shed, and toilet— were gone. Daddy seemed pleased to be able to show his little boy where he had lived as a child. They spent half an hour looking the place over.

Probably when I was in my early teens, instead of the family going to Tennessee, we started visiting Aunt Zeffie, Daddy's sister. Aunt Zeffie was Mama's favorite Cheatham relative, and the only one of Daddy's siblings to graduate from high school. Mama considered her intelligent and refined. Aunt Zeffie and Uncle Thomas lived in Wayne, Michigan, a rural area then, but now a Detroit suburb that has been renamed Romulus. They had two children, Roland, six months younger than I, and Diane, four years younger than the twins. Two more of Daddy's sisters, Aunt Ovella and Aunt Hazel lived in Detroit. They would come out to visit and bring Aunt Ovella's children—Delores Ann, Michael, and Kenny. Delores Ann was a year younger than I, and her brothers were around Diane's age. Best of all, the Beanum

Arthur Beanum sitting atop a tractor at our Michigan relatives' farm, circa 1950. Behind Arthur you can see two of the three homes in the compound, and the roof of the third.

brothers—Uncle Thomas and his siblings, Isaac and Eddie—lived in three houses that stood in a row about fifty yards apart. Within that family compound were ten children, in a range of ages that encompassed all four of us. The Beanums owned thirty contiguous acres that they farmed with their families. We loved going to Michigan and our cousins also came to visit us. Nobody had guest rooms. Part of the fun of these visits was that we children gave our beds to the adults and we slept on pallets on the living room floor. It was our version of a slumber party.

We also went to tourist destinations like Chattanooga's Lookout Mountain and Mammoth Cave in Kentucky near Louisville. I recently learned that in the 1830s black men discovered all but the first few miles of the more than 350 miles of known passageways in the cave. Because they knew the inside of the cave so well, these intrepid explorers also served as guides for tourists. They were being held in bondage at the time and no doubt preferred their underground assignments to hard labor in the hot sun awaiting them outside. At home we took jaunts to the Children's Museum, the Indianapolis Museum of Art, and Indiana's state parks. We didn't see other Negroes when we visited the museums and state parks. As an adult I learned that during my childhood these places were either customarily or officially off-limits to Negroes. Park employees had run a group of Negroes out of a state park in 1945, although the park director said those employees had exceeded their authority. So far as I can remember, the only overt act of discrimination we encountered was at Brown County State Park where James and his friend Raymond were refused entry to the swimming pool. They were disappointed, but not surprised; *racial* barriers were likely to pop up anywhere. We also knew that we were not allowed to eat or stay overnight at the state park inns, but that didn't affect us because we brought our own food and returned home after a day of frolicking.

Our trips to the state parks are a favorite memory from my childhood. Indiana has one of the nation's best state park systems. The first park was acquired in celebration of Indiana's centennial in 1916. Several of the parks have quirky descriptive names like Clifty Falls, Turkey Run, Chain O' Lakes, Potato Creek, and Spring Mill. Other parks have Indian names—Mississinewa, Pokagon, Ouabache. Over

Rosie and Reggie (front), Ronald and me at a state park, circa 1944.

the years we visited more than half of the twenty-two parks Indiana had then. We hiked the trails in the thick virgin forests, struggled up sand dunes, explored dank caves, and were fascinated by the animals, reptiles, and birds at the nature centers. After exhausting ourselves, we selected a prime spot beside a lake or overlooking a waterfall and enjoyed a bountiful meal.

After years of effort to make our childhoods memorable and their community a better place, it was gratifying to see my parents relax a bit. When all of us were grown up and gone, and the parks had been desegregated, Mama and Daddy took pleasure in driving to a state park, taking a scenic walk, then having a leisurely repast at the one of the inns.

Chapter 5

Warring Ideals

One ever feels his twoness—an American, a Negro; two souls, two thoughts, two unreconciled strivings; two warring ideals in one dark body, whose dogged strength alone keeps it from being torn asunder.

~ W.E.B. DuBois in *The Souls of Black Folk*

In addition to our relatives in Tennessee and Michigan, we had plenty of family in Indianapolis. Grandma and Grandpa, Daddy's parents, lived on the west side of town and we visited them regularly, usually on Sunday afternoons. At their house, we might see one or more of Daddy's brothers: Oliver, William Rozell, or Samuel. Daddy was the oldest remaining sibling, and they regarded him as the head of the Cheatham clan, respectfully calling him Brother. Uncle Oliver, next oldest among the males was light brown-skinned and strikingly handsome, though not so tall as Daddy. Uncle Oliver always worked, but he was not interested in acquiring things. Mama thought his first wife left him after twenty years of marriage because "he didn't have a thing to show for the money he made." Uncle Sam, the youngest, was dark-skinned and you could nearly imagine how handsome he would be if he weren't so overweight. He seemed short-tempered, but his wife Elnora was devoted to him.

Although there was about a fifteen-year difference in their ages, Daddy was closest to Uncle Rozell. They worked together in the chitlin business and he joined Daddy in volunteering at the YMCA. Uncle Rozell was also the only uncle who had children. Norma Rosetta and James William lived in Lovetown with their mother, Aunt Frances, who was divorced from Uncle Rozell when we were quite young. James William was born six months after the twins,

Daddy's family of origin, plus one, in 1937. Back row, left to right: Christy, Smith (Daddy), Lillian (Grandma), James (Grandpa), Bertha, Viola, Oliver. Front row: Zeffie, Ovella, William Rozell, James Henry (my older brother), Samuel, Hazel. The siblings are arranged in birth order. Harris Brothers Studio

and Norma was three years younger than he. We saw them regularly because we all attended the same church. Uncle Rozell was no better looking than his brothers, but women seemed to find him irresistible. And the feeling was mutual; he was a Cat. His second wife was named Anne, and they had two daughters, Jo Anne and Carolyn. We saw them fairly often while Uncle Rozell and Anne were married, but once they divorced, we didn't see them much. His third, and last wife, Ruby was a much younger woman. They adopted a son Michael who is the same age as my nephew Michael.

Daddy's older sister Christy died when we were small, and of his five remaining sisters only Aunt Bertha lived in Indianapolis, in Norwood, a neighborhood on the south side not far from us. Aunt Viola lived in Hagerstown, Indiana near Richmond, and the other three sisters were in Michigan. Mama didn't join us for the Sunday visits to our grandparents; she liked Aunt Zeffie, but otherwise she could do without Daddy's boisterous family. I also imagine she relished the rare opportunity to have some time alone.

Like many people as they age, Mama saw the past and her own generation in euphoric terms. She described it as more stable than mine with fewer out of wedlock births and "broken homes." But as I learned more about our family, I asked Mama about the several "illegitimate" children and divorces in her generation. Mama had two older half-sisters whose mother was never married to Papa Halyard, my grandfather. Daddy hadn't been married before Mama, but he already had a daughter. Mama's Uncle Shannon also had a daughter outside of marriage. So far as I know, these men did not deny parentage, or refuse to care for their offspring, but they also did not marry their mothers. And divorce was not unusual either. Only Daddy and three other of the ten siblings in his family stayed married until they were parted by death. For whatever reasons, I had many relatives with the spirit to defy convention and seek happiness in their own ways. I salute them for making the effort. Mama's younger sister, Aunt Lula said, "Even if I had met the perfect man, I don't think I could have stayed with him for the rest of my life." I came to understand exactly what she meant.

When I was about ten years old Aunt Lula bought a house on Randolph Street, two doors away from us. A few years later, my cousin Mary Ophelia Ransom, Aunt Virginia's daughter, and her husband Frank rented the house next door to Aunt Lula. I had admired Ophelia since she visited us when I was five years old. At the time, she

My glamorous cousin Ophelia and me. Taken on Randolph Street facing our house around 1944 when I was 7 and she was 20. The house behind us is where I later worked as a babysitter.

was eighteen and had just graduated from high school. She wanted to join some friends who were moving to Washington, D. C. to take government jobs, but Aunt Virginia wouldn't hear of it. Ophelia was so disappointed that Mama, who was there to attend Ophelia's graduation, invited her to come to Indianapolis. Ophelia grabbed that opportunity to get out of Woodlawn and happily returned home with Mama. To me, Ophelia was a glamorous child-woman. She towered over me the way adults did; yet seemed to treat me like a peer. I was entranced by her. Mama felt that Ophelia needed someone her own age to run around with, so she invited Fellie to visit. Fellie lived in Hopkinsville, Kentucky, and was Daddy's teenage daughter from a previous relationship. That was the first time I met my half-sister. Fellie was deemed illegitimate, a word most often spoken sotto voce. It was many years before I figured out that the word *illegitimate* could be applied to situations other than people born outside marriage. Although Mama welcomed her into our home, Fellie remained a shadowy figure whose name rarely came up. I think Daddy visited her periodically, but we saw her only two or three more times, and I never got to know her. Even now I have no idea where she and her children are.

Ophelia stayed with us from June until December, then returned to Tennessee. Four months later, she married Frank Ransom. When they moved to Randolph, she and Frank had a four-year-old daughter, Patricia Elaine, and were expecting their second child. Everybody, including me, assumed they'd have a boy and several boy's names had been suggested. When a girl was born, we had to scramble to name her. Ophelia chose Belinda, a name I didn't care for, so I suggested Denise. They named her Belinda Denise. I was thirteen at the time, and flattered that everybody called her Denise, the name I had chosen. Twenty months later Ophelia had another daughter, Margo Rochelle. With family all around, childcare was never an issue. The only time the term "babysitter" was used was when someone outside the family hired Rosie or me to care for their children. A white couple that had recently moved in across the street from us had two young sons that I sat with occasionally for fifty cents an hour. When Rosie was fourteen, she took care of a set of twin boys all day during the summers for Uncle Oliver's sister-in-law. It was Rosie's first job. She liked the idea of being a twin taking care of twins.

Cousin Nannie and her husband, Allen Brewer, bought a house next door to the couple I sat for. Nannie was Mama's younger cousin, and the fifth of Uncle Maynard's ten children. Mama and Nannie had grown up together on adjoining farms. Interestingly, except for Cousin Nannie and Allen, all the Negro families on Randolph Street lived next door to one another on the same side of the street.

Aunt Lula was my favorite relative. She was so hip! She was proud of her trim figure and often described the fancy clothes she wore to the parties and dances she'd attended when she was younger. Aunt Lula also told me about her many beaus and how she dealt with them, information that I remembered and used. She'd end these little stories with the expression, "I have *had* my fun!" I was enraptured listening to her talk about her life. I wanted to be like her—an independent, fashionable woman, with her own income, who enjoyed life. She said she had worked in a defense plant during World War II and made good money. But women and blacks had had to relinquish factory work to white males returning from the war. The federal government's Fair Employment Practices Commission "indicated that at the end of the war, [Negroes] in Indianapolis suffered a more severe setback in job opportunities than did [Negroes] in many other cities." Aunt Lula had no choice but to go back to the maid service otherwise known as day work. Single or married, Aunt Lula worked every day. She rode the bus to her day work jobs, and sometimes it was dark when she returned home. Whenever she was out after dark, Aunt Lula took out her pocketknife, opened it, and carried it in her hand covered with a handkerchief. When I asked her why she didn't keep the knife in her purse, she replied, "If somebody messes with me, I won't have time to look for the knife, then open it. This way, I'm ready for 'em." I thought that was so smart. So far as I know she never had to use the knife to defend herself. Aunt Lula was in the third of her five marriages when they moved to Randolph.

Ronald, Aunt Lula's only child, was three months younger than I. During the school year, Mama kept Ronald until Aunt Lula got home from work. He spent his summers in Tennessee with Aunt Virginia. When he was around, Ronald was my best friend and favorite playmate. We spent a lot of time together and shared confidences. Ronald had little regard for the rules laid down by our parents and was always challenging me to disobey them as well. He'd call me a scaredy-cat if

I wouldn't go along with him. I wasn't scared, and didn't want Ronald to think so, but I was concerned about disappointing Mama. She called me her good girl, unlike Rosie who Mama said, "was born hollerin' and hasn't shut up since." Ronald was the first person to encourage me to be myself and take risks.

Ronald dared Reggie, Rosie, and me to explore further and further from home and finally shamed us into going down a precipitous ravine to cross Pleasant Run Creek. The creek usually had no more than three or four inches of water, so it was possible to cross it without getting wet by stepping from stone to stone. However, after a series of heavy rains, the creek could rise to three or four feet of rushing, swirling water that could have easily overwhelmed a young child. It was only two blocks from our house, but Mama had strictly prohibited our going down the steep banks, ever. The forbidden act was exciting, and we did it over and over again. But I never stopped being uneasy about it because I thought Mama would find out. I believed she could read disobedience and guilt in my face, and more than anything I didn't want to lose Mama's regard for me.

Ronald told me about his plans to travel around the world, to go to college and become a doctor or a lawyer, to write books, to pilot airplanes. Every time we talked he had a new idea about how he would become rich and famous. When I told Mama about his dreams, she said, "That boy's not going to do a thing. He's just building air castles." To please Mama, I adopted her disdain, but I still liked to hear Ronald's plans.

When he was a toddler Ronald's dad died, and Aunt Lula had married Leonard Thompson when Ronald was about six. We seldom visited Aunt Lula's house while Uncle Leonard was there, and Ronald told me Leonard was a drunk who beat him and his mother. One night Aunt Lula and Ronald pounded on our door in a panic. Leonard was drunk and tearing up everything in his path. They spent the night with us, and Mama took the opportunity to tell her sister she needed to divorce Leonard. Aunt Lula agreed but obviously changed her mind, because things continued as they were. By the time Ronald was twelve years old he was tall and husky, and also generally considered a difficult child. Although he was smart as a whip, he was not doing well in school and had fallen two years behind me. That was when Ronald told me he and Leonard were having fights because he no longer allowed Leonard to hit him or Aunt Lula. Within a few months, Leonard moved out. Ronald was ecstatic.

Besides the drunken Leonard, Ronald may also have been troubled because he was much lighter-skinned than other members of his family. In a family portrait with his parents, his half-brother and half-sister, Ronald looked like a lemon drop in a box of dark chocolates. People of African descent come in varying shades of skin color, and in this country that has been a thorny issue. Children whose skin tone is different than other family members—either lighter or darker—sometimes feel like outsiders. Fortunately, that was not a significant issue in my family. Both sets of my grandparents had one dark-brown spouse and the other one a few shades lighter. Consequently my uncles, aunts, and cousins are a range of colors. In referring to her own children, Mama was fond of saying, "One good thing, everybody in *this* family is the same color: medium-brown-skinned—not too light and not too dark." Her alleged satisfaction with our color, however, did not prevent her from encouraging her daughters to use Nadinola. Mama specialized in mixed messages and this was one of them.

"Mama, this is bleaching cream. I don't want this stuff on my face." I think I was about sixteen when Reggie pointed out that the Nadinola Mama bought for Rosie and me to use on our faces was designed to lighten the skin. Mama had given it to us when we reached puberty, saying that it would keep our skin smooth and blemish-free. Surprisingly, I hadn't read the label, but when I did, I discovered that Reggie was right. On the color scale I was somewhere in the middle, I guess, and never felt self-conscious about my skin pigment. I knew there were guys who only dated girls who were light-skinned, and some who preferred those with darker skins. There were also folks who did not want to be seen with anybody whose skin color varied much from their own, but the people I knew—family, friends, as well as the guys I dated—spanned the color spectrum. Since I had no desire to be any lighter, I stopped using Nadinola and told Mama why. She seemed embarrassed, and insisted that she had recommended it merely to keep our skin smooth.

Negroes had an entire lexicon to identify our various skin colors. Although there were some regional differences in the descriptive terms, the variations were slight. Growing up I heard phrases and terms such as coal black, jet black, smooth black, dusty black, chocolate brown, light brown, paper bag brown, redbone, meriny, café au lait, high yella, and light, bright, damn near white. In addition to the descriptive terms for skin color, Negroes who were striving to increase or maintain their perceived social standing, had a hierarchy based on skin color differences that meant the more someone resembled whites in appearance and behavior, the higher their status. I knew one dark-skinned middle-class matriarch who insisted that her children and grandchildren select spouses who would help lighten up the family.

At the other extreme were Negroes who rejected everything about their oppressors, including their skin color. Their motto was, the blacker the berry, the sweeter the juice. Before the Civil Rights Movement of the 1960s, I rarely encountered blacks who accepted their African heritage with no regard for how they imagined whites perceived them. Women were the most devastated by these color appraisals. Education or money could ameliorate a man's color, but black women, like white women, were judged primarily on their appearance. Whatever the perspective, the emphasis on skin color is a preoccupation shared by most Americans. Not surprisingly, this fixation on skin color appears in our literature and music. A number of early Negro novels and stories were written about the difficulties of Negroes who were light enough to pass—Nella Larsen's *Passing* and Charles Chesnutt's *The Wife of His Youth* are but two of the many tragic mulatto works. Toni Morrison turned that convention on its head in her contemporary novel, *Paradise,* about Negroes who prize dark skin. A blues song, "Yellow and Brown Woman" also examines the skin color obsession,

> You can have your high yella,
> but black and brown is what I crave.
> You keep messin' up with them yella women,
> they'll put you in your lonesome grave.

I noticed that there seemed to be an unspoken rule that a Negro man who had worked hard to obtain an education, or succeeded in making money, should have a light-skinned wife to accompany his achievement. The background and education of the light-skinned woman hardly mattered, but if she happened to be educated, so much the better. The ultimate sign of status and financial prosperity was the Negro man who had an educated, light-skinned wife who, astonishingly, did volunteer work instead of taking a job. Nearly all Negro women worked outside their homes, either daily, or like my mom, part-time. That's why Negroes found it amusing that one of the primary goals of the Women's Movement in the 1970s was to liberate women to the workplace. Negro families sacrificed to educate their daughters, so that when they did go to work at least it would not be scrubbing floors and doing laundry. Madam C. J. Walker, the brilliant and enterprising black woman who became wealthy while revolution-izing hair care for Negro women, attracted legions of them to sell her products. By working for Madam Walker, either as a sales agent or a hairdresser, Negro women could earn more money than they brought home from laboring in somebody else's kitchen. Industrious agents could even make more than the few educated Negro women, and do it without first having to scrape together money for college.

Ronald had never said a word about his skin color until one morning when we were walking to school. We were twelve years old at the time.

"Mother told me that Earl Banner is my real father. That's why I don't look like anybody."

Earl Banner was a man we both knew because he occasionally attended our church, and Mrs. Banner sang in the choir with Mama. The Banners lived in Lovetown, had no children, and were consid-ered relatively well off. I thought Ronald was fantasizing again. I, too, had had fantasies that my "real" parents were wealthy and lived in a big house where I could have my own room, and everything else I wanted. But I never said any of this out loud. It was just like Ronald to put into words things I barely dared think about.

"Earl Banner? I don't believe that. Mr. Banner doesn't have any children!"

Ronald insisted that his mom had told him Mr. Banner was his dad. I didn't know whether or not to believe him. And I couldn't ask anybody because he had sworn me to secrecy. So I chalked it up to his active imagination.

I didn't remember Ronald's dad because he died when we were quite small, but their family portrait was among the photos on display in our house. I took it down to look at it again. Ronald was right! He didn't resemble the other members of his family. Not only was his skin lighter than everybody else's, but he also had curly, rather than kinky, hair. The next time I saw Mr. Banner, I took a good long look. I was shocked! Ronald did look like Mr. Banner! He might actually be telling the truth. Secret or not, I had to ask Mama about this. Unexpectedly, Mama wasn't a bit ruffled by what she would ordinarily consider an improper, womanish question.

"Yes, Lula told me about that. I don't know why she wanted to get that boy all worked up. Talkin' 'bout he was interested in his cousin. Lord knows he wasn't about to marry the girl!" Apparently, Ronald had told his mother that he liked a girl, who in fact, was his first cousin. Mama emphatically disapproved of Aunt Lula's having revealed the long-held secret.

Ronald started bragging about his dad, and what his dad owned, and how much money his dad had. I got really sick of it. Plus I was more than a little jealous of this romantic turn in his life. One day I challenged him. "What difference does it make how rich your *dad* is? It's not doing you any good!" Perhaps my taunting affected him because Ronald decided to go see Mr. Banner and ask him for some money. I learned about the visit from Mama. Ronald didn't tell me that Mr. Banner refused to talk to him except to tell him not to ever come to his house again. Ronald stopped talking about his dad. More than twenty years later, within days of his wife's death, Mr. Banner asked Aunt Lula to marry him. We were all astonished, but Aunt Lula didn't seem surprised. Mama decided that Aunt Lula had kept the relationship going over the years. Aunt Lula told Mr. Banner she'd marry him on one condition: he had to make Ronald his heir. He agreed. When Aunt Lula and Earl Banner were married just two months after his wife's death, her family was incensed. The Lovetown gossips bad-mouthed Aunt Lula for years. At the time Ronald was an adult, married with eight children, but he was delighted that at last, he was welcome in his father's house.

In Ronald's case, skin color and hair texture made him look different from his family, but as a male he didn't have to be concerned about daily appraisals of his looks based on that criteria. For girls, not only skin color but the length and texture of your hair were factored into the evaluation of your appearance. And that's where I had a big problem, especially within my family.

"I don't know what I'm going to do with your nappy head." Mama complained about how difficult it was to straighten my hair. "Your hair's so short I get cramps in my fingers trying to make it look like something." If Mama had not been cut off from her ancestral traditions, she would have known that the best way for my hair to grow was to leave it alone. In recent years, urged on by my son, I have done just that by adopting the hairstyle called dreadlocks. Now I know why most Africans did not let their hair grow; it's like having a thick wool blanket draped over your head, neck, and shoulders. In hot weather all that hair can be unbearable. Of course Mama would be appalled by my locks because they are the antithesis of straight hair.

To prepare for church on Sunday, we had the ritual of the hot comb on Saturday. In the kitchen I sat on a low seat between Mama's knees. After washing and carefully drying my hair, Mama parted off a small section and pinned down the remaining hair. To straighten my hair she used a metal comb with close-set teeth and a wooden handle. She put the metal part of the comb in the fire of the gas-stove burner. While the comb heated, she applied Madam Walker's Glossine or Dixie Peach pomade to the parted off section of my kinky hair. She started with the edges, the hair on the side of the face in front of the ears where new hair grows out first. When the comb was hot enough to straighten out the naps, but not too hot—determined by testing it on a towel, if the comb burned the towel, it was too hot—Mama pulled it through my hair. Voilà! The crinkly hair flattened out. The principle is the same as applying a hot iron to wrinkled clothes. If my hair was not completely dry, steam hissed and burned my scalp. I hated having my hair straightened. In addition to the astringent smell of sizzling hair and grease, Mama would sometimes burn my scalp, my ears, and especially my neck when she was getting at the kitchen, the hair at the bottom of the head on the neck. She said my hair was so nappy it took a lot of heat to straighten it. When she wanted it to look especially "nice," she used pullers. Pullers opened like tongs, with a knob on each business end. After the iron pullers were heated, a few strands of hair were caught between the flat sides of the knobs and pulled. It was torture.

I was the first girl born to Daddy and his siblings, and they were so dismayed by the texture of my hair they took drastic measures. Mama said Daddy's sisters cut all my hair off when I was about a year old. They believed my hair would grow back longer and more like theirs—wavy and soft. Mama had insisted that enough hair be left for a ribbon so that people would know I was a girl. I can imagine how painful that must have been for her because my hair was very much like hers. I suppose everybody was relieved when Rosie came along. She was bald for quite awhile, but when her hair grew in, it was softer, easier to straighten, and grew longer than mine. When we were older and wanted our hair styled rather than in braids, we went to a beauty shop for a professional do. Although the professionals didn't burn me, I still found the procedure repugnant. I detested making an appointment, then waiting as much as four hours to be served. I didn't like the way beauticians and their clients raved about "good" hair, meaning hair that was closer to the texture of white folks' hair, then gossiped about people after they left the shop. Moisture of any kind was devastating to straightened hair, instantly reverting it to its original kinks. That's largely why Negro girls tried to avoid perspiring, and never put their heads under water in a swimming pool. Nobody ever made a swimming cap capable of keeping our hair from going back. I longed to be rid of the constant effort to keep my hair looking "presentable," but it was absolutely verboten for a woman to be seen in public with kinky hair. In the early 1960s chemical compounds were developed so beauticians could straighten hair permanently, meaning until new kinky hair grew out. I immediately tried that.

Chemically processed hair was impervious to moisture, so it seemed like the perfect solution. I would no longer need to go to the beauty shop every two weeks, praying that my hair didn't go back in the interim. A chemical perm could last for several months, with occasional touch ups to the edges and kitchen. After a couple of years of perms, the harsh chemicals damaged my hair, leaving me with a bald patch on the right side of my head. I imagined everybody would stare at the bare spot making me an object of derision, so I bought a wig. What can I say? I was young and still wanting to fit in. I was never comfortable in that wig. The "hair" looked artificial and it felt like I was wearing a hat all the time. In warm weather it was nearly unbearable.

Finally, in 1966, two years after I left Indiana, I threw the wig away, had my hair cut, and stopped having it straightened. The Civil Rights Movement had been startled by Stokely Carmichael's call for Black Power and many of us seized that idea to recast our identity. We became black instead of Negro, and considered straightened hair to be an indicator of a slave mentality. Even James Brown stopped straightening his hair. When I began wearing my hair in its natural state, it wasn't yet widely acceptable. When I came home to visit, Mama was so dismayed that I was displaying my kinks that she asked me to wear a hat to church. When I refused, she lost her interest in my religious upkeep. One summer while I was in town, Rosie and her husband Gordon had a party at their house on Capital Avenue. Rosie asked me not to attend because she didn't want her friends to see my nappy hair. I didn't mind because Rosie's friends didn't interest me that much. However, Daddy was outraged when he heard about it, and he let Rosie know it. Cutting my hair and wearing it natural was relatively simple, and a hip political statement, but my weight was another matter altogether.

As far back as I can remember I'd heard a litany of despairing complaints from Mama about my size. "You're going to be as wide as you are tall, just like those Cheatham women."

I stood up as straight as I could and silently prayed, PLEASE, GOD, LET ME BE TALL LIKE MAMA.

When we were shopping, she'd shake her head and say, "You're so big nothing fits you right."

I lowered my head in shame. "I'm sorry, Mama."

When I was twelve Mama bought me a corset. "With that behind of yours, you've got to wear a girdle."

The girdle had stiff plastic stays inserted in the elastic band around the waist. The unyielding elastic that covered my stomach and buttocks felt like two boards strapped to my body; bending forward was so difficult that I avoided doing so whenever I could. My body was restricted from just under my breasts to an inch or so below my crotch. I lived to get home and take it off, but I never left home without it, believing that if I did, my wobbling fat would lead to public ridicule. James added to my misery by teasing that I would never have a boyfriend because I was so fat. He said the same thing about Rosie for the opposite reason; she was too skinny.

The female attendants at Rosie's spectacular rose-themed wedding where we all wore white and each carried a single rose. (l-r); junior bridesmaid, Rita Britt; bridesmaids Brenda Dickey and Betsy Campbell. Slender me, the matron of honor; flower girl, Terry Lyons; and the bride. Our cousin, Norma Cheatham, maid of honor; bridesmaids Jean Avery and Artila Wilkerson; and junior bridesmaid, Sheila Williams. Courtesy of Gordon E. Mickey

I lived and dieted with the disgrace of being fat. As a kid I ate whatever Mama cooked, and she cooked big meals to make up for sometimes having had meager meals in her own childhood. Mama encouraged us to eat heartily and never asked anybody to diet. At the same time, however, she was constantly talking about how big I was and how difficult it was to find clothing for me. Friends and family members, regularly complimented me on the way I looked, but I didn't take them seriously; I knew I was fat. I think my first real diet was the one I went on for Rosie's wedding. I was twenty-five and had been married a couple of years. My husband had picked up where Mama left off, telling me I was too heavy, except that he went a step further and told me I needed to lose weight. I was to be Rosie's matron of honor, and along with her seven other attendants, went shopping for dresses. All the other young women were sizes thirteen and under. I required a size fifteen. On the spot I decided that I would not be the biggest woman in the wedding. I ordered a size thirteen. That was in February or March. For the next several months I religiously counted calories, eating primarily salads with lo-cal dressing and lean meat. I banished desserts and bread altogether. By June, I slipped into my size thirteen with room to spare; it had to be taken in. When James came home on leave from the army, he told me I looked like I had TB. From that point on, I periodically went on crash diets to "look good" for a special event, or for some other illusory reason. Not until I was in my forties did I finally accept the idea that my size was not a hindrance, and stopped focusing on it. I had long since given up girdles and at that point I also quit dieting.

I was fifty-two when my mother died. Reggie cleaned out her house and sent each of us our pictures from Mama's collection. I looked at the pictures of myself taken over the years, beginning with some before I could walk all the way to the present. I got the shock of my life. I WAS NEVER FAT! In one photo, I looked absolutely lean, probably in my late thirties when I was on the grapefruit diet. I was a well-rounded child, but at no time was I fat. Not thin, mind you, but not fat either. I couldn't believe that I had suffered so much for so long over something that wasn't real. I had looked at every one of those pictures on many occasions, but for the first time, I could actually *see* myself. As the enormity of the fraud seeped into my mind I completely understood a phrase I'd heard many times that each person creates her own reality. Although America's standard for what makes a woman beautiful had long disparaged everything African, like so many others, my mother, as intelligent and proud as she was, had succumbed to that standard and passed it on to me. Mama—a large woman with short, kinky hair—looked at me and saw herself.

Chapter 6

Powerful Lessons

Education can be one of the most liberating forces in
the world, but it can also be one of the most oppressive.
Twelve years of segregated schooling teaches you some
powerful lessons not featured in textbooks.

~ Robert L. Green in
The Urban Challenge—Poverty and Race

Of the white families on our block, we were friendliest with the
Rickerts, but even with them our visits didn't go beyond the front
porch of either house. They had a daughter Betty, whose birthday
was the day before mine, and a son Virgil, who was the same age as
James. Betty and I played together outside, and when we were about
five we talked about soon going to school like our older brothers.
We could see School 20 from the sidewalk; it was about three blocks
away. The school was a sprawling, relatively new tan brick building,
sitting on a grassy rise on the other side of Pleasant Run Creek. I told
Mama that Betty and I were going to walk to school together.

Mama sat down and pulled me into her arms. "You and Betty
won't be going to the same school."

"How come? James and Virgil go to school together."

"No, they don't. They walk to the corner together, then James
goes to his school and Virgil goes to the school down the street."

I had no idea that James walked past the school we could see to
another smaller building farther away. I learned that all the Negro
children in that section of Indianapolis in grades one through eight
were bused to Frederick Douglass School 19 at 1624 Quill Street. We
lived slightly less than a mile from the school and weren't eligible for
a bus ride. Thirteen years earlier, we would have attended School 20
on Pleasant Run Boulevard.

Indiana has had a difficult time trying to decide whether Negroes and whites could be educated together, or should have separate facilities. Before 1843, each community made that decision—some allowed Negroes to attend school with whites while others did not. At the time, not all Negroes in Indiana were free to attend school; some were being held in slavery. In 1843, the Indiana legislature decreed that public schools in the state were for whites only. Negroes were outraged; what was the point of being free if you couldn't be educated? They set up their own schools while also petitioning the legislature to include them in public education. After battling for twenty-six years, in 1869 Negroes finally succeeded in having the legislature pass an act requiring school trustees to set up schools for colored children. These schools were to be opened only when there were enough colored children within "a reasonable distance" of each other to justify a separate school. Negroes challenged that law as well, because some children were still left without public education. Eight years later, in 1877, the law was amended to read, "Colored children shall be allowed to attend the public schools with white children" in places where there was no colored school.

In Indianapolis there were a number of Negro families like ours who lived in predominately white areas. The 1877 amendment permitted those Negroes to attend elementary school with whites. There was no colored high school in the city; every Negro who went beyond eighth grade attended the same high schools as whites. This stew of integrated high schools and some segregated and some integrated elementary schools was the way of life in Indianapolis for the next fifty years. A few years after World War I ended in 1918, the *racists* who started the White Supremacy League demanded more rigid segregation and made schools a major focus of their campaign. By 1925 whites began to clamor for a separate high school for Negroes. At the time, "there were over one thousand Negroes attending the four" Indianapolis high schools. They also wanted Negroes out of "their" elementary schools. Daddy had just arrived in the city, and Mama was still in Tennessee, when the NAACP and other groups presented a petition to the Board of Education strenuously objecting to separate schools for Negroes. The petitioners particularly opposed the construction of a colored high school. Their objections were ignored however, and a new high school was built for the exclusive use of Negroes.

In a move that was both patronizing and insulting, the Board of School Commissioners named the new building the Thomas Jefferson High School. Indianapolis's Negroes were offended by that choice and insisted that the school be named for a colored hero, rather than a white man who had held our ancestors as his property. Negroes chose the name Crispus Attucks, to honor the first person killed in the Boston Massacre of 1770, a skirmish considered the opening battle of the Revolutionary War. The board relented, and in the fall of 1927, three months after Mama and Daddy married, Crispus Attucks High School opened. All Negro students were pulled out of the other high schools and ordered to enroll in Attucks. By 1929, the elementary schools in Indianapolis were completely segregated as well. For the next twenty years the Indianapolis Board of Education operated two school systems—one for Negroes, the other for whites.

Thirteen years after this particular separation of the *races* in Indianapolis schools, Mama told me I wouldn't be going to school with Betty. I was five years old and it made no sense to me. I just kept asking the same question: "Why can't I go to school with Betty?" Mama's answers didn't satisfy me so I stomped. I cried. I sulked.

While I was still fuming about not walking to school with Betty, Mama announced that I could go to school with James. Oh, happy day! I longed to imitate whatever James was doing, so I had already gotten Mama to teach me how to read and write. At the time, kindergarten was not mandatory in Indiana. The mandate was that children must begin first grade in the September following their sixth birthday. A child could enroll in the September prior to their sixth birthday, if that birthday occured before November. I have no idea how my parents did it, but I was permitted to enroll in first grade in January 1943, four months before my sixth birthday. My disappointment over not going to school with Betty melted away. She could have the school down the street. I was going to school with my big brother!

My first grade teacher was Mrs. Earnest. One day she handed out fat red pencils and ruled paper and asked the class to practice writing their names on every other line of the paper. I wrote my name then noticed that another student was printing her name. *IS THAT WHAT MRS. ERNEST WANTS?* I was confused. But, Mrs. Ernest had said, "write," not "print." To me writing was cursive. *I KNOW WHAT. I'LL WRITE MY NAME ON ONE LINE, SKIP A LINE, THEN PRINT IT.* I filled

Frederick Douglass School #19 at 1624 Quill Street. A new structure was built a few blocks away at 2020 Dawson Street and this building was demolished. Photo by Reginald Cheatham

the page that way. I guess it was okay because Mrs. Ernest didn't say anything. I kept pace with my classmates, and in June was promoted to second grade along with everybody else.

I didn't understand why Betty and I had to go to different schools, but I knew there was something unsavory about the whole business. At the time I didn't give it a thought, but now I wonder: what did Betty's mother tell her about not going to school with me? Is that when Betty learned she was "white"? Although we were friends, I decided not to play with Betty anymore. I ran into her the summer after I completed first grade and taunted her.

"What grade will you be in when school starts?"

"First grade."

"First grade?" I repeated her words as if that were the most ridiculous thing I had ever heard. Then, with as much hauteur as I could manage, I continued.

"*I'll* be in second grade. I can read and write. Can *you* read and write?"

"Not yet."

"Well, I can. And I'll be in second grade."

Betty and I didn't talk after that.

Racially segregated schools were the most constant reminder that whites considered themselves better than us, but certainly not the only one. My family, along with many others, went to movies at black theaters—Walker, Douglass, and the Avenue—because Negroes were forced to sit in the balcony in the white downtown movie theaters. We were also refused service in downtown restaurants. Riverside Amusement Park was a looming reminder of our status. The park, located at West 30th Street and White River, not far from the homes of the city's more affluent blacks, opened in 1903. It featured a number of thrilling rides including two large roller coasters and a Ferris wheel. Lewis Coleman acquired the park in 1919 and instituted a whites only policy, although he set aside one day a year as Colored Frolic Day. His son John took over in 1939 and maintained the apartheid. I remember that we saved milk bottle caps to use for admission on our day, and Negroes packed the place. In the mid forties, we wised up and decided that if we weren't welcome everyday, we shouldn't go at all. The Colemans didn't care. They were willing to forego that day's profits rather than change their policy. The park remained off-limits to blacks well into the 1960s. They were upfront about their *racism*, displaying a Whites Only sign at the entrance.

With these restrictions all around, it was hard to believe we were equal to whites, although Mama assured us, "You are just as good as anybody else." *We* may have been just as good, but our school certainly wasn't. We passed School 20, the white school, every morning so it was possible to make daily comparisons. Their school was large and looked new, with an attractive green lawn around it. School 19 was smaller, built of red bricks that had weathered over many years and now looked dingy. Our playground was covered with gravel. Buildings that we called portables took up a significant part of the grounds at Douglass. These "temporary" structures—brought in to handle the expanding enrollment—were there when I arrived and remained for all eight years of my elementary education. When the white schools got new textbooks, their ragged, out-of-date discards were delivered to us.

Children from upper grades pretended to be Indians for this school play performed in 1946. I'm 4th from left in the front row, leaning into the camera. Emma Hoggatt is on my left. On my right are two good friends, Barbara Petty and next to her, Margie Duff. My cousin Ronald is on the right end of the second row. Emma's brother, Doyal, is 4th from left on the third row. My brother James, along with the other eighth graders, is in the last row, third from the right. His buddy, Raymond McClure is on his right.

Despite these signals that we weren't entitled to the best, we were fond of Douglass because in school we were away from white hostility, scrutiny, and disapproval. At School 19, except for two American Indian students—Doyal and Emma Hoggatt—everybody, from the principal to the janitor, was Negro. It was nearly as comfortable as being at home. The only time we resorted to the stilted behavior required to show whites that we were respectable, was when supervisors visited from the school board's central office.

Emma Hoggatt was in my class, and I wondered how she felt when we did a school play, I think it was Longfellow's "Hiawatha's Song," where we all wore costumes and pretended to be Indians. I guess we invented hair extensions for that play because the girls were told to attach braided black cloth to our own hair to make it appear longer. As we were being posed for a photograph, a teacher asked us to put our "braids" in front of our shoulders. In the picture, Emma, one of two or three girls whose long braids were actually their own hair, and the only real Indian, was the one girl who did not move her braids.

Teaching at School 19 was not considered a plum assignment. The school was on the southeast side, far from the affluent northwest section of Indianapolis where many of the teachers lived. However, our principal, Emma Mae Allison, and most of our teachers cared about us and wanted us to learn. I did my best work for the teachers I liked—my favorites were Mrs. Davis in third grade and Miss Moton in eighth grade. Mrs. Coston, who taught seventh grade, was rather stern, but I enjoyed the poems she had us memorize. I still remember most of the lines of Longfellow's "Psalm of Life," in particular the verse,

> Lives of great men all remind us
> We can make our lives sublime
> And, in parting, leave behind us
> Footprints in the sands of time.

Mama and Daddy believed teachers were the key to our salvation, just a notch below the men called by God to save our souls. Despite their regard for educators, however, they didn't hesitate to stick up for us if we thought a teacher was being unfair. And because they trusted us, we told them the truth. Mama kept a scrapbook for each of her children in which she pasted significant documents marking our lives: photos, 4-H Club awards, Summer Reading Club certificates, and our report cards. By grade four my schoolwork no longer challenged me, and I became restless; my teacher wrote on my report card, "Stop Janet from coming to school with chewing gum." Mama replied, "Janet gets the gum from Margie Duff." In grade five I became a problem; completing my assignments quickly, then chatting with the students around me, sometimes helping them with their work. Mrs. Johnson, my fifth grade teacher, wrote, "A great talker, but also a good worker." There is also a Report of Misconduct from Mrs. Johnson in my scrapbook: "Janet does nice work, but she talks and

School 19's faculty, apparently around 1941 before I started school because there are a couple of teachers I don't recognize. Front row l-r: Hazel Moore, 4th grade; Sarah Zeigler, junior high; Emma Mae Allison, principal; Ella Ernest, 1st grade; don't recognize him. Second row l-r: Another teacher I don't recognize; Caroline Davis, 3rd grade; Frances Coston, junior high; Mary Etta Johnson, 5th grade and choir director; Ruth McArthur, traveling instrumental music teacher and later, owner of the McArthur Music Conservatory on Indiana Avenue.

whispers constantly." I was sometimes sent to the principal's office for talking in class.

Going to the principal's office didn't feel like punishment because Miss Allison let me help her. I took notes to teachers and operated the mimeograph machine on which we duplicated the school paper. I was truly excited when Miss Allison let me write something to fill an empty space in the paper. I made up a joke about a girl who was following a recipe that told her to wash lettuce thoroughly before she used it in a salad. I wrote that the girl washed the lettuce on a scrub board with soap. It was my first published work! I was nine years old.

In sixth grade we had a new, young teacher, Miss Smith, perhaps in her first assignment. We could see her hesitancy and decided to take advantage. Whenever she turned her back to write on the blackboard, we went wild, making noises and throwing spitballs, pencils, and whatever we got our hands on. When she turned around, we were sitting quietly with our hands folded on our desks. We talked in class and generally showed our disdain for the hapless teacher. Although I knew my parents would vehemently disapprove, I joined the classroom anarchy. On my first report card from Miss Smith she wrote, "Janet wants to talk back, fuss and fight with her classmates." My mother's response was enigmatic, perhaps because she had little respect for an adult who couldn't control a group of eleven-year-olds. Mama wrote, "I hope the pupils are cooperating with you in your efforts to improve their conduct." On another report card, Miss Smith wrote, "Janet has been very sassy. I am sure she does not mean to be, because she is a nice child." Mama replied, "I am very sorry about Janet's conduct, but I hope she will improve." The following six weeks Miss Smith wrote, "Janet has improved since our talk. Thank you." I don't recollect what Mama said or did to make me improve. Miss Smith didn't stay at School 19; the word was that we ran her away. She was replaced by a series of substitute teachers, including Mrs. Collins. Mrs. Collins was a large, imposing woman with a gravelly voice and no-nonsense manner. Our chaotic class settled down immediately. Beatrice Bowles was a substitute who was hired to take over the class. Mrs. Bowles also exercised a firm hand. Miss Allison must have told the office that she needed experienced teachers for her unruly sixth graders. I remember these two substitutes because each of them had a child my age—Charlemae Collins and Howard Bowles—that I later met at the parties and dances we attended on the other side of town. Mrs. Rankin replaced Mrs. Coston in seventh grade, I don't remember why, and she seemed openly annoyed that she had been assigned to the south side. She specifically disliked me. On my report card she wrote, "I have been greatly disappointed in Janet this last six weeks. I hope the next six weeks will show a marked improvement." I had talked to Mama about Mrs. Rankin's attitude so she responded, "I am sure with kind consideration and more love, Janet will improve." In addition, I found the carbon copy of a letter Mama wrote to Mrs. Rankin questioning her classroom management. The letter read in part:

Janet is repeatedly sent from the room to sit in room three or in the cloak hall standing, and many times its really someone else that is guilty. I know something about children, and I know she isn't that much worse than the others…. If more time was spent in love, and kindness, and less in humiliating and stern ineffective lectures, they would learn more.

Twice a day we had recess and the children went out to the gravel-covered playground. The playing area for girls in grades one through six was on one side of the building, and on the other side for boys in those grades. When we reached junior high, boys and girls shared a small area in back of the building where they were easily observed by teachers and staff. We new teens and near teens didn't need space to play. All we did was stand around talking to our friends in gender exclusive clumps, pretending not to notice one another.

In the early grades we girls joined hands for circle games like "Little Sally Walker."

Little Sally Walker, sitting in a saucer,
(the girl in the center of the circle squats down)
Rise, Sally, rise, *(the girl stands up)*
Wipe your weeping eyes. *(wipes her eyes)*
Shake it to the east, shake it to the west
(rotates her hips one way, then the other)
Shake it to the one you love the best.
(selects the person to replace her in the center).

We also jumped rope, including Double Dutch, where the girls held a rope in each hand and with exquisite rhythm turned them in opposite directions. I rarely missed when I jumped rope and was particularly proud of my skill in Double Dutch. I played hard and sometimes fell which was always painful because the gravel usually broke my skin and made me bleed. It hardly bothered me, but Mama got upset if there was blood on my dress. My knees were full of scars. Even on the girl's playground there were bullies whom everybody tried to avoid. These tough older girls would hurt you if you crossed them, and they took offense easily. Shirley was one of them. She was an attractive smart girl, but she seemed angry all the time. Because I had started school early, I was a year younger than other kids in my grade, and Shirley was a year ahead of, so she was a couple of years older. She had never hit me, but apparently enjoyed seeing the fear in my eyes when she threatened to beat me up, and she made these threats regularly. I did everything I could to stay out of Shirley's way because I believed she was going to wipe the playground with me at her first opportunity. One day she was holding the door open as we filed in from the playground. As I got closer to the door, Shirley, in a low voice the teacher couldn't hear but all the students could, began describing what she was going to do to me after school. By the time I was directly in front of her, I was completely humiliated, but also fed up. I surprised myself when I got in her face and, as fiercely as I could, said, "I'm going to stomp you into the ground!" I could see that I had startled Shirley, but within seconds, I realized what I had done and was terrified. All I could think of for the remainder of the day was the beating I was going to get. The closer we got to the end of the school day, the harder and faster my heart raced. After school I didn't look very hard, but I didn't see Shirley. I hurried home temporarily relieved, but I knew I'd see her at school the next day. And I did, but she didn't even look at me. Shirley seemed to lose interest in me after that, and never threatened me again. I was about eight years old, but gradually it dawned on me that by standing up to her I had avoided having to fight. That was my initial lesson in the efficacy of selling wolf tickets, and first glimpse of the notion that most bullies are cowards. Although I haven't always employed this tactic right away, I've never forgotten the lesson, or had it contradicted.

The Cheatham kids were near royalty at School 19 because our parents were actively involved with the school. For a number of years Mama was president of the PTA. The classroom with the most parents at the PTA meeting received some kind of award, and the prize always went to a classroom with a Cheatham in it. Adult males were rarely seen at School 19. Except for Mr. Alexander, the janitor and Mr. Scott, the shop teacher, the staff was entirely female. So, our Daddy faithfully showing up at PTA meetings was special, and we were rewarded for it. When the points were tabulated for the award, each mother counted as one, and each father received five points. And since the majority of dads worked during the day, Daddy was usually the only father at the monthly Wednesday afternoon meetings. On Wednesdays and Saturdays Daddy finished his work at Stumpf Brothers by noon. On PTA days, he postponed delivering chitlins or mowing lawns. Instead, he came home, changed into a suit and tie, and he and Mama went to the PTA meeting.

I suppose our curriculum was the same as in all public schools, but in addition, we celebrated our own history. We learned about Frederick Douglass, the man for whom the school was named, and in the second week of February, which included the birthdays of Douglass and Abraham Lincoln, we observed Negro History Week, now Black History Month. Instead of the "Star-Spangled Banner," we sang the Negro national anthem, "Lift Every Voice and Sing." We also had a school wide choir organized by my fifth grade teacher, Mary Etta Johnson. Mrs. Johnson was an accomplished choir director who got the best out of us. The school choir was so polished that we were invited to venues around the city to perform Negro spirituals like "Go Down, Moses," "Roll, Jordan, Roll," "Swing Low, Sweet Chariot," and "My Lord, What a Mourning." We did some European music as well; one of our special numbers was Handel's "Messiah."

I was really surprised, but pleased, when in fifth grade I was assigned to the choir. Everybody else in the choir was in junior high, so I knew I had to be special. I soon found out that I wasn't there because of my wonderful voice, but I didn't care; I could still bask in being a member of the privileged group. To keep me on key, Mrs. Johnson spent quite a bit of time trying to get me to match the note she blew on her pitch pipe. I was undoubtedly in the choir because Mrs. Johnson knew she could count on Daddy to transport me and several other students to our performances. It was no coincidence that I was put in the choir the same year James graduated. Like the other students, James was in the choir because he could sing. His voice was good enough that he was selected for Attucks High School's elite a cappella choir. Another student from the School 19 choir, Richard Highbaugh, distinguished himself as a soloist at Attucks and received a music scholarship to a black college. Mama was really proud of Richard because he went to our church, and he may have been the first person from our congregation to attend college. I was impressed that something like being able to sing could get you a scholarship, although I knew that would never work for me.

Graduation day at School 19 was a major event. The eighth grade girls whose parents could afford it wore new white dresses, and the boys white shirts with ties. When I graduated, my new dress was white piqué. I also had a leading role in the class play, though for the life of me, I don't remember what play we performed. But I knew all my lines and Mama and Daddy were proud of me. I think graduation was a big deal because it was the only commencement ceremony many students expected to have, and many of their parents, like Daddy, had never even completed the eighth grade.

When the school day ended, we had to cope with the world outside, which often meant fighting with the white kids on the walk home. Since we attended two different schools based on skin color, we used the same criteria to draw battle lines. So many children had been hurt in this long-standing tradition of fighting between the *races* that specific routes to and from our separate schools were laid out in an effort to keep us away from one another. However, there were a couple of blocks on State Street that couldn't be avoided by either group. The whites were told to stay on one side and we on the other; nobody was to cross the street. And we didn't, unless somebody threw a rock or yelled nigger, in which cases all but the timid and the ridiculously obedient ran across the street and kicked ass. I never hesitated to join the fight. We also fought among ourselves, but we quickly closed ranks when the real enemy attacked. When I was ten and James fourteen, he had a fight with a white boy that became a serious problem.

One night there was a rapid banging on the front door that woke me up. On his way to the door, I heard Daddy say, "Who could that be at this time a night?" I think it was around eleven o'clock. I peeped through the curtain that separated my bed from the living room and heard a loud, stern man's voice say, "Police. We're looking for James Cheatham."

POLICE? OH, MY GOD! I was immediately terrified. My heart started to pound.

"Smith, what is it?" Mama called out from her bedroom, sounding upset.

"I'm his father. What do you want him for?" Daddy spoke to the policeman, ignoring Mama's question.

"He's under arrest for stabbing Vernon Sparks."

Daddy was stunned. "What...? When?"

"Earlier this evening. We're taking him down."

"Wait a minute. I'll get him."

The policemen didn't come inside. Daddy went to get James and I couldn't hear what they said. A few minutes later, James came out and went away with the police. Daddy dressed and left immediately afterward.

WHAT ARE THE POLICE GOING TO DO TO MY BROTHER? Mama got up and looked in on us. I pretended to be asleep because I didn't want her to know I had heard anything.

The following morning, James's not being there wasn't mentioned because he was always gone by the time Reggie, Rosie, and I were getting ready for school. I was too nervous to say anything about what I had heard the night before, plus I could see that Mama was anxious. When we got home from school, James was there, and that was unusual because normally, he worked after school. Mama and Daddy kept most of the distress away from the three younger children, but James told us what happened when they weren't around.

The day before, James finished work at 6 p.m. and took the bus home. Instead of getting off the bus at Randolph and Prospect, he rode two more blocks to Harlan Street to visit his buddies. Between Prospect and Orange Streets, there were three Negro families on our block, and about a dozen Negro families in the same block of Harlan Street. These were the only Negro residents within the eight square block area bounded by Churchman Avenue on the east, State Street on the west, Prospect on the north, and Orange Street on the south. We had lived on Harlan before we moved to Randolph and James had friends there. When James stepped down from the bus, it was around 7 p.m. and dark on a warm evening, September 24, 1947. A group of white boys were standing near the corner where the bus stopped.

"What are you doing over here, nigger?"

"None of your business. I didn't come to see you."

"Well, you better get home before we make it our business."

"I'll go home when I get good and ready." James was uneasy and put his hand in his pants pocket. He didn't want to appear fearful, but he was alone, and there were five of them. When one of the boys stepped up to him, James pulled out a knife and swung it wildly. The boy hollered and collapsed, clutching his chest. The other white boys took off. James had cut the boy on the chest and arm. Lawrence "Sippy" Orr, one of James's friends, could see the face-off with the five white boys and was running up the street to help. By the time he reached James, it was all over. James and Sippy knew that cutting a white boy was a grave matter, so they fled. All of the boys lived in the area, so James knew the police would be told where to find him. As soon as he got home, he took the knife he had used and hid it in our pantry. He put a smaller, more innocuous-looking knife on top of his dresser.

A couple of years earlier, James and his buddies had seen a huge fight between the older boys in the neighborhood, Negroes on one side, whites on the other. They were using knives, sticks, and broom handles as weapons. At the colored Y where he worked, James met boys his age from other parts of the city. He was surprised to learn that in the Negro neighborhoods on the east and west sides, the Negro boys fought each other. On the south side where we lived there were so few Negroes that the battles were between the *races*. James and his pals decided they should get knives in case they had to fight. From time to time, they gathered in a macho ritual of oiling and sharpening their knives. The boys wanted the knives to open easily and be effective if they had to use them. The blade on James's knife was six inches long and as sharp as a razor, but he had never used it. Since it was not a switchblade, he kept a matchstick stub between the blade and the handle so he could open it quickly with one hand. When the police asked for the knife he had used, James gave them the small penknife on his dresser. Other than James and his buddies, nobody knew about the other knife, and he kept that secret for more than fifty years.

The story in the newspaper the next morning did not mention James's name. He was referred to as "the 14-year-old attacker." It was also reported that the police arrested the attacker and turned him over to juvenile authorities. In fact, the police took James down-town to jail; undoubtedly thinking that a Negro who stabbed a white deserved the worst possible treatment. When they told Daddy they were "taking him down," they meant just that. My skinny adolescent brother had to spend the night in a cell crowded with grown men who were thieves, murderers, and rapists. Bunk beds were stacked four high in the large room, but not nearly enough for all the men inside. James could see only one toilet. The area reeked of the sweat, urine, and spiritual decay of the countless men who had occupied the lockup. As usual, except when acting jobs are passed out in Hollywood, Negroes were the majority of the inmates. One colored man tried to reassure my terrified brother, who had no idea what was going to happen to him, or how long he would be there. From time to time, a man's name was called and he'd leave. There would be a rush to the vacated bunk, if the departing man had been so lucky. Finally, James spotted an empty bunk on the top of one tier; he climbed up and fell asleep. He said that night was possibly the worst of his life.

In the meantime, Daddy was waking up his friend Henry J. Richardson Jr., a Negro, and possibly Indianapolis's shrewdest lawyer of any color. Attorney Richardson got James released to Daddy the following morning.

I learned later that after James came home nightriders started terrorizing our family. In the old South, they came on horses with torches, but these modern riders were in cars, driving past our house, leaning on their horns, and calling for James. Daddy called the police, but they didn't show up for three days. My parents must have been out of their minds wondering at which moment the house would be stormed, shot at, or burned. Daddy got a gun and his brothers, either Uncle Oliver or Uncle Rozell, took turns at the house when Daddy wasn't there. Looking back, I am amazed that each man assumed he could hold his own against a group of irate whites. I suppose they knew that nightriders are willing to kill for the principle of white supremacy, but not willing to die for it. Rosie, Reggie, and I slept through the night riding, and went to school everyday, but we knew something was going on because there were more people in and out of our house than was customary. There was also a lot of low talking and sighing, and Mama cried more than usual in church.

When the police showed up three days after Daddy's initial call, they picked up James and took him to the juvenile detention center! They told my parents it would give the neighbors time to cool off. Undoubtedly, the police had told the outraged whites they would be locking James up because the night riding ended immediately. Interestingly, despite their wrath that a Negro, for a change, had gotten the better of a fight, not one of the nightriders had had the courage to stop his car and get out. Like Shirley, these bullies were cowards.

Although James couldn't attend school or go to work, he was not locked in at the detention center. In the two weeks he was there, he ran errands for the boys who actually were being detained and made a little money.

Vernon Sparks, the boy James cut, was taken to General Hospital. We were told that if the cut had been half an inch higher, the knife would have punctured his heart. Thank God for that half-inch! The newspaper reported Sparks as saying that the attacker called him out of a snack shop and threatened to kill him. According to the newspaper, Sparks also said that James "had been after him for a long time, but [Sparks] didn't know why." James didn't even know Sparks; he had seen Sparks out and about, but otherwise they had had no contact. James had lived in that neighborhood all of his life, and he was not stupid. Even if he felt like doing so, he would not have gone out *alone* and publicly menaced a white boy.

Attorney Richardson argued that James was defending himself from an older, larger boy. Also, Richardson said, James was a good kid, never in trouble, and a high school student. Sparks, on the other hand, was sixteen and a dropout. Richardson also emphasized that we were a solid, churchgoing family, and that James worked after school at the Senate Avenue YMCA. The Y was the colored branch of the main YMCA, and a bulwark of the Negro community. The director, Faburn E. DeFrantz, was a prominent Negro leader. Mr. DeFrantz, R. K. Smith, and other YMCA staff wrote letters extolling Daddy as a dedicated volunteer, and vouching for James's character as a boy who was raised in the Y. Needless to say, James needed all the help he could get; Negroes have been lynched for much less.

Aside from the night in jail and two weeks at juvenile detention, James was not incarcerated. He was given probation and ordered to reimburse Sparks for his medical expenses. James's salary at the Y was ten dollars a week. Between November 8, 1947 and January 17, 1948, he purchased five ten-dollar money orders payable to Vernon Sparks that he gave to C. T. H. Watkins, the Negro probation worker. When he received the fifth payment, Mr. Watkins's gave James a receipt saying Paid in Full. Mama pasted all the receipts in James's scrapbook. James said the older Negro guys who had had pitched battles with the whites over the years pulled him aside and patted him on the back. The white boys in the neighborhood never challenged James again.

Annual father-son banquet at the YMCA, circa 1944. Daddy must have been on the program since he (4th from left) is sitting at the head table flanked by Grandpa and James.

I thought it was awful that white folks forced James to pay some cracker who had started a fight with him. For me, it was further evidence that white people were the enemy. At ten, I had no sense of how much worse things could have been, especially if Sparks's account had been believed.

Daddy kept the gun for several years, until he finally gave in to Mama's pleas to get rid of it.

"Smith, the way you fly off the handle with these white folks, you're liable to *kill* somebody. And then where we would be?"

"As crazy as these crackers are, you got to be able to protect yourself."

Mama was also concerned that one of us would find it and get hurt, or worse. Reggie did locate the gun and showed it to Rosie and mc in Daddy's hiding place in the chifforobe in their bedroom. It was large and silver with an engraved handle. Just looking at the gun made my legs quiver in fear, but Reggie wanted to pick it up. I warned him that if he touched it, I'd tell Mama. Reggie left the gun alone, or at least he did while I was around.

Two years after this disruption in our family, the delicate relationship between the *races* underwent yet another shift. In 1949 the Indianapolis Public Schools (IPS) were integrated, again. This time students entering first grade and high school were ordered to attend the school closest to them, without regard for skin color. School 19 was in the middle of a neighborhood that was largely white, which meant that it would no longer be a Negro school. The whites in the area were aghast that their children would be going to "that colored school." To appease the affronted parents, the school board allocated money to spruce up the building. When we heard that our school was being done over, we had to see it for ourselves.

The rickety "temporary" buildings were torn down. Workers rolled out sod, painted walls, and installed new furniture and brighter lights. My stomach began to twist when I saw the massive effort to make things nicer for the white kids than they had been for us. There it was, a concrete, visual image to reinforce the daily message drilled into our psyches: "Whites, being superior, deserve something better than Negroes have." Something tender drained out of me as I watched improvements taking place for the white children that our PTA had requested in vain for years. Even with the changes, many white parents would not send their children to what had been a colored school.

We learned that the Negro principal, teachers, and staff were removed and placed in schools where the neighborhood children were Negro. The building remained, but our beloved school was gone.

Chapter 7

Hard Work and Talent

No matter what you may or may not have, …. people understand hard work and talent—and it can prevail.

> ~ Maxine Waters, member of the
> U. S. Congress from California

Other people talked about idle hands being the devil's workshop, but my parents *believed* it. It seemed to me that work was holy for them. That notion was reinforced when I was reading one of Mama's journals and found a note about the value of work.

> *Every boy or girl as soon as they learn how to work should have a little task to do each day before and after school and begin to earn their own support after they have completed their education. No one should be dependent on no one else if he is able to work. For as Dr. W.E.B. DuBois said, "Work is heaven, Idleness Hell, and Wage is the Well Done." Work, work. Everybody should work for his or her self. A good honest work won't hurt anybody.*

We were not allowed to do nothing. Every minute that we weren't in school or doing homework, Rosie and I helped Mama wash and iron the family laundry, cook the meals, do the dishes, and keep the house clean. If Mama caught me sitting still daydreaming she said I was lazy. And she loaded the word with such disdain and loathing that it became more weapon than adjective. I once heard her making amends for a man's infidelity by saying, "Well, at least he works."

I was happy for warmer weather, but I dreaded spring because that meant pulling the house apart for spring-cleaning. I think we cleaned every item in the house, including closets and drawers. The thing I hated most was cleaning wallpaper. Each of us was assigned a section of the wall and given a wad of doughy, bright green wallpaper cleaner. I rolled the acrid smelling cleaner into a ball, then used it to rub the winter's coal soot and dust off the wallpaper. I'd keep turning the ball of cleaner to find a clean, green spot, and when it was black through and through, I pulled a fresh wad of cleaner out of the can. My arms got tired of the seemingly endless job because we had to rub hard to get the wall clean. I could have been reading a good book, but there I was rubbing on a wall. After what seemed like an eternity of rubbing walls, Mama decided that wallpaper was no longer fashionable. Whoo, what a relief! Daddy steamed the paper off and hired Mr. Watkins to paint the walls. Watkins was an American Indian who lived near our Aunt Bertha in Norwood, a black neighborhood not far from us. In addition to painting houses, he was also a root doctor, who had earned Daddy's permanent loyalty when he cured Uncle Rozell of syphilis after several university-trained physicians had said he would die, or at best be an invalid. Daddy sought Watkins' help again when it appeared that the twins were going to expire from whooping cough. Reggie still remembers how foul tasting the thick black liquid medicine was, but it worked. I was just grateful to see Watkins painting our walls so I would never again have to clean wallpaper.

We took up the rugs, carried them outside, threw them over the clothesline, and beat the dirt out. We also put our mattresses and pillows outside in the sun to air; I looked forward to the smell of sunshine in them afterwards. We sorted and straightened out the unheated back porch where we did the laundry in warmer weather. It was a relief not to have to drag the wringer washing machine into the kitchen and set up the rinse tubs there. That always made it difficult to do anything else in the kitchen, and even getting to the bathroom was a problem. On laundry day in winter, we had a simple meal—a pot of white beans cooked with fatback or ham hocks, salad, and cornbread. All four of us helped with the annual cleaning, but Mama didn't ask for help with her other spring ritual.

Mama prepared and tended to her flower gardens alone. I used to watch her while she worked in her flowerbeds. I didn't ask, but I wanted to know what she was thinking because she looked as if her thoughts were far away. She had a similar expression when she was quilting. At the end of the day when Mama finally sat down, she made quilts. She put her current project on her lap, stretched on the large round wooden quilting hoops, and made the tiny, neat stitches that held the quilt together. All of Mama's quilts had definite color and design patterns. And to get the colors she wanted, she sometimes traded pieces of fabric with other women. Interestingly, Mama never taught Rosie or me anything about gardening or quilting. And we didn't ask; we had enough to do. I did enjoy examining the quilts' cheerful, bright colors and identifying fabric that matched window curtains or dresses that Mama had sewn.

In addition to maintaining her own home, Mama occasionally did day work to buy something we needed for school, like the *Book of Knowledge* that she purchased on the installment plan. It was a set of heavy, eight-by-ten illustrated books. Each letter of the alphabet was in a separate book, though a few letters like X, Y, and Z, shared a volume. I used that set of encyclopedias all the time and looked forward to the annual arrival of the *Year Book,* which included information about events from the previous year. Mama had an older, smaller set of encyclopedias that she apparently purchased before we were born. I read them occasionally, but they were out-of-date and didn't have pictures. Mama added more day work when the twins and I were in high school, to cover the expense of daily bus fare and lunch money for three teenagers. The middle-class white families that hired her by the day to clean for them lived on the far north side of Indianapolis. Mama had to leave early and take two long bus rides to reach their homes. She detested washing, ironing, scrubbing, and cleaning for them. It was a sacrifice she made for us, and she told us so.

Daddy did whatever he could to earn "an honest dollar" as well. He often said he worked eight days a week. In the spring and summer when he didn't sell chitlins, Daddy augmented his income by doing yard work, simonizing cars, and washing windows. My brothers' household chores were the garbage and trash duties and, surprisingly, they did turns with the dishes, an inside-the-house job usually reserved for the females. After he started working at the Y, James was exempted from household chores, aside from keeping his room clean. Reggie helped Daddy with his yard work—at home and away. One of the things that was an enigma for me as a child was that the word *office* was ubiquitous, not only in the books I read, but also in the comic

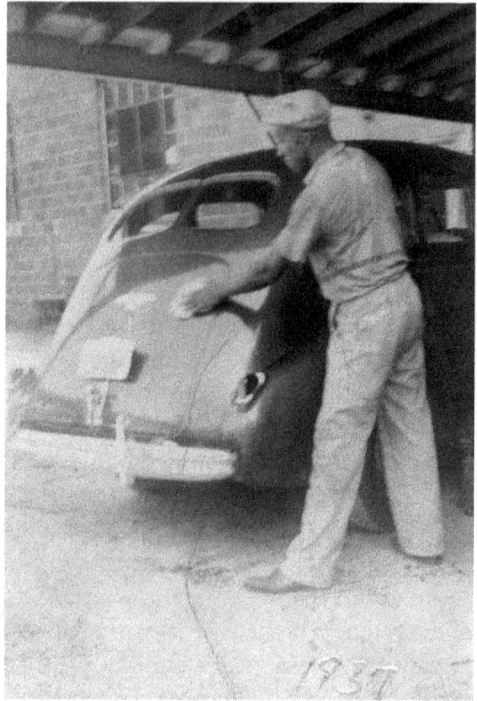

Daddy doing one of his extra jobs. One of the rare pictures with a date, 1937.

strips. Dagwood Bumstead referred to his office all the time. I couldn't understand why there was so much written about offices when I had seen only one, the principal's office at school. My parents and the other adults I knew did not work in offices. I was a teen by the time I got it.

Mama started talking to me about doing day work when I was around twelve years old. I was shocked. It had never occurred to me that I would be anybody's maid. Besides, I heard her fussing about cleaning up after lazy white folks and that did not make me eager to follow in her footsteps. Talking back wasn't allowed, so I kept my feelings to myself. Rosie was always being switched on the legs for talking back and I didn't want Mama to hit me, or worse, give me a talking to. I'd rather have a whipping than listen to Mama talk about how hard her life had been. She'd begin by saying, "I don't understand how you children can be so ungrateful and disobedient. When I was your age I didn't have a loving mother, a decent home, and plenty of food to eat." I felt bad that Mama's life had been tough, so I tried not to upset her.

A neighbor, whom I'll call Mrs. Galt, came to our door one day and asked Mama to clean for her. Mama said she was busy, but then I heard her say she would send me instead. I was horrified. *ME? CLEAN HOUSE FOR ONE OF OUR NEIGHBORS? ESPECIALLY NOT THE GALT'S;*

THEY LIVED IN THAT RAGGEDY HOUSE BY THE ALLEY. WHY SHOULD *I* BE A MAID TO THOSE POOR CRACKERS? I wanted to beg Mama not to send me to clean for them, but I knew she wouldn't listen, so I didn't say anything. I felt so bad I wanted to cry. Mama could tell that I didn't want to do it, but she didn't care.

"You've got to start earning some money and this way you'll be close to home in case you need help with something. So just prepare yourself. I told her you'd come on Saturday."

This was the worst thing Mama had ever done, making me be a maid for the trashiest family on the street. It felt like an admission that we were inferior to whites, like they said. I would have done anything to get out of it, but I had no choice. The following Saturday I trudged down the street to my first job. When Mrs. Galt opened the door I could see her junky living room—dirty clothes, a bare floor, and broken-down furniture. It was a mess! Mama was right about these people being lazy. I did not want to go in there, but what would I tell Mama? Then three nasty children came running out, and I got an idea.

"Miz Galt, my stomach's hurting real bad, so I won't be able to help you today. I'm sorry." I wanted to run off her porch, but I moved slowly since I had said my stomach was hurting. Mrs. Galt's house wasn't nearly as nice as ours; it needed paint and repairs, and there was no grass or flowers in the yard. Why should *we* be working for *her*?

I took my time getting home because I knew Mama would be mad. I was right.

"What are you doing home? You couldn't have cleaned anything this fast."

"Mama, Miz Galt's kids call us niggers. I'm sorry, Mama, but I can't work for somebody who calls me a nigger. I just can't!"

"Girl, you listen to me. You never know what somebody's calling you; they don't always do it to your face. You want new school clothes don't you?"

"Yes, ma'am."

"Then you've got to get a job. We're not educated people. And you better learn, young lady, that Negro women without education cook and clean."

"Yes, ma'am."

But Mama didn't send me to clean for a neighbor again.

I agree that children should help out at home; otherwise, they begin to think of parents as their servants. However something was missing for me. I couldn't articulate it, but it seemed we were busy all the time just so people could see how industrious we were. I longed for a vision to accompany our diligence. If we were going to work nonstop, shouldn't there be some goal—a better house, more education, or our own business—that we were working toward? Or, was hard work simply the magic that kept us from being pulled back into slavery or sharecropping?

With hindsight I can see that working hard just to survive was what my parents knew best. Hard work was their ally in the struggle against *racism* and scarcity. Oppression and poverty have a way of stifling hopes and disfiguring dreams. Rather than seeking some possibly unattainable future goal, Mama and Daddy labored to make the present better. They also practiced the Christian values they preached. Although the family income barely brought our ends together, Mama and Daddy were not interested in money that had not been earned honorably. When James was about fifteen, he won $110 shooting dice, and proudly brought the money home to help out. Daddy wouldn't touch it, and told James to take it back. We were also taught by precept and example to make charitable contributions, not only giving at church, but also sharing our limited funds with others less fortunate. Each child was given a nickel, dime, or quarter—depending on age— to put in the collection plate at church. When we started making our own money, we were encouraged to give more. If a man lost his job, Daddy slipped him a few dollars, and Mama prepared food that we took to the family. All the clothing in our family was handed down from the older to the younger children. But if we had clothing that none of us could wear anymore, we laundered it and passed it on to the needy. Any child who came to our door selling something, or asking for help, was never turned away without a donation. This principle of sharing with the needy continues to be a reflexive action with me. No matter how limited I perceive my income to be, I always give a portion of it away. Mama was equally adamant about saving money. Her mantra was, "If you make a quarter, save a nickel." She believed fervently in having a rainy day stash, but she rarely considered any day rainy enough to go into her savings. Daddy saved money as well—until he had enough to buy whatever new toy he had his eye on. For most of my life I was an adherent of Mama's financial philosophy, but I've given that up in favor of Daddy's way of operating.

My parents were as generous with their time as with their resources. Daddy's volunteer schedule was particularly hectic; when he wasn't working, he was at a meeting. In addition to the Southeast Civic League and the church, he was active in Fidelity Lodge #55 F & A M (Free and Accepted Masons). Daddy was their financial secretary for about twenty-five years. Many times I recall seeing him working on his record books. The lodge kept re-electing him because he could be trusted to turn in the dues he collected, and he kept scrupulous accounts. Daddy trained a young man from Lovetown, Oliver Duncan, to replace him. Then in 1965 Daddy was free to be elected to the lodge's highest office, worshipful master. Daddy was also a notary public, a member of the NAACP, and of the Southside Democratic Club.

Most of Daddy's volunteer work though was as a top fund-raiser for the Senate Avenue (later the Fall Creek) YMCA. Faburn E. De Frantz, whom Daddy called Chief, had been executive secretary of the Y since 1916. Under his leadership, membership grew from 350 to over 5,000 by the time he retired in 1951. It was the largest Negro Y in the world, and the largest Y, Negro or white, in Indiana. DeFrantz was also an active leader in the local Struggle. In response to critics of his activism, he said, "As long as I stay in this town, I shall see to it that the Negro is in the picture of what is going on."

Daddy must have become involved with the YMCA in 1929 because in 1959, noting his thirty years of service, he was registered in the Y's Leadership Fellowship. In a 1934 Y campaign kick-off photograph, Daddy is on the front row. He was elected to their board of managers in 1953, and was chairman of the board from 1967 to 1969. The Y was almost as important in our family as the church, and Daddy put in hours raising money in their annual drives to finance memberships for boys who couldn't buy them. Mama often said, to Daddy and to us, "Those YMCA folk don't care a thing about your Daddy. They're just using him 'cause he's a hard worker." However, she quickly let strangers know who her husband was. And after Mama died, we found several pages she had written lauding Daddy's accomplishments. James and Reggie learned to swim because Daddy took them and a car full of boys from the south side to the Y on Saturdays. Learning to swim was not easy for Negroes in Indianapolis. There were no pools in the public schools, and of the few Negro city parks, only Douglas had a pool. Douglas Park was in a Negro neighborhood on the east side of town at Twenty-fifth Street and Martindale Avenue (now Andrew J. Brown Avenue). That was quite a ways from where we lived. As the name implies, the Young Men's Christian Association was then for males only, so Rosie and I never learned to swim. I don't know whether or not the Phillis Wheatley YWCA had a pool because we weren't involved with the YW.

The YMCA had a variety of clubs and programs for boys of every age including The Life Builders Club and the Self-Starters. Reggie said Life Builders focused on character development, and in Self-Starters each boy donated twenty-five cents a week to help needy families. I

The Senate Avenue YMCA's 1949 campaign teams preparing for a fund drive. Uncle Rozell, captain of team 2, is second from the left on the front row. At first I wondered why Daddy (5th man from the left on the front row) didn't have a sign, but then I noticed the banner centered above the men. Daddy is a member of the executive committee. The man with the white hair, third from Daddy's left, is Joseph H. Ward. Dr. Ward often accompanied Faburn DeFrantz when he called on Herman B Wells at Indiana University.

This photo of "A Top YMCA Family" was taken for the cover of the February 22, 1958 issue of The Y's Man, a weekly newsletter mailed to members. We're in the living room of our house on Randolph Street.

participated in a couple of their coed clubs, Tri-Hi-Y and the Inter-Collegiate Club. I'm sure those clubs had lofty goals as well, but what I remember about our meetings is that I met some cute guys. Mama always said I was boy crazy. Maybe she was right, but at least her prediction that men would be my downfall didn't come true. In 1958 our family was featured on the cover of the Y newsletter, *The Y's Man*. Above a family photo was the caption, "A Top YMCA Family." We were all adults at the time. James is not included because he was married and also away in the army. After identifying each of us, the article went on, "This fine family is making plans for the YMCA Family Membership Service. The Cheatham family is typical of YMCA families wherein the children were raised up in the YMCA program." The article continued with a description of our past YMCA activities and current pursuits.

The Senate Avenue YMCA in 1913 when it was new. (l-r): George Knox, publisher of the Freeman; Madam C. J. Walker, a major donor; Freeman B. Ransom, attorney; Booker T. Washington, President of Tuskegee Institute; Alex Manning, publisher of the Indianapolis World; Joseph H. Ward, physician, who sixteen years later worked with Daddy at the Y. The two men on the right are YMCA executives R. W. Bullock and Thomas Taylor. A'Lelia Bundles/Walker Family Collection/ madamcjwalker.com

Not only was the Y important to our family, it was a major pillar of Indianapolis' Negro community. The four-story brick building at the corner of Senate and Michigan in which the Y was housed had been completed in July 1913. Madam C. J. Walker, the hair care entrepreneur, donated $1,000 to the campaign for the new building. Madam Walker had come to Indianapolis in 1910 to build a factory to manufacture her products as well as open a school to train hair culturists. She was born Sarah Breedlove in 1867 on a Louisiana plantation, where her parents had been enslaved. She married at age fourteen, and by eighteen gave birth to her only child, Lelia, later known as A'Lelia Walker. After Sarah was widowed, she joined her brothers in St. Louis where she worked as a laundress. She moved from there to Denver as a sales agent for Annie Malone, another black entrepreneur who sold hair care products. In Denver, Sarah married a newspaperman, Charles Joseph Walker, and had a dream in which the healing formula for a scalp conditioner was revealed to her. Using that formula, Madam C. J. Walker founded her own business to sell Madam Walker's Wonderful Hair Grower. She traveled throughout the country promoting her products, and training sales agents. In the process, she became a wealthy woman. She was also a social activist and a generous philanthropist. Madam Walker once commented, "There is no royal flower-strewn path to success. And if there is, I have not found it for if I have accomplished anything in life it is because I have been willing to work hard." When the Senate Avenue YMCA was dedicated in 1913, Booker T. Washington came to Indianapolis to speak at the ceremony. Madam Walker hosted him in her home.

Daddy met a number of educated, successful people at the Y and during the course of his other volunteer work. He talked about them, but none of them ever came to the house. I couldn't understand why until the day I heard Mama speaking to Daddy in an unusually loud, angry voice.

(l-r): Dr. Harvey Middleton, chairman of the board of management, presents Smith Cheatham (Daddy) with a plaque inscribed "For Service to Youth, Senate Avenue YMCA, February 21, 1958." Annie Cheatham (Mama) and my brother Reginald, share the moment.

"I am *not* going to the Smiths for dinner. If we stick our feet under their table, the next thing you know, they'll want to come over here. And this old, raggedy house is not fit for entertaining people like that."

Daddy came out of their room looking angry and hurt, and walked out of the house. I felt bad for him. R. K. Smith was the Boy's Department Secretary at the Y and one of Daddy's dearest friends. Mr. Smith and his wife had invited my parents to their home for dinner, but Mama refused to go. Except for having attended a couple of Daddy's lodge functions, Mama limited her social engagements to family, church, and school activities. She didn't believe her clothes were good enough for what she called high-class affairs. I believe Mama was more ashamed of not being as well educated as the YMCA people than she was of her clothes. Although some of the people Daddy met at the Y guarded their perceived social standing, and wouldn't have considered socializing with my parents, not all of them felt that way.

Around the time I started high school, I began to accompany Daddy to some events Mama considered out of her class. I especially liked the Monster Meetings. (These public forums were so named because the term Big Meeting was already being used at another venue.) The purpose of the Monster Meetings, begun in 1904, was to "encourage free discussion of all subjects of human interest," and "provide Negro youth an opportunity to see and hear social leaders from an inspirational perspective." These forums hosted a variety of nationally renowned speakers, and some local leaders. W. E. B. DuBois himself had spoken on March 9, 1941 on "The Economic Plight of the American Negro." DuBois was the first black to earn a doctorate at Harvard University in 1896, and was a leader and chronicler of the Struggle for decades. He was one of the founders of the NAACP and editor of their organ, *The Crisis.* He also wrote the classic *The Souls of Black Folk,* as well as numerous other books and studies on African Americans. Other Monster Meeting speakers were Tuskegee's wizard with plants, George Washington Carver; NAACP director of legal defense, and later U. S. Supreme Court Justice, Thurgood Marshall; Percy Julian, honor graduate of Indiana's DePauw University, and pioneering research chemist; and Eleanor Roosevelt, widow of U. S. President Franklin Roosevelt, and a powerful white ally in the Struggle, as well as a board member of the NAACP. There were also periodic debates on such topics as socialized medicine and solutions to the *race* problem. No doubt Daddy bought some of our books at the Monster Meetings because one of their speakers had been Lillian Smith, author of *Strange Fruit*, a book we had at home. I felt grown-up and important hearing the famous speakers, and having my dad introduce me to some of the people I'd heard him talk about. Chairs were set up in the Y gymnasium, and the lectures were held on Sunday afternoons, free and open to the public. The place was usually packed. I remember hearing Mordecai Johnson, first black president of Howard University, who was always the initial speaker in the series that began in November and ended in March. Dr. Johnson reminded me of a Baptist preacher, which, I found out, he was. I also heard two national executives of the NAACP, Walter White and Roy Wilkins. I listened closely to the speakers and don't recall ever being bored. In December 1958, when I was twenty-one, I went with Mama and Daddy to a Monster Meeting where Martin Luther King Jr. spoke. That meeting was moved from the Y to Cadle Tabernacle, the largest auditorium in the city. In my recollections, I have a hard time distinguishing King's speech that day from countless others I subsequently heard on television. What I do remember vividly is the skill Reverend Ralph Abernathy displayed in talking people out of their money. He spent twenty minutes or longer after King finished, pleading with the audience to donate to the SCLC (Southern Christian Leadership Conference), then a two-year-old civil rights organization.

The most memorable Monster Meeting for me occurred when I was fourteen. The speaker, Dr. Nilkanth Chavre was an international scholar from India who had lived with Mahatma Gandhi. Near the end of his speech, he called me up to be his model as he demonstrated how to wrap a sari. It was an easy choice for him; I was the only teenaged girl sitting near the front of the audience. I wasn't a bit reluctant to go on stage in front of that huge group of people; in fact, I enjoyed the attention.

One of the impressive people I met that Daddy had talked about a lot was Henry J. Richardson Jr., the lawyer who defended James after his fight. Daddy truly admired Henry J, as he called him, and regularly regaled us with stories about his triumphs. Richardson had come to Indianapolis from Alabama as a teen. On his own he worked to support himself while completing high school, college, and law school. After receiving his law degree in 1928, he immediately became a feisty and outspoken politician. In 1930 he was appointed a temporary judge in Marion County Superior Court, and in 1932 he won a seat in the Indiana legislature. Richardson was not the first black to serve as a state lawmaker, however; James Hinton, a Republican was elected to the lower house in 1880 and three other black Republicans subsequently joined him before 1900.

Richardson, a Democrat, made an impact during his three terms. In 1933 he wrote the first fair employment practices law in the country. He also helped change the state constitution to permit Negroes to serve in the Indiana National Guard. I often read and heard about Richardson's insistence that laws prohibiting Negroes from exercising their rights as citizens be changed or abolished. My favorite story, though, was how he contrived to move into a fabulous house set back from the street on a wooded lot on North Illinois Street near forty-second. Daddy showed us the house and it looked like a mansion to me. It was not only in a neighborhood that was all white, but it was a more ritzy address than the white people Mama did day work for. Richardson had a white friend pretend that he was interested in buying the house. The realtor probably assumed that the colored man tagging along was his client's employee. The white man bought the house, then immediately sold it to Richardson.

One perplexing idea that I repeatedly turned over in my young mind was how did Henry J, and others that I read about, manage to achieve so much when they were Negroes just like us. I knew how much my mother longed for an education, so I asked her why she hadn't gone to college. She said she didn't have anybody to help her.

Chapter 8

Being Invisible

I am invisible, understand, simply because people refuse to
see me.

~ Ralph Ellison in *Invisible Man*

Just as I thought, whites had everything. Even the Negro doctors
and lawyers in Indianapolis didn't live like the family my aunt Viola
worked for. Aunt Viola was Daddy's sister and a maid for Donald
and Dibbie Teetor and their family in Hagerstown, Indiana. In the
summer of 1950, I worked with her on the Teetor estate. Donald
was president of the Perfect Circle Piston Ring Company, a business
owned by his family. The family name had originally been Dieter. The
first Dieter to come to the U.S. from Germany was Jorg, who arrived
in Philadelphia in 1729. The name evolved to Deeter, then to Teeter,
and finally, in 1913, Teetor. The Dieters were members of the plain
living Dunkards, or Pennsylvania Dutch. In the early 1820s, Abraham
Teeter left Pennsylvania to settle in eastern Indiana where he started
a bicycle shop. That business became the Railway Cycle Manufacturing Company and by 1926 evolved into Perfect Circle Piston Rings,
a business that continued until "the last factory door in Hagerstown
was closed" in 1995. At its peak in 1943, the company, with plants in
nearby towns like Tipton and New Castle, had 6,455 employees. The
"star" of the Teetor clan was Ralph Teetor, whose loss of eyesight at
age five did not impair his vision. He was a brilliant mechanical engi-
neer with a number of automotive and aviation inventions, including
Cruise Control for automobiles.

Mama had jumped at the chance to have me work with Aunt
Viola for the summer. I didn't have any idea what I would be doing,
but I was ready to show the world that as a teenager, I was all grown
up. Leaving the family to go off to spend the summer with Aunt Viola

would be a signal that I was no longer a child. On top of that, I'd be making eighteen dollars a week! I wanted to be like James, who had money from his after-school job at the Y. He not only bought his own clothes, he had money left to buy candy and pop, and go to the movies anytime he wanted. By helping Aunt Viola, I'd have my own money too!

Aunt Viola was the third of Daddy's six sisters and she was considered the family beauty. Her skin was light caramel in color, and her wavy hair was soft and easily straightened. She smiled often, showing her straight white teeth, and had a dry sense of humor. Aunt Viola was a firecracker, way more worldly than Mama. She had been divorced a couple of

Aunt Viola. This is how I saw my aunt— jaunty and fashionable. I'm guessing she was around thirty in this photo. Harris Brothers Studio

times, didn't have any children, and owned a car. I liked my aunt, although I could tell that Mama didn't exactly approve of her. Aunt Viola was fortyish when I went to work with her, and recently separated from her latest husband, John. They had been working for the Teetors four or five years—she as their maid, and he as their butler. He must have abused Aunt Viola in some way. When he left the Teetor's employ, their son Tom said he was told to drive him to Indianapolis and drop him off where he would be unlikely to run into Daddy and my uncles. There was a family story that a couple of my uncles had thrown a previous husband of hers down a flight of steps after he had hit Aunt Viola. With John gone, Aunt Viola needed help serving the family.

When school let out, I packed my things, Aunt Viola picked me up, and we drove away. I didn't look back; I was on my way to a major adventure.

On our arrival at the Teetor estate, my eyes were overwhelmed trying to take in the whole spread. Aunt Viola drove through huge iron gates down a long driveway. I couldn't believe the size of their massive house, and the fact that they had *three* cars. I had heard and read about rich people, but never expected to see this rare species up close. The Teetor house where I was to work was so big it made me think of a museum. The "yard," like the state parks we had visited, had acres of woods, a tennis court, and a log cabin in the woods. One of Donald Teetor's nephews described the estate where he grew up. "In 1930 Lothair, Donald, and Herman moved into their three new homes at Woodside, the eighteen-acre compound they had constructed. ...They surrounded the estate with a secure iron fence with heavy gates...that were locked at night [with] an armed night watchman patrol[ling] the grounds. One driveway served all three houses." A half-mile or so separated each of the three mansions and all three men worked for the family business in Hagerstown, a burg sixty miles east of Indianapolis. Much of the town's population of about two thousand was employed at Perfect Circle.

The Donald Teetor house seemed enormous to me with tons of rooms including a huge living room that was divided into two seating areas with chintz-covered couches, and I don't know how many chairs, tables, and lamps. The dining room was capable of seating ten, comfortably. And there was a guest bedroom with adjoining bathroom that had a black sink and black bathtub. I saw what I thought was a smaller dining room, but Aunt Viola said it was a breakfast nook. And then there was a little bathroom without a tub that she called a powder room. Upstairs was the master bedroom suite, which dazzled me. I entered the double doors and saw the largest bed in the world. The huge bed, probably a precursor to king-sized beds, turned out to be two single beds hooked together. Aunt Viola showed me how to unhook them so I could put on fresh sheets, and hook them back together. *Inside* the bedroom was a bathroom. That bathroom had a long counter with two sinks, a bathtub, and a separate shower. The toilet was in its own little room! On the other side of this outsize bathroom was another bedroom. Also on the second floor were two dressing rooms, two more bedrooms, and another full bathroom. Dramatically lit artwork was everywhere in the house, contributing to its resemblance to the Indianapolis Museum of Art.

This is the Teetor family home where I worked during the summers of 1950 and 1951.
Courtesy of Connie Teetor Rodie

Don Teetor's nephew corroborates my memory of this house. "Don's living room was spectacular, the size of a small basketball court with a cathedral ceiling two stories high, and a fireplace one could literally walk around in without bumping one's head. The hand hewn beams had been salvaged from a mill…. The theater organ [purchased from a Chicago theater that was being demolished] was a bit oversized for any home and had to be played at a subdued volume…. Don became very knowledgeable about fine art and …assembled an impressive collection. His home, hung with old masters framed in Baroque frames and lit with little picture lights, was impressive."

The kitchen in this opulent home was headquarters for Aunt Viola and me. And what a kitchen it was! It had lots of workspace, two stainless-steel sinks, a garbage disposal, and a dishwasher. I didn't even know a machine could wash dishes. I wished we had one at home. With the garbage disposal we could scrape leftover food, except for bones, into the sink, run some water, then turn it on. That was it; the food went down the drain. I guessed the appliances—stove, refrigerator, dishwasher—were custom-made because they were black rather than white. The servants' eating area was a small sunny room with a table and two chairs right behind the kitchen.

I couldn't understand why the whites in my neighborhood didn't live like the Teetors. After all, *racism* wasn't holding them back.

There were only four people living in that enormous house: Donald, his wife Dibbie, and their two children. Their son Tom, age twenty-two, was about to marry and move to Cincinnati, and their eighteen-year-old daughter Connie had just completed high school. Mr. Teetor, who was forty-seven at the time, was tall, with white hair, and a little full around the middle. Mrs. Teetor, at age forty-five, was small and trim, just a little taller than Aunt Viola, and Aunt Viola was about my height—all of us several inches shorter than Mama. Mrs. Teetor wore glasses and had light brown hair—Aunt Viola said it was dyed and that it should have been white like Mr. Teetor's. Tom was tall like his dad, except his hair was dark, and Connie was blonde and perky.

The Teetors' house had servant's quarters—a small room with a double bed and a tiny bathroom, up the back stairs—but Aunt Viola lived in the cabin in the woods. Initially I thought the cabin had been the children's playhouse, but I learned that it was built to house servants who desired more privacy. The dark brown log cabin was about two hundred yards from the back of the house with two bedrooms, a living room, a kitchen-dining room, bathroom, screened-in porch and a garage for Aunt Viola's car. The cabin was about the same size as my family's home; however, at the cabin I gloried in the fact that I had my own room. Another unexpected joy was a bookcase filled with titles I hadn't yet read.

Except for their presence in the dining room when I served meals, I didn't see much of the family after our initial introductions. I cleaned the downstairs before they came down for breakfast and did the upstairs after they had left for the day. What little I knew about them came from cleaning up after them, plus whatever bits of information Aunt Viola shared. However, so far as I was concerned, they were the *real* white people.

From time to time, Mrs. Teetor stopped in the kitchen to talk with Aunt Viola. She was usually in a hurry, but I never figured out why she was so busy. She didn't have a job and certainly didn't lift a finger around that house. Aside from her occasional visits, the kitchen was our territory and apparently off-limits to the rest of them.

Although Mrs. Teetor signed my checks, I worked for Aunt Viola. She woke me up every morning a little before six o'clock, which felt like the middle of the night to me. I didn't get up that early for school and this was summer vacation. I quickly washed and dressed because by 6:15 we were walking in the kitchen door. I went straight to the closet to get the dust mop, dust rags, and vacuum cleaner. My morning job was to fluff the pillows on the couches, dust the hardwood floors and every piece of furniture, and vacuum the carpets in the living and dining rooms before the Teetors came down for breakfast. When the couch pillows were smashed and lumpy and the ashtrays full, I knew they had used the living room. At other times, the room looked exactly the way I had left it the day before, but Aunt Viola insisted that I do the same cleaning routine no matter the condition of the room. I thought that was silly, but did as I was told.

At 7:30 we served breakfast. After breakfast I helped clear the table and clean the kitchen. While Aunt Viola prepared lunch, I made my rounds upstairs—making beds, scrubbing bathrooms and putting out fresh towels, dusting and vacuuming. Aunt Viola believed in nonstop work, just like my parents. From the time we arrived in the morning until after the lunch dishes were put away, we barely paused, except to gobble down some food.

In addition to cooking the Teetors' meals, Aunt Viola did the laundry, including starching and ironing Mr. Teetor's and Tom's dress shirts. Unless we took on an occasional job, like polishing the silver, we went back to the cabin after lunch and rested for an hour or so. We returned to the house around 3 p.m. On the afternoon shift, we prepared dinner, served it, and spit-shined the kitchen before going home for the evening. We couldn't leave though until we were dismissed. Sometimes, particularly if the Teetors had company for dinner, they sat around the table talking until nine or ten p.m., buzzing us for coffee and drinks.

We actually sat down to eat dinner and sometimes got through it without being buzzed into the dining room. Mrs. Teetor didn't ring a bell or pull a cord like I had seen in movies. She used her foot to press a button underneath the carpet at her end of the table. That way no one knew when she called for her servants; we just appeared to clear the table at the precise moment they were all finished eating. We didn't work on Thursdays, Sunday afternoons, and those Saturday evenings when the Teetors went out. At least on Sundays I didn't have to clean the house and make the beds.

I had no idea I could work so hard. I should have apologized to Mama because compared to this my chores at home were frivolous. Our entire house could nearly fit into the Teetors' living room. I could see why the Teetors didn't clean the place themselves; it was too damn big! Despite this adventure not being exactly what I had hoped for, I did everything I was told as well as I could and didn't question Aunt Viola. It wouldn't do for her to tell Mama I was being sassy. So far as my parents were concerned, the worst thing we could do was behave in front of other people like we didn't have good home training. When I wasn't working, I was reading. I read *Gone with the Wind* that summer and knew exactly how Mammy felt scurrying around to serve Miss Scarlett.

I loved my aunt, but she needed her coat pulled about the way she acted around white folks. She did way too much bowing and scraping for my taste. First of all, I couldn't believe that the Teetor children, who were not that much older than I was, called her Viola. Even if their parents hadn't taught them any better, Aunt Viola should not have let them get away with it. But worse than that was the day Mrs. Teetor stopped in the kitchen as we were about to leave for our afternoon break. I was sitting in our eating area waiting for Aunt Viola and reading the newspaper. When Mrs. Teetor came in, I spoke to her and went back to my reading. When she left, Aunt Viola lit into me.

"Don't ever sit down when the Teetors are in the room!"

"Don't sit down? ...Why?"

"If you're sitting down, they'll think you have nothing to do. Stand up and look busy. They're paying you to work."

ARE YOU CRAZY? THE TWO OF US ARE KEEPING THIS BIG-ASS HOUSE SPOTLESS, COOKING THEIR MEALS, WASHING AND IRONING THEIR CLOTHES AND THEIR LINENS, MAKING BEDS, AND FOREVER CLEANING BATHROOMS. WHY WOULD THEY THINK WE DON'T HAVE ENOUGH TO DO?

"Yes, ma'am." Unbelievable! I knew then I would never make it as a maid.

Before that incident, Aunt Viola had seemed amused by the fact that I liked to read. I had heard her telling friends, "She reads all the time," with what I thought was pride. I was disappointed and hurt that she had a different attitude for whites. I guess white folks only respected Negroes for working, not reading. What really dug at my soul, however, was the implication that I had no value except in my ability to keep the place clean. As a person I was inconsequential, invisible.

I had gone to work with Aunt Viola in early June as soon as school was out. By the end of the month we had packed for the annual trip to the Teetors' cottage on Lake Wawasee, a hundred miles away in northern Indiana. When I heard cottage, I thought it would be a cute little place with a lot less work than that massive house I had been cleaning every morning. I couldn't have been more wrong! The cottage had more beds to be made than their house because they regularly had houseguests at the lake. In addition to two full bathrooms, each bedroom had one or two face bowls with mirrors. My bed-making rounds included scrubbing all the face bowls and the bathrooms. There were four Teetor family cottages at the lake, and my memory of endless bed making was reinforced when I read a description of one of those cottages, "It had seven bedrooms...[and] anticipating many house guests,... each bedroom [was equipped] with two double beds which gave the cottage a sleeping capacity of twenty-eight." We got a "break" at the cottage because the Teetors and their guests tended to sleep late there. We *served* only two meals a day. For breakfast we set out fruit, rolls, and coffee so that food was available whenever they decided to roll out of bed. I didn't notice the "break"; I was busy making beds.

Although Lake Wawasee was a few yards beyond the front door of the cottage, it existed as little more than an abstraction for me. All day long I was busy, and by the time we finished working, it was nearly dark, and I was too tired to do anything except go to bed. One afternoon I was upstairs on my rounds when I heard voices and laughter through the open window. I looked out and saw a clear blue sky, bright sunshine, and the lake with a few sailboats on it. It looked like a picture post card. Connie and her friends were outside fooling around on the pier and getting ready to go out in the Teetors's motorboat. I watched them for a few minutes then returned to making beds and scrubbing sinks. A few days later Connie asked if I would like to take a ride in the boat.

Aunt Viola answered for me. "Oh, no thanks, Connie. She's got too much to do, but it's awful nice of you to ask."

I had never been in a boat and thought this was probably my only chance, but I didn't say anything.

"Come on, Viola. We'll be back in a few minutes." Connie was already pulling me toward the door. I was happy because I knew Aunt Viola wasn't about to stop her.

The Teetors were invariably polite, but they only talked to Aunt Viola, so I was surprised that Connie knew I existed. I rarely saw her, but when I did she was smiling and happy. And why not? If I were white and rich I'd be happy all the time too. Connie put me in a lifejacket, helped me into the passenger's seat of a small motorboat, and got behind the wheel. Then she astonished me further by talking to me.

"How old are you?"

"Thirteen."

"So you'll be in eighth grade next year, right?"

"I start high school this fall."

"Really? Ninth grade?"

"Yes."

"You must be smart if you're starting ninth grade already."

I liked that Connie thought I was smart, but I felt embarrassed and out-of-place in my gray-and-white maid's uniform and lifejacket. Connie, of course, was dressed for the occasion in a swimsuit and sunglasses. Despite my uneasiness, I enjoyed the short boat ride; it was a respite and, more important, I was being recognized as a *person*. I doubt Connie realized that her kindness reinforced my latent feeling that I deserved the same respect the Teetors took for granted.

In the summer of 1952, a year after I last worked for the Teetors, I was reminded of Connie's gesture when I received an invitation to her wedding. I was flabbergasted. The wedding was going to be in Indianapolis on a Saturday. I didn't recognize the name of the church or the location, but Mama knew where it was. I hadn't been to many weddings, and I'd certainly never seen an extravaganza like I expected a Teetor wedding would be. About a week before the wedding, Aunt Viola called me. She was very curt, as if she was upset about something.

"Are you going to Connie's wedding?"

"Yes ma'am."

"Well, wear a white dress."

"I was going to wear my Easter dress."

"Is it white?"

"No, ma'am, it's blue. Mama says that only the bride wears white at a wedding."

Aunt Viola hesitated for a moment as if she wanted to say something, but changed her mind. Then in a harsh tone she said, "We're wearing white. Wear a white dress and I'll give you an apron when you get there. And be there no later than two thirty." She hung up.

My heart dropped. I had been invited to the wedding so I could work? Mama instructed us to never show that we had been hurt, but I wanted to scream with anger! Why send an invitation? Why not just call and ask me to work? I felt like throwing something breakable against a wall, but I knew that wouldn't go over well in the Cheatham household. I casually told Mama what Aunt Viola had said.

"I figured that's why they sent you that invitation. And even if it wasn't, Viola wasn't going to have you sitting in a pew while she was working. How much are they paying?"

"I forgot to ask." I could care less about the money I just wanted to see the wedding. And I sure as hell didn't want to wear a maid's uniform again.

The wedding was scheduled to begin at 3:30, but Aunt Viola wanted me there an hour early. On the day of the wedding I left home at one o'clock wearing the ill-fitting white dress from my elementary school graduation. Mama told me which bus to catch from downtown and where to get off. I caught the correct bus but got off at the wrong stop. I became so lost and confused that I never found the church and missed Connie's wedding altogether. I still don't know whether or not Connie invited me as a guest, or to work. And aside from that brief motorboat ride, my scrubbing and cleaning went on as usual that summer.

As the Fourth of July approached, I began to get excited. At home we always went on a picnic or had a barbecue, and I wondered how we would celebrate here at the lake. When I asked Aunt Viola what we were going to do, she said we wouldn't be off until about four in the afternoon. *WHAT? WE HAVE TO WORK!* I couldn't believe it! Not only did we have to work, but every bed in the cottage was in use for the holiday. I know because I made them up. I also helped Aunt Viola prepare tons of potato salad, coleslaw, rolls, and about a dozen chickens for frying. I already felt horrible about working as if it were any other day, but Aunt Viola made bad matters worse. After we had taken the food out to the Teetors and their guests for their picnic, I looked at the pieces of chicken left behind for our dinner. Aunt Viola had not set aside one decent piece for us to eat. Not a leg or breast, not even a wing.

"Aunt Viola, there's nothing here except necks and ribs. You forgot to keep some good pieces for us."

"Girl, they bought that chicken for them, not us. What would they think if they walked in here and saw you eating a drumstick?"

"That I was trying to keep up my strength so I could do all this work."

"Don't you sass me!"

I didn't understand Aunt Viola. Didn't the Teetors want us to eat well? How would they ever know anyway? Were they counting the chicken pieces? That was the worst day of my summer as a maid. I wrote to Mama about it.

Several days later, Aunt Viola asked, "Janet, are you getting enough to eat?"

UH OH. MAMA MUST HAVE SAID SOMETHING TO AUNT VIOLA. "Yes ma'am."

"If you're not getting enough to eat, tell me. Don't be writing home. There's nothing they can do about it."

"Yes, ma'am." After that I kept my discontent to myself.

Even my paycheck didn't bring me any joy. There was no place to buy anything, and my friends weren't there to go to movies with me. I sent my checks home to Mama who put the money aside for school expenses. The summer of 1951, after my freshman year in high school, Aunt Viola was eager to have my help again, but I didn't want to go back. Mama wasn't having it.

"Do you want new school clothes?"

"Yes, ma'am."

"Then you've got to work."

"Yes, ma'am."

I continued to do the best job I could, but in my soul, I knew that I had to figure out some way to insure that my future would not include a career as a maid. I was not at all happy being the phantom who kept dirt at bay without disturbing the Teetors' thoughts or their field of vision. And even though I was a Negro, I thought I was supposed to be happy.

My summers with Aunt Viola were not all work and disappointment, however. I learned several things that proved useful as I got older. Aunt Viola was known to be a great cook, and I enjoyed the cooking tips and helping her prepare meals. I was introduced to unfamiliar foods that we didn't eat at home like asparagus, tomato consommé, and filet mignon. I also learned how to set a table with a full complement of dishes. There were wineglasses, water glasses, and after dinner, brandy snifters. Dinner plates, salad plates, bread plates, and all kinds of forks—dinner, shrimp, dessert—and butter, dinner, and steak knives. No wonder we had to bring in the food; there was no room on the table after I laid out all that china, crystal, and silverware. But, for whatever it was worth, when I dined in fine restaurants as an adult, I knew which fork was for what.

Aunt Viola also talked to me about sex, asking if I had ever had any. I told her I had not. She didn't tell me to wait until I was married, but until I was older, seventeen or eighteen.

"When you're older, you'll know more about what you're doing. Then, if you get in trouble, you'll know what to do."

"Get in trouble?"

"Infamilyway. You don't want to have a baby until you *want* a baby."

Aunt Viola continued. "If you ever do get in trouble, let me know and I'll tell you what to do."

I had heard Mama and Aunt Lula sighing about girls who were infamilyway and not married. After I began menstruating—on New Year's Day, five months before my eleventh birthday—Mama warned me that I was now a woman and could get infamilyway if I messed with boys. I had no idea what she meant, nor did I understand what was happening to me. When I used the toilet and found the rusty stains in my panties, I figured I had hurt myself somehow. I put on a clean pair and ran back outside to continue playing. Every time I used the bathroom, I put on a clean pair of panties. Mama found the several pairs of soiled panties when she did the wash. Somebody came and got me out of class because my mother was on the phone.

Mama didn't even say hello, "Are you still menstruating?"

I didn't know what she was talking about. "What?"

"I found your bloody panties. Are you still bleeding?"

"Naw. Not anymore."

"Well, you let me know the next time it happens."

"Okay." *THE NEXT TIME IT HAPPENS? WHY WOULD IT HAPPEN AGAIN? I JUST HURT MYSELF WHILE I WAS PLAYING.*

But it did happen again. When I told Mama she handed me a box of sanitary napkins and a belt and said, "Here. Use these."

I literally had no idea what to do with the strange items. "How? What am I supposed to do?"

Mama showed me how to put the belt on and where to fasten the pad to the belt, but she was clearly upset, even angry. And she warned me again about messing with boys. When I asked Mama what messing around with boys meant, her harsh reply was, "Just don't be messin' with 'em!" The only thing I could think of was not letting boys touch me while we played. Once a boy hit me and I was absolutely terrified. *OH GOD! AM I INFAMILYWAY NOW?* I was in a panic for a few days, then I forgot about it. I was so embarrassed by the nasty business, that I didn't tell any of my friends. A couple of years later when they started menstruating, I found out from them that I had to "do it" with a boy to get infamilyway. I wasn't sure what that meant either, but I knew it took place secretly, not on the playground. By the time Rosie got her period I was a sophisticated fourteen and saved her the agony I had experienced.

I would rather have died than shame Mama and Daddy by getting infamilyway, but it was comforting to know that if it happened, I could talk to Aunt Viola. All I heard from Mama on the subject was, "Keep your panties up and your dress tail down."

Not only did Aunt Viola speak openly about verboten topics, but I was not banished when her friends came over. At home, when adults came to visit, we children were called out so the company could remark on how much we had grown. Then we were told to go play, which meant, "Do not come back in here until the company is gone." Aunt Viola hung out with the servants of other wealthy families in Hagerstown and at the lake. When they got together on their days and evenings off, they always brought the latest records to play on the Victrola. And they partied hard—eating, drinking, dancing, and laughing while listening to the blues. They drank the same expensive whisky as the people they worked for and ate food prepared by women who cooked for the wealthy.

They also played cards, an activity forbidden by my parents, who thought a deck of cards was an instrument of the devil. I felt really risqué playing cards. Aunt Viola and her friends played poker, gin rummy, and, my favorite, bid whist.

Poker they played for money, but the whist games were just for fun. In whist one set of two partners competed against another pair of players. Sometimes trumps were whatever suit the dealer turned up as the last card in the deck. Most of the time we bid the number of books above six we hoped to make. A card from each player made a book. All fifty-two cards were dealt—thirteen to each player—and the highest card in each suit won the book unless a player had nothing in the suit and played a trump. Asa, who had been a Pullman porter before he was a chauffeur, was the best player. The Negro Pullman porters played during their runs, and added their own modifications to the game, which had originated in Britain. Asa talked so much trash that he kept everybody off-guard. He had something to say about every play.

"That mess ain't goin' nowhere!" he'd say when he trumped somebody's ace.

"Try some of this!" and he'd slap his winning card on the table so hard sometimes it made you jump.

Although they taught me how to play all their card games, I usually preferred to read when they were having a game. Sometimes when they needed a fourth for whist, they'd call on me and pair me with Asa, to handicap him, I guess. I was just glad that I didn't have to play against him. A few times when I wasn't playing, Asa would call me in and whisper his strategies to me. He showed me how to count trumps, when to play my best card, and when to slide. He taught me how to figure out what cards the other players had from the way they played, and how to play so nobody knew what cards I was holding. He also gave me suggestions on what to do when I had a lousy hand.

I loved the way Aunt Viola and her friends let it all hang out, and made up my mind that I would have fun like that when I was an adult. However, as much as I enjoyed their parties and playing bid whist, I had had enough of being a maid. Anticipating that Aunt Viola would want my help for a third summer, I signed up for summer school. I was in my second year of high school, and told Mama I wanted to go to college. I had no expectation of actually doing so, but I was determined not to spend another summer busting my hump. I figured Mama wouldn't pull me from summer school to work as a maid. I was right. When Aunt Viola came over, I heard Mama say with great pride that I wouldn't be available. "She's going to summer school to get ready for college."

Chapter 9

Some Times Are Worse

There are no good times to be black in America, but some times are worse than others.

~ David Bradley, author of
The Chaneysville Incident

In junior high, my girlfriends and I had started drooling about going to high school. We were looking forward to meeting new boys from all over the city. James seemed to me to be having the time of his life at Crispus Attucks. He went to parties, attended ballgames, and sometimes brought home new friends from exotic neighborhoods that I had never seen. These intriguing older boys didn't notice me, but I knew that James met them at Attucks, where I would soon be going. When my parents heard me rhapsodizing about Attucks, they interrupted. There was something they needed to explain, *again*.

"You won't be going to Attucks. Manual is the closest high school to us."

"What do you mean I won't be going to Attucks? Why not?"

"Manual is our closest high school." Mama repeated that meaningless statement. "What's *Manual*? What does *Manual* have to do with it?"

"That's the high school you'll go to."

"What do you mean? Manual? I'm going to Attucks. I *have* to go to Attucks. Where did Manual come from?" I had never heard of Manual, and didn't want to hear anymore about it. "You can't make me go to Manual!"

"Watch your mouth." Mama felt I was sassing her, but the idea that I would not be going to Attucks made me nearly hysterical.

"I could talk to Andrew Ramsey. He can probably get her in."

Daddy offered to help. Mr. Ramsey was Daddy's lodge brother and the chairman of Attucks's foreign language department.

Mama wouldn't hear of it. "We worked too hard to integrate these schools not to take advantage of it. How would it look, after all we've done, if our own daughter didn't go to one of the white schools? She's going to Manual."

What was this madness? When I was five I was barred from going to a nearby school because of *segregation*. Now I was *dying* to go to Attucks and Mama said I couldn't because of *integration*. I couldn't believe I'd have to go to some dumb *white* school and be integrated. Dammit! My life was ruined! I couldn't possibly have any fun in a white high school.

When World War II ended in 1945, Negroes who had saved democracy in Europe accelerated their demands for democracy at home. Negroes in Indianapolis were embarrassed when Gary, Indiana outpaced the state capital by ending segregation in their schools in 1946. Indianapolis, alone, was the largest northern city with segregated schools. Rosalyn Richardson's son, Henry J. III, was ready for first grade in 1946 and she took him to the neighborhood school three blocks away. School officials told Mrs. Richardson that her son had to take a two-mile bus ride to a colored school. Mrs. Richardson and another black parent, Willa Taylor, asked Virgil Stinebaugh, superintendent of the Indianapolis Public Schools, to intervene and allow their children to enroll in the neighborhood school. Stinebaugh refused. The two affronted mothers decided enough was enough. They organized a citywide campaign to desegregate the schools. The NAACP, sororities, fraternities, lodges, church groups, and my parents immediately cooperated. Even the national NAACP, in the person of Thurgood Marshall, offered their assistance, both legal and financial. Marshall, who later was appointed a justice of the U. S. Supreme Court, was then the NAACP's chief counsel.

Stinebaugh announced, "Segregation is the established policy of the Indianapolis Public Schools and will be enforced." Although it has been Indianapolis's way to blame the Ku Klux Klan for segregated schools, "the Klan was merely one of the architects of Indianapolis's segregated schools. The policy of segregation was instituted before Klan-supported candidates took office, continued while they were in position, and was maintained after they were ostensibly removed from the school board." Not long after Stinebaugh made his pronouncement, Attorney Henry J. Richardson Jr., Rosalyn's husband and Daddy's pal, presented a desegregation plan to the Indianapolis Board of School Commissioners. A few months later the state legislature nullified Stinebaugh's reiteration of the segregation policy by passing yet another law specifying how the *races* should be educated in Indiana. The new law stated that in September 1949 all students entering elementary school, their first year of junior high, or high school, would attend the school closest to their home, regardless of *race*. The black community's general exultation was expressed in a bold headline triumphantly proclaiming, "[Governor] Schricker Signs School Bill."

So far as elementary schools were concerned, the new policy made little difference because most Negroes lived in two sections of town that were overwhelmingly colored. (Even when the *racial* composition of neighborhoods changed, the Indianapolis Board of Education proved "especially adept in gerrymandering school districts to maintain *racial* exclusiveness.") High schools were another matter. Crispus Attucks, the Negro high school, was located in one of the colored areas and would remain a Negro school. However, there were a number of Negro students like me who did not live near Attucks, and we would be scattered among the other six high schools.

The same year that *racial* barriers were being cautiously removed from the schools, two other events made it clear that schools were not the only places where *racial* segregation was the order of the day. Two black couples were arrested for breaking "an unwritten law against 'colored and white mixing.'" The two "white" women were actually light-skinned Negroes, and the men were a juvenile court judge and a dentist who was a highly regarded local politician. Although the charges were dropped, and the people arrested had broken no laws, the arresting officers suffered no penalties. Whatever the trumped-up charges were, they undoubtedly would have been carried forward if the people arrested had not been prominent members of the community.

Another example of Indianapolis's petty ignobility toward Negroes occurred in August. A Negro employee of a Haag's drugstore was fired because she sold a sandwich to her brother, and he ate it inside the store. The manager of the store denied that was the reason for the employee's termination but did admit that it was company policy not to serve Negroes. The manager was quoted as saying, "We have all white trade here, and the girls have been informed that Negroes are not to be served."

This was the *racial* climate in the city when I enrolled at Manual High School in 1950, the second year of this latest version of school integration. I had been cheated out of going to Attucks, so I wasn't any happier to be at Manual than they were to have me. Not only had James been lucky enough to go to high school *before* desegregation, but Mama's evening classes were also at Attucks. Attucks High School was a cherished institution in the Negro community. Since our schools were virtually the only places where Negroes could put their college degrees to use, Attucks's staff was the best educated in the school system. Teachers were recruited from around the country and within seven years after the school opened, "the sixty-two member faculty held nineteen master's degrees and two Ph Ds. Every teacher had at least a baccalaureate degree."

My sister, Rosie, did a study of Russell A. Lane, Attucks's long-time principal, for her doctoral degree. She described Lane as committed to educational excellence, and a taskmaster. Lane encouraged his teachers and students to obtain additional education and set the example himself with five degrees, including a bachelor's from the Ivy League's Brown University, and a J D from the Indiana University Law School. During his tenure as principal from 1930 to 1957, Lane made Attucks a first-class institution. The Negro community packed the school auditorium for professional-grade student performances, and their graduation exercises were so popular, they were held at the 10,000-seat Cadle Tabernacle. I had spent my life idolizing Attucks, but in the name of integration, I had to forego that dream for Manual High School.

Unlike Gary three years earlier, and Boston twenty years later, Indianapolis's whites didn't organize to stop Negroes from enrolling in "their" schools. However, that didn't preclude my feeling completely alone and isolated at Manual. The faces I encountered among the crowd of students in the hallways between classes were white, strange, and not particularly friendly. There were so few Negroes that we rarely saw one another; I was the proverbial fly in buttermilk. When I was a freshman in the second year of integration, I'd guess there were no more than forty of us Negroes in a student body of seventeen hundred. My graduating class of two hundred sixty included fifteen Negroes. Three other Negroes—Laura Noel, Esther Quarles, and Rosalind Trabue—were in my physical education class, but I was alone in all my other classes. I already knew the girls in phys ed: Laura was my writing buddy, and Rozzie, Esther and I attended the same church. I was right; Manual would not be any fun.

We Negro students had been advised to be "little Jackie Robinsons," meaning that no matter what happened, we were to be pleasant and cooperative so that whites wouldn't regret having us there. Nobody cared that I regretted being there. Some of the white students were cordial. Others asked to touch my skin or my hair to see what they felt like. In an effort to be nice, I allowed it a few times, but I was offended. What did they expect me to feel like? At least nobody asked to see my tail. Another insult added to my injuries was that I was assigned to English 1R for retarded students. I was mortified, but didn't complain because I was trying to do my best Jackie Robinson. My teacher's name, like much of my Manual experience, has been so deeply suppressed I can't call it up. I'll call her Miss Wren. I believe she was a slightly built older woman. Miss Wren gave us careful instructions for the simple in-class assignments that I completed in minutes. In a few days she realized I didn't belong there.

"I think there's been a mistake. You shouldn't be in this class for slow learners. I'll have you transferred. "

What a relief! I was embarrassed at being in the dumb class and bored as well. "Thank you, Miss Wren." I waited patiently for my transfer, and when weeks passed with no further mention of it, I asked Miss Wren about it. She said the office wouldn't allow her to transfer me.

I couldn't believe it! What was I supposed to do after I finished the second grade busy work she passed out everyday? I spent several days immobilized by resentment, mentally cataloging the reasons why I hated Manual High School. After my initial frustration dissipated, I decided to use the class time to do homework for my other courses. When I finished serving my time in English 1R, Miss Wren gave me an A+, and recommended me for English G, the honors classes. Surprisingly, I was assigned to English honors for the remainder of high school, a pleasure that almost made up for the stigma of taking home economics classes. In English honors we spent our time reading and writing about literature rather than studying grammar and diagramming sentences. There were no Negro writers in our texts, but I enjoyed reading James Fenimore Cooper, Charles Dickens, George Eliot, and Shakespeare. I wonder how often a student went from retarded to honors English in one semester?

I have no idea why I was put into an English class for slow students. Perhaps I didn't score well on the Stanford Achievement Test I was given in eighth grade. I have no doubt that it was culturally biased because there were many questions on it that made no sense to me. I had hoped that tests like that would be discarded as a measurement of student ability and potential; however educational systems are relying on them more than ever. The testing lobby must be very powerful.

All the teachers and staff at Manual were white. It would require more years of struggle to convince the Indianapolis school board that Negroes were capable of teaching white students. One of my English teachers, Miss Allen, surprised me with a final grade of B. I had made A's on nearly all of my papers and exams, so I didn't understand the grade. When I asked her about it, she insisted that I had received occasional A's, but mostly B's and C's on my work. Clearly Miss Allen had not considered the possibility that Annie Cheatham treasured every school paper that her children brought home. And there was no way that Mama would lose a paper on which her child had received an A at a white school. When I told Mama that I thought Miss Allen's grade was unfair, Mama collected my papers and went to see her. Miss Allen protested that changing grades was just not done, but somehow she found a way to change my B to an A.

My guidance counselor, whom I'll call Miss Barnhart, advised me on the classes I needed to meet the requirements for graduation. Miss Barnhart was a lanky, joyless woman who didn't seem to like her job. Near the end of freshman year, when we were to declare a major, Miss Barnhart said I should major in home economics.

"Home economics is cooking and sewing, right?"

"Yes. It will prepare you for domestic work."

No way! I didn't have the faintest idea what I would do as an adult, but I knew that it would not be cleaning white folks' houses.

"I don't think I want to do that. I'd like to major in English."

She responded impatiently, "All students take four years of English. You need another major in addition to English."

"So what else can I major in?"

"Home economics is the best major for you." Miss Barnhart refused to discuss it any further.

I was outraged and couldn't wait to tell Mama. I knew she wouldn't want me to prepare for domestic work. You could have knocked me over with a feather when Mama agreed that a home ec major was a good idea. How could she believe I should be a maid? I didn't need school to learn how to cook and clean; I had already spent a long summer with Aunt Viola doing that for the Teetors. I didn't understand how Mama could betray me like that. Mama told me that domestic work would be my employment, as it was hers, so if home economics courses would help prepare me for that, so much the better. I bitterly resented the idea that *anybody,* let alone my own mother, thought my only choice in life was to serve and clean up for white people. I majored in home economics because I didn't have the courage to defy the school and Mama, but every day I spent in those classes, I was ashamed.

My sister Rosie in her senior year at Manual.

This was another of Mama's mixed messages. I grew up listening to her say that she longed for me to attend college, but she insisted that I learn to be a domestic servant. She hoped I would be a professional career woman but claimed that marriage and children were the highest calling a woman could have. Inwardly I raged against these psychic leashes, but I didn't say anything. In many ways I was Mama's living, breathing doppelgänger: her first–born daughter who resembled her, and shared her interests in books and writing. I think she vacillated between wanting me to have the life she longed for and not wanting me to be hurt if, like her, I was unable to fulfill my dreams. At other times when she actively discouraged my desires, she was probably overcome with resentment seeing me accomplish things that were impossible for her.

Two years later when Rosie was told to major in home economics, she absolutely refused. She knew I was pissed off about it, plus Rosie never hesitated to challenge Mama. Rosie knew that a white classmate planned

Charles Kenneth Barker. Courtesy of Charles K. Barker

to become a secretary and was taking typing and shorthand classes. Rosie decided she would do that as well and asked to major in business. When Manual balked at letting Rosie take business classes, Mama called the principal and told him she would take the issue to the school board and the NAACP. They backed down immediately. As usual, Rosie's rude defiance got more from Mama than I ever did by being tractable.

At least Rosie and I were directed to the courses we needed to graduate. Reginald, Rosie's twin, never even had a counselor assigned to him. Reggie took whatever he wanted until Rosie started telling him what courses he needed to graduate. Charles Kenneth Barker, a friend from my elementary school, was in my class. Charles doesn't remember having a counselor either, but he knows he was directed to take four years of shop. I know that in the 1950s many people—black and white—expected black boys to drop out of high school and go to work at their earliest opportunity, so it may have been a school policy not to discuss graduation requirements with Negro males. Charles also remembers being surprised to see in the school yearbook that Manual had career days. None of us were directed to career day activities. Manual's neglect didn't stop Charles. He credits his electrical shop teacher, Mr. Hully, with initiating an interest that led to a career in computers. After graduating from Manual, Charles obtained a degree in computer technology from Purdue University. He worked at IBM for several years, was adjunct faculty at Indiana-Purdue University's Indianapolis campus, and retired as a senior vice president and CIO of information systems for an insurance company.

Five days a week, all day long, I was in high school surrounded by the enemy. Not only that, but I was supposed to be *educated* inside the enemy camp. And the people teaching me, I believed, at *best* thought I was inferior to them, and possibly even hated my guts. Despite the circumstances, my parents insisted that I be on my best behavior. I was to study hard and get good grades so I could show the people who probably hated me how industrious and intelligent Negroes could be. On the other hand, I was taking classes to improve my skills as a domestic servant. I was confused and angry. I felt as if I had been dropped off in a strange, hostile city without a guide or a weapon. To protect myself as best I could, I sharpened my ability to detect *racism*.

Mary Jane Grace, who taught the cooking class that was my first home ec course, had a distinct Southern accent. When she announced she was from Georgia, I was instantly on alert. I had read *Strange Fruit* and *Twelve Million Black Voices,* so I knew what to expect from a Southerner. *Strange Fruit,* published in 1944, is an uncompromising novel confronting the evils of *racism* in the story of a love affair between the *races*. The author Lillian Smith was a Georgian and perhaps the first white southerner to write about the brutality of the Southern way of life. Richard Wright wrote the text for *Twelve Million Black Voices,* published in 1941. The book is a collection of pictures by a variety of photographers that depict some of the misery of black life in America in the 1930s. The pictures ranged from rural housing barely fit for human habitation, to city storefront churches, but the photos that seared my memory were the ones of Negroes who had been lynched. I remember the pictures of bodies hanging by nooses from trees, and other charred remains that were unidentifiable. These burned and mutilated bodies were the strange fruit in the title of Smith's novel and in the song made popular by Billie Holiday. These two books convinced me that Southern whites were rabid *racists*.

And Miss Grace lived down to my expectations. On the very first day, she told the class that I would clean up after our cooking exercise the next day. I could not believe it! Just because I was the only Negro there, did she really think I was going to be the class maid? She was out of her mind! After class I approached Miss Grace and spoke quickly before I lost my nerve.

"I'm not cleaning up after we cook. You think I'm supposed to clean up after everybody just because I'm a Negro."

Miss Grace looked startled and sputtered, "Oh no." She couldn't seem to think of anything else to say. I guess a Negro had never talked up to her before. Her silence empowered me, so I kept talking.

"This isn't Georgia. Up here I don't have to be the one who does the cleaning."

With that I left the room. I was shaking because I didn't know what might happen to me for sassing a teacher. Maybe they would take me out of her class; or better yet, kick me out of Manual. Nothing happened. At the next class meeting Miss Grace had posted a list indicating that a different girl was to clean up every week. The list, arranged in alphabetical order by last names, included everyone except me. I don't know if it was a coincidence or not, but I noticed that there were no names earlier in the alphabet than Cheatham. I'm not sure if Miss Grace actually thought it was my place to do the cleaning or if, due to the alphabet, I was just the first person assigned. I do know that the list was posted *after* I talked to her. From then on I took sewing classes. I much preferred cooking to sewing, but I wouldn't risk being asked to clean another kitchen.

I doubt the white girls in the home economics classes were told to prepare for domestic service; they were likely preparing to be homemakers. Manual had a Future Homemakers of America (FHA) club whose membership was all white and all female. Of Manual's eighty-nine teachers, ten of them taught home economics—more than the number teaching music and art combined. There is a picture in *The Ivian*, the school yearbook, of a Foods class—all girls—displaying their "homemaking abilities." Boys who learned to cook were preparing to be chefs. It was the 1950s.

Some teachers gave me special attention of a more positive bent. I remember the pride I felt when Mr. Van Arsdale announced in geometry class that I was the only student with a perfect score on an exam. He was considered one of the toughest teachers at Manual, and my classmates were appropriately awed. (One day Mr. Van Arsdale brought his redheaded identical twin boys, Tom and Dick, to school. Those little boys later distinguished themselves as All-American basketball players at Indiana University, and All-Stars in the National Basketball Association.)

Mrs. Siener, my speech teacher, worked on my pronunciation until my long, soft vowels were shorter and crisper. When I said the number five, instead of rhyming it with *have*, I made it rhyme with *hive*. My music teacher, Miss Trent, promoted me to first-chair cellist in the school orchestra and encouraged me to take private lessons. Interestingly, in the yearbook picture of the orchestra, every one of the five black students is seated on the last row. I don't know what pretext was used to get me on the back row; I should have been sitting down front to the left of Barbara Henn, where I sat when the orchestra performed. Playing in the school orchestra introduced me to classical music. I found pleasure in attending the free concerts for students, and enjoyed sitting in the hushed darkness listening to the sometimes soaring, sometimes soothing sounds of the Philharmonic Orchestra of Indianapolis.

As I had expected, there was no social life for me at Manual. We didn't even listen to the same popular music as the white kids. White girls were swooning over Frank Sinatra and Bing Crosby while I was agog about Billy Eckstein and Nat "King" Cole. Although whites and Negroes basically operated in two separate worlds, we dressed similarly in sweaters, plaid skirts with a large safety pin attached, and saddle oxfords with our socks rolled into a donut around our ankles. The few Negro boys at Manual were mostly the same ones I had known in elementary school, and they were too familiar to be appealing. Some daring souls crossed the color line to date, but only in secret. I barely noticed the white boys, but if I had been attracted to one, no way would I have considered *sneaking* with him. Although several of the white students were friendly and talkative in school, we did not see one another off-campus. The lack of social interaction with my white classmates, plus being excluded from most school activities because of my *race*, left me with no emotional attachments to Manual, no school spirit. Manual wasn't a part of my real life, my Negro life.

Despite my feelings, I was on the honor roll from time to time because Mama did not like her daughters to bring Cs home, and Daddy was paying fifty cents for every A. I felt I should have been invited to join the Masomas, but I wasn't. The Masomas was an honorary orga-

(l-r) Rosalind Trabue, Barbara Petty, Lewis Moore, and Helen Baker in front of Manual High School at the beginning of our senior year in 1953. Photo by Janet May Cheatham

nization serving school and community for senior and outstanding second-semester junior girls. The selection criteria were not publicized, but it was a prestigious group, and all the members were high achievers. I had a good idea why I was not one of the chosen ones, but decided to ask anyway. I went to see Helen Tipton, an English teacher who was the club sponsor.

"Miss Tipton, why haven't I been invited to join the Masomas?" I named two students whose grades were similar to mine. "Both of them are members, so I don't understand why I'm not a member."

Miss Tipton had a ready answer.

"You're not taking college prep courses, Janet. To be a Masoma, you must be enrolled in the college prep program."

COLLEGE PREP COURSES? WHAT THE HELL IS THE COLLEGE PREP PROGRAM? IS IT JUST FOR WHITE STUDENTS? NOBODY HAD EVER SAID ANYTHING TO ME ABOUT COLLEGE PREP. I didn't want Miss Tipton to know that I had no idea what she was talking about, so I thanked her and left. I didn't know where to go or who to ask about college prep. There weren't any black teachers, not even a black secretary or janitor. So I pushed it out of my mind. It was just one more thing Negroes weren't allowed to do. The guys were even barred from playing on the varsity sports teams! High-achieving Negro students were not recommended for the National Honor Society either. My discomfort at Manual notwithstanding, I did engage in a few things outside class. My activities in the yearbook are listed as "Ivian Agent 4; Operetta 3; Orchestra 1-4; Special Assistant 4; Vaudeville 1-4." It's not surprising that most of my extracurricular involvement was performance oriented. Negro students were encouraged to participate in music-related activities. I don't remember what a special assistant was, but a number of students had that designation. When I participated in vaudeville performances I noticed another interesting *racial* difference. The white girls prepared by applying leg make-up, to make their legs appear darker, I guess. I didn't ask. We Negro girls were busy putting lotion on our legs so they wouldn't appear ashy.

A major reason Negroes gave for wanting to integrate the schools was that it would improve the quality of education for us. Ironically, my classmate Charles and I agree that we could have received a better education at Crispus Attucks than at Manual. Attucks's language offerings—Greek, Latin, French, Spanish, and German—are indicative of their more comprehensive curriculum. Manual offered only Latin and Spanish. And, more important, Attucks guidance counselors would not likely have told a mathematics whiz like Charles to take shop, or directed me to home economics to train for domestic service. But if they had, in the Home Economics Department at Attucks I could have learned to make hats!

Many of the girls in my high school classes longed to get married. Margie Duff, one of my closest friends in elementary school, dropped out at fifteen to marry. She appeared happy, but it seemed tragic to me. I had no idea what I would do, but not once did I fantasize about a future with a husband and children. I recall being startled when Marie Schrader said she was not going to college. In our senior year Marie, her steady boyfriend, Wayne Brehob, and I

E. Franklin Fisher, the man who changed the arc of my life.

were in the same chemistry class. I thought Marie was as smart as her boyfriend, who *was* planning to attend college. I couldn't understand why an intelligent white girl, who I thought had more opportunities than I could ever hope for, did not aspire to a career.

E. Franklin Fisher was assigned to counsel the junior class to prepare us for our final year in high school and beyond. Mr. Fisher was an imposing figure, tall, with receding black hair and slight paunch, always crisply professional. I thought he looked more like a businessman than a guidance counselor. In my first meeting with him, he had a pointed question.

"Why aren't you taking college prep courses? With these grades you should be preparing for college."

"Miss Barnhart said I had to major in home economics." *HE THINKS I CAN GO TO COLLEGE! I KNEW I SHOULDN'T BE TAKING HOME ECONOMICS.*

Mr. Fisher didn't respond to that, he looked down and checked my record for a few minutes. "It's too bad there's not enough time for you to take a language. But you've taken some solid courses—honors English, chemistry, algebra, geometry—and done very well in them. I think we can still fix this."

Maybe Mama's fragile dream that one of her children would go to college could come true! But in my family graduating from high school was a significant achievement. Of the ten children in Daddy's family and three in Mama's, there were only two high school graduates, including Mama, who had just earned her diploma. Nobody even talked about college except Mama, and for her it was more yearning than expectation. The main objective in our family was for everybody to get a job as soon as possible and become self-supporting. Staying in high school until you graduated was a luxury, acquiring more prestige than practical outcomes. Graduating from high school didn't usually help Negroes get better jobs; sometimes a college degree didn't either. And in my family, going to college was out of the question. Nobody had money for that.

Mr. Fisher recommended a full load of courses for my senior year to bulk up my transcript. I was taking only the few courses each semester that I needed to graduate. The earlier I got out of school, the more hours I could work at my after-school job. The additional courses Mr. Fisher wanted me to take would shorten my work hours and take-home pay, but Mama didn't mind. She started getting her hopes up that I might go to college.

Mr. Fisher wasn't done. At the beginning of my senior year, he called me out of class. "Why didn't you sign up for the S.A.T.?"

"I didn't know I was supposed to." I had heard about the test, but didn't think it had anything to do with me.

"If you do well on the S.A.T., you could get a scholarship. Don't you want to go to college?"

"Oh yes, I just didn't know…."

"Today is the last day to register. It costs twenty-five cents. Do you have any money?"

"No sir."

Mr. Fisher gave me a quarter and told me to go sign up.

As he expected, I scored well enough to receive a work-study scholarship to the Indiana University Extension in Indianapolis, now IUPUI, Indiana University-Purdue University, Indianapolis. Just like that, without fanfare or premeditation, the arc of my life changed. At the time, I had no concept of what Mr. Fisher had done, but over the years I often recalled the words he wrote in my yearbook: "T'is better to aim high and fail/Than to aim low and succeed!"

Twenty years later I was back in Indianapolis working as the Ethnic Studies Consultant for the Indiana Department of Public Instruction, now the Department of Education. I read that Mr. Fisher was retiring from the school system, and by then, of course, I was fully aware of what his intervention on my behalf meant. I wrote him a letter, thanked him for what he had done, returned the quarter, and enclosed a copy of my resume. He wrote back immediately and told me how grateful he was to receive my letter.

In January 1998, I was living in Chicago when I received a call from the president of the Manual High School alumni club. He was calling from Indianapolis to tell me that I had been selected as Manual's Alumna of the Year. The ceremony, he said, would be held May 2, and he wanted to be sure I could attend. I told him I could.

I was stunned by his call and didn't think of any of the questions that later circled my mind. Why had they selected me? Whose idea was this? Were they trying to be funny? I had assumed that Manual High School and everybody connected with it were as oblivious to me as I was to them. Later, I received a congratulatory letter with a request for the names and addresses of people whom I would like to invite to the event. The letter helped me accept the reality of what I was inclined to dismiss as a mistake or a hoax. After graduating from Manual I had no desire to participate in alumni activities and hadn't been anywhere near the school since Rosie and Reggie graduated. My family kept the alumni association current on my whereabouts, but I always tossed the mail in the trash. Now Manual wanted to honor me. It made no sense.

I'd graduated forty-four years earlier, but when I began to think about Manual, I realized that I was still seething about the rejection and humiliation of my high school years. As the alumna to be honored that year, I would be expected to give an acceptance speech expressing my gratitude. What a crock! Gratitude? Hardly. Initially, I thought of writing and telling them exactly why I would not accept the recognition. Then I decided my refusal would be more dramatic if I did it at the event. With that idea in mind, I enthusiastically began to write an "acceptance" speech.

Emmerich Manual High School was originally established as the Industrial Training School in 1895. In 1899 Industrial Training became Manual Training, and in 1916 it was named the Charles E.

Emmerich Manual Training High School. Emmerich was the first principal of the school; "Training" was later dropped from the name. Negro students were routinely enrolled at Manual until 1927, when all Negroes were pulled out of the other high schools and sent to Attucks. The Manual alumni began recognizing an alumnus of the year in 1962. In 1998, I was the thirty-eighth alumnus, the ninth woman, and first black selected to receive the accolade.

It was good that I had a few months to work on my speech. Going back over my high school years was an excruciating experience that I needed time to process. The first drafts I wrote were angry and scathing. I wanted everybody connected with Manual to know how mean-spirited they had been and how my life had been affected by their cruelty. After writing each tirade, I discarded it. None of them felt *right*. Finally, I recognized that Manual had not ruined my life. My high school experiences were traumatic and infuriating, but they had prepared me for life in America, where people who look like me are outnumbered and regularly marginalized. I barely noticed the predominately white neighborhood where my family lived because everything else in my life was all-black—elementary school, church, social occasions. Manual High School immersed me in a series of situations in which I was either the only black, or one of very few. Manual was the laboratory in which I lived the axiom that African Americans learn early on, "When you're black, you have to be twice as good as whites to get half as much." Looking back, I realize that it was school officials, faculty and staff, not the students, who were intent on marooning us. Most of the students were oblivious to the few Negroes in their midst. I was deeply wounded by my high school experiences, but the injuries were life enhancing, not life threatening. As uncomfortable as it was at the time, I know now that high school was neither the abyss nor the apex of my life.

I was nervous about my speech because I planned to tell the truth about my painful years at Manual, and I didn't know how that would be received. I would be breaking the ultimate taboo of American society—talking about *racism* in the presence of blacks and whites. But I was determined not to dissemble. I described some of the overtly *racist* acts, like my being counseled to take classes that would prepare me for domestic service, and how it felt to be alienated. I also praised Mr. Fisher's intervention. I closed by saying, "I am actually grateful to

Manual for teaching me about the world that awaited me. My experiences here prepared me for what was coming and consequently, I was better able to cope with it."

When I finished most of the black people and a few whites in the audience of about three hundred jumped to their feet with applause. After twenty seconds or so, most of the remaining audience also stood and applauded. The applause lasted for several minutes. I was astounded. At best, I had expected a restrained, polite response. About half the audience was black—my family and friends, and former Manual students from a range of years. I believe the former students from my era felt a sense of relief hearing our silent suffering finally being openly discussed. The president of the alumni association, who had introduced me, quickly left the stage without a word. There were a few other white alumni who had been cheerful and friendly at the earlier festivities who refused to look at me. Several whites, however, lined up to shake my hand and tell me they had had no idea what black students were going through. Others thanked me for telling the truth.

"Janet, I hope you realize you've just fixed it so they will never again give the award to a black person." Reggie teased me as we left the auditorium.

The night before I had been invited to the fiftieth reunion of the class of 1948. Someone at the reunion gave me a letter from Mr. Fisher. In the letter he congratulated me and explained that he was ill and would not be able to attend the award presentation. He died not long afterward.

A few years later I learned that Earl Major, who was a member of the Manual alumni board, had presented my credentials and suggested that the board give me the award. He said they agreed unanimously. Earl is a black man and the son of the late Alvis Major and his wife Mary Anna, long-time friends of our family. Earl graduated from Manual in 1982, twenty eight years after I did. By then the school had several black faculty and a large number of black students. Mary Anna admitted to some discomfort during my speech because, she said, "My children had such wonderful experiences at Manual."

Chapter 10

Passing the Baton

If each of us will do it and spread it around, we can open up some jobs. Too often we don't pass the baton along.

~ Bob Jones, entertainment industry lawyer

Near the end of my sophomore year I signed up for summer school to avoid a third summer of scrubbing and cleaning with Aunt Viola. However, that didn't mean I wouldn't have to work. Early in my junior year Daddy found a job for me—working as one of the student pages at the Indiana State Library downtown. The library regularly employed students as part-time workers, but no Negro students had ever been hired. In fact, there was only one other visibly Negro person working in the library. In 1952 Negroes who worked in downtown Indianapolis, no matter how much education they had, were either sorting mail at the post office, operating elevators, working as stock clerks, or as janitors. All white-collar jobs, even entry-level positions like bank tellers and salesclerks, were reserved for whites. A local white newspaper said, "Indianapolis incorporates the worst aspects of the southern and northern patterns in Negro employment, either no jobs at all, or only the most menial with no chance for advancement." Through a variety of organizations, and using every strategy they could think of, many Negroes and some whites were working to open up better employment opportunities for us.

My father was one of those activists, and, in a conversation with William R. Hill, a founder and board member of the Senate Avenue YMCA, Daddy learned that Hill's wife, Gladys, was looking for a smart colored student to work at the library after school. The Hills, like my parents, were dedicated to the Struggle to Uplift the *Race*. Mrs. Hill's African ancestry was invisible to the naked eye; consequently, she had been working at the library long before they gave any thought to hiring Negroes. She hadn't lied about her *race;* she just let her employers assume what they would. Once inside, she paid attention to job openings and told other Negroes about them. When these qualified applicants weren't hired, the NAACP had proof that a public, tax-supported institution was refusing to hire Negroes. And Mrs. Hill kept black applicants coming, piling up the evidence.

Finally, the library relented and hired Vera as a secretary in the Traveling Library Department. Vera was Mrs. Hill's niece and, like many of the early Negroes hired in downtown offices and stores, she was female, attractive, and light skinned. To the casual observer, she appeared white. The first brown-skinned person hired at the library was William Porter, who ran the shipping room. As the only Negro man in the library, Mr. Porter knew that he would be closely watched to see if it was safe to have black males in what was essentially a white female work environment. Unsurprisingly, Mr. Porter was not a tall, strapping black buck, but a short, round man who walked with a limp. Like Jackie Robinson, Mr. Porter understood that if he were deemed acceptable, it could pave the way for the employment of other black males. He was more than up to the scrutiny. After sorting the mail, Mr. Porter delivered it to every department in the library. Like Santa Claus, minus the red suit, he made his rounds with a smile, twinkling eyes, and a friendly comment for all. Everybody in the building knew him, and, more important for the Struggle, everybody *liked* him. To preclude white folks' proclivity to call him Willie, Bill, or possibly boy, when asked his name he always responded, "Mr. Porter." And that's what everybody called him.

Daddy took me to the library to meet Mrs. Hill before I applied for the job. If I had not known that she was a Negro, I wouldn't have guessed it. Mrs. Hill was a slender woman, possibly aged fifty, a little taller than my five feet four and a half inches. She had straight dark-brown hair that she wore pulled back and twisted into a knot on her neck. At our initial meeting she wanted to be sure I understood the responsibility of being the first Negro student to work in the library. She said I should set an example of punctuality, hard work, and re-spectfulness so that other Negro students would be hired. I knew the drill. They were basically the same marching orders I received before going to Manual. Mrs. Hill also mentioned that my enrollment in a predominately white high school was to my advantage. I guess she meant the people reviewing my application would know I was experienced in the art of being surrounded by white folks. At age fifteen I became the third person known to be a Negro hired at the library. By then, many people had figured out that Mrs. Hill wasn't entirely of European origin. A few library employees had seen her colored husband pick her up from work, and others were aware she was pushing for Negroes to be hired. That made four of us in a staff of about sixty.

Library pages worked in every department, but significantly, I was assigned to help Mrs. Hill. Both she and Mr. Porter worked in a large, cavernous room on the first floor, a few feet from the building's rear door. The walls were made of smooth beige concrete blocks, and the bare floors were also concrete. The shipping room, where packages and mail were delivered and shipped, was separated from our work area by a row of bookshelves that were probably ten feet high. It was not lost on me that three of the library's four Negro employees worked in the back of the library, out of public view, but I didn't care. I was ecstatic to have a job that didn't require any scrubbing, dusting, or bed making. On top of that, I could indulge my love of books! I also felt pretty special because I was the *first* Negro page. Initially Mrs. Hill's demeanor was stern; I think she felt the pressure of having brought in the first Negro student and she was nervous that I might disappoint vigilant whites. After I had worked there a few months, she softened appreciably. Mrs. Hill even became complimentary about how quickly I learned and how polite I was. Having been carefully trained by my parents on how to behave around adults, I yes ma'am'd Mrs. Hill until she was sick of it. She finally asked me to leave off the ma'am.

It was our responsibility to prepare books to be shelved after they had been cataloged. That meant I got to see all the new books. Eventually, Mrs. Hill trusted me to take books home after they had been processed. We stamped Indiana State Library on the copyright page and on page twenty-six of every book, and on the top and bottom of the closed pages. In the back of the book we pasted a pocket and inserted the circulation cards. We also wrote the call number on the spine in white ink, covered the dust jacket in plastic, and taped it to the book. It didn't take long for Mrs. Hill to instruct me on how these routine tasks should be performed, so while I processed the new books, she spent much of her time binding old books that were falling apart. After a while, she also taught me how to do the repairs, but I much preferred handling the new books. During my breaks, I browsed in the closed stacks and found other works by black authors whose names I recognized from books we had at home. My favorite discovery was Langston Hughes's collection of short stories, *The Ways of White Folks*. The books Daddy brought home about Negroes were all nonfiction and poetry. Hughes's stories were the first fiction I read with recognizable Negro characters in credible Negro–white relationships. I also discovered new authors during my meanderings through the library stacks. I particularly enjoyed historical novels and read every Frank Yerby work I could find. Yerby wrote more than thirty popular books that sold over fifty million hardcover and paperback copies around the world. His first novel, *The Foxes of Harrow*, published in 1946, was made into a movie. It was many years later that I found out Yerby was black. At the time I assumed he was white because his main characters were of European descent. However, he also featured Negroes in his intricate plots, particularly the ones about the antebellum South, and that was one of the reasons I enjoyed reading them so much. Yerby grew tired of America's *racism* in 1955 and moved to Madrid where he died in 1991.

In addition to my new job, another momentous event occurred the year I turned fifteen: our family finally got a television set. It was a mahogany console with possibly a twelve-inch screen. The first time I saw television was at my best friend Laura Noel's house. I was maybe twelve or thirteen years old. Laura lived on Harlan Street and her family had the first television among the black families in the neighborhood. Word spread quickly about the startling new invention. On weekends the Noel living room would be crowded with neighbors looking at the amazing black and white moving, talking pictures on their tiny nine-inch screen. I remember seeing Milton Berle at the Noels' house. I didn't find him particularly interesting. By the time we got a set, everybody had one. Our family usually gathered on Sunday evenings to watch *The Ed Sullivan Show*. In the 1950s, there were only occasional black faces on television, so we stopped everything to watch when we knew one would be on. Negroes did not appear in sponsoring ads at all. It was the late 1960s before blacks began to appear sparingly in commercials. I saw Eddie Anderson in the role of

Rochester on *The Jack Benny Show*, and as a family we watched Nat "King" Cole hosting an eponymous short-lived fifteen-minute show in 1956. I thought Rochester was a bug-eyed stereotype, but Cole represented how we preferred to see ourselves on television. He was dapper and smooth, and his voice just laid me out! NBC had to sponsor Cole's show because corporations were afraid of losing customers if their brand was attached to a show starring a Negro. A few years later I saw Richard Pryor for the first time doing a Rumpelstilskin bit on *Sullivan*. He was hilarious. I was a Pryor fan from that moment on.

Rosie, Reggie, and I were attending a predominately white high school, but our social life was in the Negro community of which Indiana Avenue, from New York to around Tenth Street, was the center. While I was growing up, you could find nearly anything you wanted on the Avenue—clothes, pawnshops, restaurants, groceries, dry cleaners, and nightlife—at places like the Cotton Club, George's Bar, and the Sunset Terrace. Three institutions important to our community were also located there: the Walker Building; the Negro weekly newspaper, the *Indianapolis Recorder*; and the McArthur Music Conservatory. The Walker Building, built of tan-brick, was a block long and four stories high. It had opened in 1927 and was set in the triangle made by the intersection of the Avenue and West Street (now Martin Luther King Jr. Street). It was the capstone of the Avenue. In addition to being the headquarters of the hair care business founded by Madam Walker, the building also housed a beauty culture school, professional offices, the Casino Ballroom, and a theater—with an Egyptian-themed décor.

In those segregated days Indianapolis had several colored movie theaters. The Indiana Theater was at 112 Indiana Avenue, five blocks south of the Walker at 617. On the east side of town were the Park and Douglas theaters near Douglas Park. The Park was at Twenty-fifth and Martindale (now Andrew J. Brown Avenue), and the Douglas was on Nineteenth, near Martindale. Like most movie theaters of the time, they offered double features and a newsreel. The major difference at our theaters was that the second of the two features often had an all-colored cast. The colored feature movies were such classics as *Cabin in the Sky* with Ethel Waters, Lena Horne, and Eddie Anderson; and *Stormy Weather* with Lena Horne, Bill "Bojangles" Robinson, and Cab Calloway, both released in 1943. Another popular

movie was *Imitation of Life,* a white 1934 movie that starred Clau-
dette Colbert, and had two black actors—Louise Beavers and Fredi
Washington—in major roles. Washington played the light-enough-
to-pass daughter of Beavers who played the maid of Colbert. When
it was initially released critics of both colors assailed the movie for
its stereotypical portrayals of the two black women, however, it was
regularly re-played in colored movie houses. I saw the 1959 remake
that starred Lana Turner in the Colbert role, Juanita Moore in the
Beavers role, and a white actor, Susan Kohner, in Washington's role.
The remake lessened considerably the cloying servility of the maid,
and enlarged the role of her tragic mulatto daughter, making her
more defiant. Since it wouldn't do to have an impertinent Negro on
the screen, Hollywood gave the part to a white woman. Rosie and I
found the movie immensely annoying because the maid was good,
loyal, and wise beyond belief, and her high yellow daughter whined
too much about not being white. We agreed that if she had stopped
chasing after whites, some well-fixed black man would have snapped
her up and pampered her beyond her wildest dreams. Despite its
many shortcomings, I believe Negroes liked to watch *Imitation of Life*
because it was one of the few films that actually conceded, however
obliquely and perversely, that America had a *race* problem.

The colored theaters sometimes also screened film shorts, like
Fight That Ghost starring the Negro comedian Pigmeat Markham, or
Hot Chocolate with the debonair Duke Ellington leading his band, or
Cab Calloway performing his popular song, "Minnie the Moocher."
We took advantage of nearly every opportunity to see movies with
black actors. I remember seeing and loving *Song of the South,* a Dis-
ney adaptation of the Uncle Remus stories blending animation and
actors. I had to forgive myself for enjoying a movie set on a sweet-
ness-and-light plantation with black people who wanted nothing
more than to serve the master. It was 1946; I was nine years old and
taken in by the music, the bright colors, and the animation.

When I was a little older, I saw *Pinky, Lost Boundaries,* and
Intruder in the Dust. All of these movies, released in 1949, con-
fronted the issue of *race* and starred black actors. Ethel Waters was
the colored woman with the high-yellow daughter in *Pinky.* Another
white actor, Jeanne Crain, played the part of the passing-for-white
black woman. Mel Ferrer, a white male actor, did the pretending-to-

be-black-passing-for-white honors in *Lost Boundaries. Intruder in the Dust* was my favorite by far, possibly because the Negro was dignified, did not rue being black and, with the help of whites, managed to avoid being lynched. Many years later I read the William Faulkner novel on which the movie was based. In the book the innocent man was killed, which, of course, was the more probable outcome.

I first saw the handsome and elegant Sidney Poitier when I was thirteen. He played a physician in *No Way Out* released in 1950. Although I cringed at the unfair way Poitier was treated, I was gratified and delighted to see a black man on screen in a role that did not require bowing and scraping. The 1951 remake of *Show Boat*, however, reiterated the images of the 1936 version with again, a white actor, Ava Gardner, playing the light-skinned black character. It infuriated me that the movie moguls refused to give these parts to the many light-skinned black actors desperate for work. Of course, I know why they did it. These passing-for-white characters were interacting too closely with other white performers. Hollywood did not believe America was ready to see blacks and whites in intimate, peer relationships, so they cast whites in the black roles. Watching Hollywood's version of *racial* issues in the 40s and 50s, you could easily assume that every light-skinned black person wanted to pass for white, which certainly was not the case.

By 1953, when I was sixteen, major studios were producing black movies that did not employ stereotypes. I took pleasure in watching Dorothy Dandridge and Harry Belafonte in *Bright Road,* and the following year saw them again in *Carmen Jones.* The movie that had the biggest impact on me during that period, though, was not a black one. It was *New Faces,* a talent showcase that included Eartha Kitt. I was mesmerized by Kitt and read everything I could about her glamorous life in Europe. Kitt was an uncommon woman who spoke several languages and stepped to the beat of her own drummer.

On the top floor of the Walker building, deejays spun records at teen dances in the Casino, with its sparkling revolving ball. The dances at the Casino were considered more classy than the ones at Northwestern Community Center, at Twenty-fourth Street and Northwestern Avenue, about two miles north of the Avenue. The Casino's status was evident in the price as well. The Friday night dances at Northwestern were twenty-five cents; the Casino dances cost fifty cents. Also, we sometimes went to after-parties in that part of town—parties that started after the dances were over at 10 p.m. However, some of the best parties were held at our house.

Mama and Daddy encouraged us to have friends over and helped us get ready for the parties. They were also discreet. Once the party started, they kept an eye on things without hovering. Parties with only a few people sitting around not dancing were considered lame. A really good party had all the right people and plenty of dance music. Slow records could take the life right out of a party, so we played lots of fast tunes like "Money-Honey" by Clyde McPhatter and the Drifters, "Sixty-Minute Man" by the Dominoes, and "I Got A Woman" by Ray Charles. To give the dancers a rest, we offered occasional romantic ballads like "The Glory of Love" sung by the Five Keys and "Crying in the Chapel" by the Orioles. Dancing stopped at our parties only when the house was so packed people couldn't move, even then the music blared on. A good party also needed dim lights and refreshments—punch, chips, some dip, and maybe cookies—nobody expected a meal. Mama dressed up our punch by floating chunks of ice cream in it. Our most memorable party was held one summer in the backyard. We had a big crowd and The Five Diamonds, a popular local singing group who had released a record, not only came to the party, but they sang for us! When I played the Spaniels' "Goodnite Sweetheart" everybody knew it was time to go home.

These social occasions were primarily about boys and girls getting together, but you had to know the latest dance steps or you would be considered square and hardly noticed. To make sure we mastered new dance steps, my siblings and I played records at home and practiced. I wasn't one of those dancers that people gathered in a circle to watch, but I managed not to embarrass myself. For the latest dance music, we listened to radio station WLAC-AM. *Randy's Record Hi-Lights* was broadcast from this Nashville station at 10 o'clock seven nights a week. Of course, we could only listen on non school nights, but nothing thrilled me more than hearing "Blues after Hours," the song Gene Nobles, the deejay, always played at midnight. To this day when I hear that song, I think about that program. You could hear all the best rhythm and blues and gospel on WLAC, and find out which records you wanted to buy. Our first record player only played 78s, but we later got a hi-fi that played 78s, 33s and 45s. The sponsor of the program, Randy's Record Shop of Gallatin, Tennessee, was touted as "The World's Largest Mail Order Phonograph Record Shop," but we bought our records at music shops on Indiana Avenue.

Music was an integral part of our lives. Rosie and I belonged to the Tempé Music Club, founded by Mrs. Sadie Hardiman, a staunch supporter of her son David's musical ambitions. Mrs. Hardiman started the music club under the auspices of the Indianapolis Music Promoters, founded in 1919 as a branch of the National Association of Negro Musicians. The Indianapolis Music Promoters encouraged their members to study music, perform, and to further the musical talents of young people. David, who played trumpet and is now a bandleader in San Francisco, was being trained at the McArthur Conservatory where Rosie and I were also taking lessons—she in piano, and I on the cello. In my sixth grade instrumental music class, the teacher asked if I'd like to learn to play the cello. I agreed because the cello was something different; everybody else seemed to play the piano, a wind instrument, or violin. I liked the mellow sound of the cello so much that I played it throughout high school. I never had my own instrument; the public schools supplied the cello and allowed me to bring it home for practice. Miss Trent, my high school music teacher, was keenly disappointed that I didn't plan to audition for the orchestra when I went to Indiana University. But my interest in music was, and remains, more appreciator and spectator than student and performer. In my soul I have always been a writer; I didn't have the fervor required to become a skilled musician.

The McArthur Conservatory trained a number of Indianapolis's accomplished musicians, including Larry Ridley, Jimmy Spaulding, and Slide Hampton and other members of his musical family. Freddie Hubbard hung out with the McArthur students, but he studied at the Jordan Conservatory with Max Woodbury, the principal trumpeter of the Indianapolis Symphony Orchestra. Freddie was a devoted musician and it showed in his skillful performances. I dated him sporadically for about a year, and it was he who introduced me to modern jazz. I spent many nights listening to him play with the Jazz Contemporaries at George's Bar. Larry Ridley, the bass player, managed the business affairs of The Jazz Contemporaries, and had obtained the gig for the teenaged group. At the time Freddie was sixteen and I was seventeen—all of us too young to be in a nightclub. He and the other

The Jazz Contemporaries were playing at George's Bar when this picture was taken on Indiana Avenue around 1954. (l-r) Larry Ridley, Freddie Hubbard, Walt Miller, Jimmy Spaulding, Paul Parker.

musicians in the Jazz Contemporaries were so good that nobody cared about their ages. Maybe I was overlooked because it was expected that their girlfriends would show up, but we weren't allowed to drink. I was so moved by their passion for the music that I learned to love jazz.

Freddie left Indianapolis for Chicago around 1956, a year after I went to Bloomington to attend Indiana University. Freddie was in the Windy City briefly before moving on to New York where he played with Art Blakey's Jazz Messengers, as well as working with John Coltrane, Dexter Gordon, and other acclaimed musicians. Freddie has been described as one of the great jazz trumpeters of all time, and is also a celebrated composer. I didn't see him again until 1970, shortly after I moved to San Francisco. Freddie was playing an engagement at the Both And jazz club on Divisidero, and I went to hear him perform. I had no idea what to expect because he had become a well-known figure in the intervening years. Freddie immediately recognized me in the audience and dedicated a song to his home-girl. After the show, he blew off the groupies so that we could catch up. The next day, Freddie showed off his success by taking me to dinner at a high-end restaurant on Fishermen's Wharf. Back in Indy neither of us could have imagined we'd ever be dining so grandly. In 2006 Freddie was awarded a National Endowment for the Arts Jazz Masters Fellowship. He died in 2008.

I ran into Larry again on IU's campus where we both were students. Larry also went on to have a distinguished career teaching as well as performing. Dr. Ridley is professor of music emeritus at Rutgers, the State University of New Jersey, and continues to perform with the Jazz Legacy Ensemble.

By the time Freddie and I started going out, I had learned to drive. Not long after I went to work at the library, Daddy picked me up from the beauty shop where I had just had my hair straightened. On the way home, he stopped the car and got out. I didn't know why Daddy had pulled over. He walked around and opened the passenger door.

"Scoot over."

I slid over to the driver's side, not understanding why.

"Go ahead. Drive."

I was stunned. I had no idea what to do first. "What do I do?"

"I thought you said you wanted to learn to drive. Go on and drive."

"I do want to learn, but what do I do first?"

"Haven't you been watching me?" Daddy's voice was edged with irritation. "The first time I let James behind the wheel, he drove right off. He had been watching me." Daddy's words were clothed in disdain for female inability to handle mechanical things like cars. His efforts to teach Mama to drive had been such a disaster that they didn't talk about it.

On the two-mile ride home I labored to keep the car on the right side of the street while I coordinated shifting gears with the use of the clutch. All the while, Daddy was telling me what to do in a fierce voice. He was not a happy man, and I was tight with fear. What if I didn't get it right and never learned to drive? The fact that my usually approving father was angrily disappointed with my ineptitude did nothing to relax me. When we finally lurched to a stop in front of our

The stick shift 1950 Studebaker in which I learned to drive. Here Reggie poses beside the car parked in front of our house on Randolph Street around 1952. Reggie was about thirteen, so he wasn't driving yet.

house, Daddy curtly told me to get out of the car so he could park it closer to the curb.

Despite his obvious disgust, Daddy took me to get a beginner's permit and kept up the lessons. Within a few months I learned to drive our 1950 Studebaker smoothly, and unlike James, I never wrecked the car. At the time I had no idea why Daddy was so motivated to teach me to drive, but I shortly found out.

It was eight months before my sixteenth birthday when Daddy gave me my first lesson. As soon as I turned sixteen, I took the driving test and easily passed. Once I had a real license, Daddy passed on to me the responsibility of being family chauffer. He was sick of spending his weekends and evenings dropping off and picking up his teenage children. He drove to work, to his meetings, and then handed the keys to me. I was the one who took Mama to the grocery store and choir practice, and the three of us around town to our social engagements. Sometimes, I even dropped Daddy at a meeting, leaving him to get a ride home so I would have the car to take another family member somewhere else.

James had taken care of these duties and drove himself and his friends around until he joined the army. At the time he wasn't yet eighteen, so he had to obtain a parental signature before he could be processed. After crashing the car for the second time in a couple of months James knew he was permanently grounded, and that Daddy would be furious. He went straight to the army recruiter's office. My parents received the news about the damaged car at the same time they learned he was going in the army. Mama was distraught at the thought of her first-born leaving home so suddenly, but Daddy quickly signed the form. He had already told James that if he wrecked the car again, he couldn't drive anymore. A few months later, we found out that James had another reason to want to get out of town.

One day Mrs. Stevenson, a woman we didn't know, came to our house with her visibly pregnant, sixteen-year-old daughter, Joan. That was when we found out that James was to become a father. Mama wrote long letters trying to convince James to marry Joan, but he wouldn't consider it. Failing that, Mama insisted that he provide for

My nephew, Tony (left) and his cousin Bryan McClure, probably in the winter of 1953 when they were two and a half. My guess is that my parents stopped by to give Tony the Christmas present he's holding, then took this picture.

his child. The army would not send monthly allotment checks to Joan unless James went to court and asserted his paternity. James did just that the next time he was home on leave, so Anthony O'Neal Stevenson legally became a Cheatham. He was born May 30, 1951. Twenty days after my fourteenth birthday I was an aunt. We also learned that James's buddy, Raymond McClure, had fathered a child, Bryan, with Joan's sister, Mildred. For her own reasons, Joan sometimes would not allow Tony to visit our family. After I started driving, and when Joan permitted, I picked Tony up and spent an afternoon with him being a doting aunt. By then he was a cute, big-eyed, potty-trained toddler and I adored him.

James left for the army in November 1950, two months after I started high school. Daddy was stuck with the driving duties for nearly three years until I was old enough to become the family cabbie. Driving family members—and this sometimes included aunts, uncles, and cousins who lived on the block—to their various errands and appointments was the price I had to pay if I wanted the car on weekends. Being at everybody's beck and call became mighty tiresome, but you couldn't put a price on the prestige of being a teenage girl with a car. Several boys drove cars, but I was the only girl my age with wheels.

Mrs. White, an older woman who knew our family, saw me picking up my friend Laura Noel, who lived across the street from her on Harlan. She told Daddy that by allowing me to drive his car, he was just making it easy for me to get infamilyway.

Daddy replied, "I see girls getting infamilyway who don't drive, so I guess driving a car is not the only way for that to happen."

When Daddy told me about this exchange with Mrs. White, I understood that he trusted me not to do anything stupid, and I would not let him down. On my own I decided not to allow boys, no matter how cute or persuasive, to ride in Daddy's car. It was not a difficult decision because I couldn't use the car unless I took Rosie and Reggie with me, and each of us often brought along a friend or two. So, the car was usually packed with folks sitting on top of one another. When Daddy traded the Studebaker for a new 1956 Dodge, it was totally used up. The odometer had gone as far as it could—100,000 miles— started over again and was halfway to its second 100,000.

After I had been working at the library a couple of years, and both Reggie and Rosie had their driver's licenses, I took on an additional job. I saw a coat that I had to have in the window at L. S. Ayres & Company, a department store downtown. It was cashmere, a deep red, almost burgundy, with a mink collar. It was very expensive—one hundred dollars—but I knew that if I worked at Ayres, I'd get a discount. Since I bought my own clothes, it made sense to save some money by working in a department store. And if I was going to work in a department store, it might as well be Indianapolis's finest, which Ayres was. The only positions available to a colored girl at Ayres were in the stockroom, operating the elevator, or cleaning up after hours. I applied for the elevators and was hired to relieve the full-time operators when they took breaks.

The library closed at 5 p.m. and I walked the six blocks to Ayres and worked from 5:30 until 7 p.m. when the store was open in the evenings—usually Thursdays—and all day on Saturdays. In late November and December the store was open several nights a week so I worked more. Ayres had a bank of eight elevators operated by attractive black women in matching tailored dresses. It was a prestigious position for uneducated Negro women whose other employment opportunities were primarily day work and similar labor-intensive jobs. The elevator operators were the only visible Negroes working in the store.

I put that fabulous coat in layaway and finished paying for it before Christmas. It only cost me eighty dollars, so I saved twenty and made some extra cash while doing so! I loved that coat and it looked good for years. I finally gave it to my mother when I decided that it was no longer fashionable.

I could barely wait to leave school everyday and get to my library job. Over the next ten years the Indiana State Library became my bulwark. I worked in a variety of positions—from elevator operator to professional librarian—part-time when I was in school, and full-time when I wasn't. I periodically became frustrated and looked for other employment, but the library would come up with a promotion that was better than whatever other possibilities I had, so I continued to work there until I moved away from Indianapolis. Apparently, I behaved well enough as the test Negro that other black students were soon allowed in. One was Leo Grissom, from Attucks High School, who assisted Mr. Porter in the shipping room. As I encouraged friends to apply for jobs at the library, two more Manual students were hired: my younger brother, Reggie, and my classmate, Helen Baker.

Chapter 11

What a Feeling!

Oh, my Lord
What a feeling,
When Jack Johnson
Turned Jim Jeffries'
Snow-white face
Up to the ceiling.

~ from "My Lord, What a Morning" by Waring Cuney

When I was twelve I went to my first high school basketball game. I could see that James was excited about basketball, so one night I asked to go with him. James was sixteen, and the last thing he wanted was me tagging along. Daddy, my hero, told James that if he wanted to use the car, he'd have to take me. Yea!

Needless to say, James was pissed and he let me know it. "You'd better get one of your friends to go with you 'cause I don't want you anywhere near me at the game."

I called Rosalind "Rozzie" Trabue and asked her to go with me. Rozzie was a petite, cute, light-brown-skinned girl with plump cheeks and a husky voice. Mama liked Rozzie because she was quiet and not fast, and since we went to the same church, our parents knew each other well. I envied Rozzie's expensive-looking clothes; she wore a different dress to school every day. And she had more than one Sunday outfit. I had three school dresses and one Sunday dress. Both her parents had jobs. Everybody said that Mr. Trabue made good money at the Chrysler foundry, and Mrs. Trabue worked five days a week in a school cafeteria, or maybe it was in a stockroom at a downtown department store. There were just two kids in their family, Rozzie and her younger brother, Roderick.

I was a kid who couldn't wait to grow up, so I was jacked up about going to a high school game with my big brother and his friends. Rozzie was excited too. In the car when one of James's friends asked how old I was, I answered, "Thirteen." No way would I be the only one in the car who wasn't a teenager.

Attucks's basketball games were played at Tech High School and other venues because the school's auditorium stage served as their basketball court and it had a seating capacity of only eight hundred. That night the game was at Tech, which was about four miles from where we lived. We had passed the school many times. I don't recall who Attucks was playing that night, but I know it wasn't Tech. In 1949 the only city high schools that would schedule games with Negroes were the Catholic high schools, Cathedral and Sacred Heart. As soon as we got inside, James ditched Rozzie and me. As he hurried away, he said, "Meet me right here as soon as the game is over." Whatever thrill I got from watching the game has slipped from my memory, overwhelmed by what happened afterward. When the game ended, we returned to where we had entered, but couldn't find James in the exiting crowd. The building emptied and still there was no sight of James. We were stranded. I had a moment of panic that soon passed, but Rozzie was terrified. There was no need to be upset; it was just another part of the adventure.

"Don't worry, Rozzie, I know the way home. We can walk."

Rozzie was horrified. "I'm not walking. I'm going to call my father."

"Rozzie, please." My tone was meant to convey that this was an ordinary circumstance that she was making too much of. "Come on. It's not that far."

Very reluctantly, Rozzie agreed to walk home, but she was decidedly uneasy about it. We had been walking about fifteen minutes when Rozzie spotted a phone booth and ran up to it before I knew what was happening. By the time I reached the booth, she was already talking to her dad. When Rozzie hung up the phone she said, "Daddy'll be here in a few minutes."

I responded with disgust, "Okay, Rozzie, if you're such a 'fraidy cat, I'll just walk home by myself."

"Janet! You're not leaving me here by myself. You better wait 'til Daddy gets here." Rozzie was yelling as she grabbed my arm.

"Okay, Rozzie, I'll wait with you." I couldn't understand why she was frightened, but I stayed with her until her dad arrived.

Mr. Trabue arrived quickly, and the car barely stopped before Rozzie opened the door and jumped in. I turned to continue my walk. "Janet, where are you going?" Mr. Trabue's emphatic question was meant to stop me in my tracks, and it did. "Girl, get in this car."

I would no more have disobeyed Mr. Trabue than my own father. I climbed into the back seat. When we got to my house we all went inside and Mr. Trabue told my parents what had happened. Mama and Daddy were appalled and kept apologizing to Mr. Trabue. They couldn't thank him enough for coming out to pick us up.

Because James went off and left us, it was a very long time before he got to use the car again. And Mama was furious that I tried to walk home through an unfamiliar white neighborhood. She said that two young girls walking the streets at nine o'clock at night was dangerous. "You have no idea how lucky you are that nothing happened. Girl, you don't have the sense God gave a goose." Not for the first time, Mama was exasperated by my foolhardiness. She never understood why I felt completely safe no matter where I was. Mama saw danger lurking everywhere, but I didn't expect bad things to happen. If something came up, I'd figure out what to do. If I couldn't work it out, then I'd call Daddy. I knew he could handle anything.

That was the last high school game I saw until I was in high school.

Despite that inauspicious beginning, I loved high school basketball and immersed myself in Hoosier Hysteria. Basketball is still my favorite sport, although I now prefer to watch the NBA teams. It was my good fortune to be in high school at the same time as Oscar Robertson, the Big O. I followed his career all the way to the Hall of Fame and consider him one of the best ever to play the game. My basketball timing was excellent on two other occasions as well: I moved to Boston the season before the Celtics got Larry Bird, another Hoosier, and I relocated to Chicago the same year the Bulls drafted Michael Jordan. The Big O, Jordan, Bill Russell, Magic Johnson, and Bird make up my all-time favorite team. Watching any one of those guys take over a game to ensure victory was like being able to see inside the mind of an artist as the creative process unfolds.

I celebrated each of the Chicago Bulls six NBA championships, and joined other fans in Grant Park to applaud the team. However, none of those contests matched the wild excitement and satisfaction of witnessing Attucks win Indiana's high school championship. I would be much older before I understood the depth of my parents' determination to thrive while also fighting intractable *racism*. However, I got a concrete lesson in the power of perseverance watching the Attucks basketball teams struggle to win a state championship. With all the might and authority of the city and the state aligned against the Negro school—and, we felt, against all Negroes—the effort was protracted. It lasted from 1950 to 1955. Finally, the Big O, along with his teammates, and using his skill and his will, carved out victory after victory to bring the Crispus Attucks Tigers and the city of Indianapolis their first state championship. I was right there in the whirl of the whole endeavor, from my first year in high school through my first year in college.

Attucks's successes were sweetened by the fact that the school had been barred from playing in the tournament less than a decade before they made it to the Final Four the first time. The Indiana High School Athletic Association (IHSAA) was founded in 1903 to encourage and direct athletic programs in the state's high schools, and they conducted tournaments that culminated in state championships. IHSAA membership was not available to Negro, Catholic, and private schools, and membership was a requisite for tournament participation. In 1927, the year Attucks first opened, a delegation of black leaders went to the association seeking to have the new segregated school admitted. Arthur Trester, head of the IHSAA, told them that only public schools were eligible for membership in the IHSAA, and Attucks, he said, was not *really* a public school since it catered only to Negroes. Trester's word was law so there was no appeal. He denied that his policy of barring Negro schools had anything to do with *race,* because black players on teams from predominately white schools had participated in the tournaments.

At one time there were eight all-Negro high schools in the state. They were located in Jeffersonville, Madison, Mount Vernon, New Albany, Princeton, and the state's three largest were in the cities where the majority of blacks lived: Evansville, Gary, and Indianapolis. In most of the state's small towns, there weren't enough Negroes to warrant separate schools so they attended schools that were overwhelmingly white. As early as 1930 the Washington, Indiana team that won the championship had a black player, Dave DeJernett. Several other

Negroes playing on teams in small Indiana towns were in the tournament long before black schools were admitted to the IHSAA. Three Negroes who played on those small-town teams before 1950 later had Attucks connections. George Crowe, the best player on the Franklin team that played in the 1939 championship game, was the first Negro to be named Mr. Basketball. Eleven years later, his older brother Ray, who had played for Whiteland High School, became the coach at Attucks. Bill Garrett, who succeeded Ray Crowe as head coach at Attucks, led his Shelbyville team to the championship in 1947. Garrett was also named Mr. Basketball, and became the first Negro to play at Indiana University.

Being named Mr. Basketball was a distinct honor. The coaches and athletic directors from all over the state traditionally selected the best senior player without considering skin color. In addition to other Negroes to be so honored, I recall that within the space of four years, there were three blacks selected for the honor. In 1953, while I was in high school, Hallie Bryant was named Mr. Basketball, next was Wilson "Jake" Eison of Gary in 1955, and Oscar Robertson in 1956.

In 1941 Senator Robert Brokenburr, the lone Negro in Indiana's upper legislative body, proposed a law to open IHSAA membership to the excluded schools. The black weekly newspaper urged its readers to write their state representatives in support of Senate Bill 181, and W. Blaine Patton, a white sports editor, wrote an open letter asking that the bill be passed, but it was rejected. The following December, the association passed a resolution to include Negro, Catholic, and private schools, effective August 15, 1942, nearly over Trester's lifeless body. Nevertheless, the IHSAA described Trester, who ran the association from 1913 until his death in 1944, as "a man who had a positive outlook on life…who possessed courageous integrity—passion for truth with an unbiased attitude."

For a long time I thought Catholics were nicer than other white people and that their schools played Attucks out of religious piety. I had no idea they were pariahs just like we were. When James was enrolled at Attucks from 1946 to 1950, *after* the IHSAA had opened up its membership, the other city high schools still refused to play Attucks's sports teams during the regular season. Attucks's teams traveled a lot to find opponents: they played other Negro schools, sometimes going out of state, and teams in small Indiana towns.

Negroes who lived outside Indiana's major cities were largely isolated in rural areas or small towns. The Crowe family, who lived in the appropriately named Whiteland before they moved to Franklin, was the only black family in that area. Many white villagers around the state saw Negroes only when the Attucks team came to town. Although they knew the Negroes would leave when the game was over, groups of blacks still made some of them nervous. One small-town resident said, "As nearly as I can remember, I had never seen a black person in Huntington. When the high school scheduled Attucks for a game, why I just had to go. I guess you could say I was curious. When I got to the game and saw all of those buses full of black people, I don't mind saying that I was a little scared. I don't know why I was scared."

Throughout the state everybody got pumped for the basketball tournament. My adrenaline still surges when I think about how much we anticipated it. My friends and I telephoned each other, planning what to wear and discussing which boys we hoped to see. Around the state at different sites, high school teams played three rounds—sectional, regional, and semifinal games—leading to the Final Four. All the Indianapolis rounds and the finals were held at the Butler University fieldhouse (now the Hinkle Fieldhouse), on the north side of the city. When it opened in 1928 the field house, with more than 10,000 seats, was the largest basketball arena in the country, a distinction it held for twenty years. It is one of only twenty-six Indiana landmarks listed in the National Register of Historic Places. We went to all the games, except the finals; those tickets were impossible to come by. In the Indianapolis sectional, there were two games on both Wednesday and Thursday nights, and games all day on Friday. On Saturdays, when only four teams were left, there were two games in the afternoon, then a break of two or three hours before the sectional championship game was played that night. We usually took a lunch on Saturday to preclude the long trek home during the three hour or so break between the afternoon and evening games. Our fervor began on the city bus that took us to the field house. It felt like everybody on the crowded bus was an Attucks fan, and we bonded in a jubilant expectation of victory.

Negro girls all over the city scrambled to go out with Attucks basketball players. One of the reasons we had good parties at our house was because girls knew team members would be present; my sister and a couple of our friends dated Attucks players. The guys came to our parties because they knew there would be lots of girls. One night the very shy Oscar Robertson himself came with a group of friends.

The state high school basketball tournament began in the freezing cold of February, but even mounds of snow couldn't weaken our enthusiasm. We knew there would be plenty of heat in the field house. In 1954 Rozzie and I were seniors and feeling quite grown up as we neared graduation.

"Do you think the team will go all the way this year?" Rozzie was particularly interested because she was dating, and later married, Ludwig Johnson, who was on the basketball team.

"We will. We've only lost two games this season." I was confident that in our last year of high school, we would finally win the championship.

"Well the referees could cheat us again." Rozzie was thinking of how the officials nearly always called games in favor of our opponents.

I responded with a fury fueled by impotence. "They *can't* keep doing that! Look at all the uproar it caused last time." I knew, however, there was nothing Negroes could do about the way the white referees cheated.

We were students at Manual High School, but for us, "we" meant the Crispus Attucks Tigers, not the Manual "Redskins." If there had been Negroes on Manual's varsity basketball team, we may have felt conflicted, but there weren't, so we felt no loyalty to the school we attended. In our freshman year, 1950-51, Attucks's new coach Ray Crowe led the basketball team to an 18-1 record. With a record like that, we thought Attucks was good enough to win the championship. Sure enough, they made it to the Final Four! We exploded with excitement. Indianapolis's white authorities were shocked that Attucks was in the championship round after just eight years of playing in the tournament. Most of the city hadn't taken the team seriously. After all, it was just a Negro team with a Negro coach from a Negro school. Indiana's top-ranked schools didn't play Attucks, so the fact that they had an excellent season record didn't mean much to basketball mavens. But when the Negroes actually made it to the championship round, the city anxiously took notice. Oscar's brother, Bailey "Flap" Robertson, was a member of that team, and Oscar remembered that, "in the days before the game, the mayor of Indianapolis met with

Principal Lane and Coach Crowe, worried about blacks starting a riot in the streets in the event of an Attucks victory."

In the afternoon game of the final round, the referees did everything they could to ensure that Attucks lost. As a result, Evansville Reitz, a Catholic school, won 66-59. The *Recorder* reported that, "The Reitz team was helped along its way to victory by the officials who rendered some very questionable decisions against the Tigers." When the game officials had to choose between two social outcasts, they favored the white one. We were not surprised, but our spirits deflated as we watched the white referees display their bias. It was the fifth time an Indianapolis high school had made it to the Final Four and come up empty. Although the Attucks Tigers didn't win the championship, they were still heroes to Indianapolis's black community. Nearly every Negro in Indianapolis, no matter what high school they attended, or had attended, was supporting the Attucks Tigers.

The following year Attucks had another impressive record of 19-1. They were ranked third in the state and we had high hopes again, but they didn't get out of the sectional. They won their first game with Cathedral 55-49. But in their next game, where the *Recorder* described the officiating as "doubtful," Attucks lost to Tech 63-60. There was no point in going to the regional and semifinal games. That year's tournament is memorable only because I met my first boyfriend, Claude "Teeter" Anderson, an Attucks student, on the bus ride to the sectionals. I was completely smitten with Teeter, who, although only fifteen years old, was allowed to drive his father's new Pontiac. One day when he picked me up, I had him drive down Harlan Street so my friends who lived there could see us. We had a great time for a year or so, but eventually went our separate ways.

In 1953, when we were juniors, Attucks racked up some impressive margins in the tournament beating Southport, a rural school south of Indianapolis, 106-64 to win the sectional, and winning the regional over tiny Amo 72-46. Bursting with anticipation again, we decorated Daddy's black Studebaker in green and gold crepe paper streamers to let everybody know we were Attucks fans. The team won the first game of the semifinal round. We only needed one more victory to be in the Final Four for a second time! Again, the referees blocked us, this time helping Shelbyville win the game. "With the score tied at 44, Shelbyville stalled." John Bridgeforth knocked the ball away and went for the shot, but a Shelbyville player fouled him. Instead of calling the foul, the referee called a jump ball. Attucks won the jump and Hallie Bryant drove for the basket. Two Shelbyville players sandwiched him, knocking Hallie down, but he got the shot off anyway. Winford O'Neal tipped in the errant shot and the referee blew his whistle. Good, we thought, Hallie will get two free throws. To our utter amazement, the referee, waved off O'Neal's tip-in, called a foul on Hallie, and gave Shelbyville two free throws! Shelbyville won the game with those free throws, 46-44. The *Recorder* said, "Stan Dubis's [the referee] capricious act reversed the outcome of the game."

That blatantly unfair call broke our hearts. Rozzie and I sat in the stands after the game sobbing, our hopes crushed by the referees. Losing was tough enough when a better team beat us, but the pain was unbearable when we had to watch white officials cheat us out of a victory. Years later Coach Crowe said, "After that Shelbyville game, I began to realize with even greater clarity how difficult it was going to be to win a championship. I was discouraged, but I wasn't about to give up." We all concluded that Attucks could win a championship only if they had a team good enough to build a margin so big it took the officials out of the game. It was another way of reiterating our mantra, "If a Negro wants to compete with the white man, he has to be twice as good." I *hated* crackers! They would never let us win.

Attucks's basketball teams were mediocre before Ray Crowe began coaching, but he never had a losing season. He ended his seven-year career at Attucks having won an incredible eighty-nine percent of his games, with a record of 179-20. The high-achieving all-black team with an intelligent, dignified black coach was such a visible refutation of white superiority that the referees were compelled to intervene. The game officials' peers no doubt would have soundly castigated them if they had *not* given Attucks's opponents every possible break. Indianapolis's Negroes had nowhere to turn. The power of the white officials to take games from Attucks was absolute.

There was only one black referee in the state, Bernard McPeak. McPeak had moved to Indiana from Pennsylvania, where he had fifteen years' experience refereeing high school games. The IHSAA certified him, but the all-white Indiana Officials Association (IOA) voted not to accept him as a member. Clayton Nichols, president of

My brother, Reggie, refereeing a high school basketball game between Crispus Attucks and East Chicago Washington, circa 1966.

the IOA, at the time, admitted that despite his efforts to persuade the membership to accept McPeak, he was turned down by a vote of 40-7 "because of his color." The white men who refused to take McPeak into the IOA were the same ones calling Attucks's games.

My younger brother, Reggie, passed the test to become a basketball referee in 1957. However, the IHSAA would not certify him. To become certified, they said, Reggie had to belong to an organization that sponsored training clinics. The only group that offered such clinics was, you guessed it, the for-whites-only Indiana Officials Association. Not to be denied, Reggie and John Patterson, another aspiring black referee, created an organization of their own—the Fall Creek Officials Association—founded at the YMCA in 1960. (The colored YMCA formerly on Senate Avenue had been replaced in 1959 by a new and larger building at Tenth and Fall Creek Boulevard.) To gain experience so they could sponsor their own training clinics, the fledgling association volunteered to referee high school scrimmages, a practice later imitated by the white officials. During the height of the Civil Rights Movement in the sixties, the white Indiana Officials Association decided to accept black members, but Reggie wasn't interested. Although he refereed high school basketball games for twenty-five years, my brother never joined that group.

It took the high school athletic association even longer to add some color to their staff; in their seventy-fifth year, they hired their first black and second female. In 1977 Mildred Morgan Ball, my close friend from college, was named assistant commissioner. Prior to joining the IHSAA, Mildred had spent seventeen years as a physical education teacher in the East Chicago, Indiana school system.

Once Attucks became a winning team, they attracted huge, mostly black, crowds that brought in lots of cash for them and their opponents. Schools that had previously shunned games with an all-black team scrambled to add Attucks to their schedule. In 1953-54, my last year in high school, *for the first time* all the Indianapolis high schools played Attucks during the regular season. Arsenal Technical High School was one of those latecomers. Tech was the largest high school in the city, with around four thousand students, and usually had a very good team. Tech and Attucks were the only Indianapolis schools in the 1950s to make it to the championship round of the state tournament, so they had an intense rivalry. With a little help from the referees, Tech had beaten Attucks in the 1952 sectional, so when Attucks beat Tech 53-46 to win the sectional in 1954, my friends and I jumped up and down squealing our delight and singing Attucks's victory chant, the "Crazy Song," emphasizing the line, "They can beat everybody, but they can't beat us!" Finally, we thought, in our senior year Attucks would win the whole thing!

In the next round Attucks beat Alexandria 64-18 to win the

Mildred Morgan Ball, circa 1977 when she became assistant commissioner, Indiana High School Athletic Association.

regional title. We moved on to the semifinal, where Attucks was scheduled for the second daytime game. This was never a good thing. The team playing in the second game had less time to rest for the evening contest, and Attucks was already shorthanded because two of their best players—Willie Merriweather and Winford O'Neal—were out with injuries. Attucks barely managed to beat their first opponent, Columbus, 68-67 in a mentally and physically draining game. That night, still fatigued, they lost to Milan 65-52. Milan had played its first game earlier in the morning. At the time Milan, a tiny rural town in southeastern Indiana not far from Cincinnati, had a high school enrollment of 161 students. They were decided underdogs in nearly every game they played. In the finals the following week, Milan used a slow motion, ball-holding strategy to win the championship. People could hardly believe it when little Milan beat mighty Muncie Central, 32-30, on a last second shot by Bobby Plump. The smallest school ever to win the state basketball championship had defeated a basketball powerhouse that had previously won four championships and had twelve hundred students. Nearly everybody in the state celebrated the improbable event. Milan was treated to a noisy victory parade through the city, and for several laps around Monument Circle.

We weren't interested in the celebration because our team had missed another opportunity at the championship. However, as disappointed as we were, we took some solace in the fact that Attucks had lost to Milan without the help of the referees.

After we graduated high school, Rozzie went away to Indiana University's Bloomington campus. I was still at home, working part-time and taking classes at the university's Indianapolis extension. In February of 1955 I went to the tournament games with Rosie, who was dating Bill Scott, a member of the Attucks team. This team was savvy, athletic, and experienced. The injured players had healed and Attucks looked unbeatable. They were ranked number two in the state having played the top schools during the regular season and lost only one game. We cheered loudly in the sectional when Attucks smashed Manual by fifty-one points. That victory felt especially good, as though it somehow made up for the things we were excluded from at school. Attucks easily won the Indianapolis sectional, the regional, and their first game in the semifinal.

Then came the game everybody had been waiting for. Muncie Central was ranked number one in the state, also had only one loss, and was always proficient. This was the team that had barely lost the championship game to Milan the year before. Sportswriters and fans believed that the winner of the Attucks-Muncie game would win the state championship. The game lived up to expectations: It was close all the way and the highest scoring game in the history of the Indianapolis semifinals. However, thanks to sixteen-year-old Oscar deflecting a Muncie pass in the last-seconds, and his scoring twenty-five points, Attucks won by one point, 71-70. We were delirious with joy! Our squealing and screaming muffled the "Crazy Song." For the second time in five years, Attucks would be in the Final Four!

In the finals, Attucks beat New Albany in the morning, and Gary Roosevelt, another all-black school, won over Ft. Wayne North. For the second year in a row, history would be made in Indiana. With Attucks and Roosevelt playing each other for the championship, it was assured that, for the first time ever, an all-black team would be state champion. Stan Dubis, the notorious referee who cancelled the Attucks victory over Shelbyville in 1953, was one of the officials assigned to call the game. However, the referees' traditional bias was moot because there was no white team for them to favor. Attucks could actually win! In the more than fifty years of the tournament, no Indianapolis high school had *ever* won the championship. And Attucks did win, easily, 97-74. My Lord, what a feeling! The Crispus Attucks Tigers had become *the first* high school in the city—black, white, or other—to win the state championship. We watched the game at home, and as soon as it was over we drove to the victory bonfire at Northwestern Park and celebrated wildly! What a feeling! What a feeling! Later, we found out that the Attucks team had been allowed only one quick turn around Monument Circle before being directed back to the black neighborhood. Indianapolis's very first state champion did not unleash the same joyous frenzy that Milan's victory had. We were not surprised at the city's lack of elation about Attucks, about us, but it still hurt.

In 1956 Attucks topped the previous year's achievement and made history again. They beat Lafayette Jefferson 79-57 to become the first *undefeated* team to win the state title. In two years Attucks had lost only one game, with a record of 61-1. While the team was piling up forty-five wins in a row, Oscar was breaking individual scoring records.

After winning two state championships with Attucks, Oscar Robertson played for the University of Cincinnati. At Cincinnati, he was the first player to lead the NCAA in scoring three years in a row. The Big O played professional basketball for the Cincinnati Royals and won an NBA championship with the Milwaukee Bucks. He is the only NBA player to have averaged double figures in points, assists, and rebounds for an entire season. Robertson also demonstrated his leadership off the basketball court, serving as president of the NBA Players Association from 1965 to 1974. He led negotiations that won long-withheld concessions from the owners, like having trainers travel with the team, paying players for exhibition games, and a hospitalization and medical plan.

Indiana's *racial* traditions remain intransigent however. The Indiana Basketball Hall of Fame recognizes teams on the fiftieth anniversary of their winning the championship. In 2004, because of Milan's historic achievement, they passed a special resolution to induct the entire team into the Hall of Fame. On the fiftieth anniversary of Attucks's historic achievement in 2005, no such resolution was offered, and Roger Dickinson, executive director of the Hall of Fame, said none was planned. Bill Hampton, a member of the Attucks championship team, said, "What Milan did was special, but how is [it] more historic than what we did…? We were the first black team in the nation to win a title like that, and back then we didn't get the respect we deserved. But this is fifty years later. It seems like nothing has changed." He and several other team members decided not to attend the Hall of Fame recognition event. Hampton went on to say, "If it [inducting the team] happens after [our complaints], we'll know it wasn't from the heart."

The acclaimed 1986 film, *Hoosiers,* starring Gene Hackman, was inspired by and based on Milan's unlikely accomplishment. The closest Hollywood has come to Attucks was Ray Crowe's cameo appearance in *Hoosiers* as coach of the interracial team that lost to the little rural school. By casting Coach Crowe in that role, the filmmakers were using wild poetic license. There were no black coaches of interracial high school teams in 1950s Indiana; the few black coaches in the state were at all-black schools.

One week after Hampton's statement appeared in the newspaper, the Attucks team that had overcome all the forces arrayed against them to win Indianapolis's first state championship, was inducted into the Indiana Basketball Hall of Fame.

Chapter 12

The Cost of Ignorance

People who think education is expensive have never counted the cost of ignorance.

~ Andrew Young, former U.S. representative, U.N. ambassador, and mayor of Atlanta

I had hoped to be a speaker at my high school graduation. Mrs. Siener, my speech teacher, told me I was a good speaker and suggested that I enter the senior speech contest. At Manual, instead of having the valedictorian address the audience, seniors competed for the privilege. This was to ensure that the student speaker was someone who savored the task, and would do a commendable job. I relished the challenge and knew my parents would be thrilled if I won. I don't remember what I chose as my subject, but I worked hard because I planned to win. When I finished speaking before the senior class, they gave me sustained applause. As they left the auditorium, a few, both blacks and whites, congratulated me, assuming I had won. I also thought I was the winner. However, this wasn't a hundred-yard dash; faculty judges made the final decision. And they, undoubtedly aghast at the idea of a Negro speaking at graduation, selected two white students, one of whom later expressed his surprise at having been chosen. I was asked to give the closing prayer. I was furious. When I got home, I exploded.

"This is not fair. I'm not doing the *benediction*. I'm not a preacher!"

"Oh, yes you will. Somebody has to represent us. They could've left you off the program altogether. The day will come when they'll be happy to have a Negro speak. For now, we have to take what we can get." Mama believed that a Negro doing *anything* at a white high school event was a step forward in the Struggle to Uplift the *Race*.

The month before my June 1954 graduation, we received some encouragement for that Struggle. The U.S. Supreme Court in *Brown v. Board of Education* ruled that segregating students by *race* in public schools was unconstitutional. Charles Hamilton Houston had a strategy in mind to get to what would become the *Brown* case. Houston, who had been the first black editor of the Harvard Law Review in 1923, was a Howard University law professor, and Special Counsel to the NAACP. A part of his preparation included picking up a movie camera and heading south. Houston documented the inequalities between the ramshackle structures where Negroes were educated and the sleek buildings in which whites received their education. His photographic record revealed the mockery of the court's earlier "separate but equal" edict.

The Fourteenth Amendment was added to the U.S. Constitution after the Civil War to guarantee *all citizens* equal protection under the law. Twenty-nine years later, and fifty-two years before the South African government created apartheid, the highest court in the United States established a policy of *racial* separation in the 1896 *Plessy v. Ferguson* decision. In that case the court ruled that segregation of the *races* was acceptable, so long as the facilities for Negroes were equal to those of whites. Just like that, the protection of the Fourteenth Amendment was wrenched away from people of African descent. In 1954, when *Brown* declared that separate was inherently unequal, it gave Negroes, and those who supported our fight for fair treatment, a great spiritual boost. For the first time in fifty-eight years, the federal government was officially on our side in the Struggle. The *Brown* decision had little significance in Indianapolis because the schools had been *legally* desegregated five years earlier. But, as I learned at Manual, desegregation is not the same as fair and equal treatment.

After high school I could no longer be a student page. However, the State Library offered me a clerk-typist position so that I could continue working there. I was elated. I had an adult job without having to look for it. That summer I worked full-time and saved for college. The idea of going to college excited and scared me. It was exciting to be doing something few Negroes did, and that nobody in my family had ever done. (In 1950 only 2.5 percent of Indiana's Negroes and 5.5 percent of whites were college educated.) But I was scared because in fairly rapid succession I had gone from being a maid, like my mother and my aunts, to a prestigious office job in downtown Indianapolis, to suddenly getting ready for college. If Mr. Fisher hadn't intervened, instead of heading for college, I'd be settling into a career as an office worker, grateful to have escaped domestic servitude. The real worm in the apple of my college venture, though, was that I didn't have Daddy's support.

"It don't make sense for you to go to college. All you gonna do is marry some no-'count man and take care of him." Daddy didn't want a dime of his money spent on educating a girl who would be a wife and mother like every other woman.

"She needs an education so she can take care of herself without cleaning houses like I do." Mama's voice was matter-of-fact, concealing her contempt for what she considered Daddy's backwardness.

"Cleaning houses is an honest living." I couldn't understand Daddy's attitude because he had always extolled learning. Fortunately, his disdain was short-lived. Once I enrolled at Indiana University, he was bragging all over the place that his daughter was getting an education and was going to be somebody.

Daddy's initial scorn had complicated roots. My father and his siblings grew up in the Southern sharecropping system, where even an elementary school education for Negroes was actively discouraged. The landowners knew that education would give the workers information and ideas that could undermine the exploitative system. They were right, of course. It was my Aunt Ovella's additional years in school that had enabled the Cheathams to start making money before Daddy left home. Scoffing at book learning helped Negroes curry favor with the boss, and, additionally, kept as many hands as possible laboring in the fields. I also believe that Daddy, who took enormous pride in providing for his family, felt financially impotent because he didn't have the money to pay for a college education. He may also have feared that I would fail; after all, this was a new experience for everybody. Or, he could have thought that if I succeeded, a college degree would set me apart from the family. I wasn't conscious of it at the time, but I wondered if an education would separate me from the people I cared about. Some of my kinfolk were quietly in awe of the anomaly; others warned me not to get a big head and start thinking I was better than everybody. For many years I beamed with relief when relatives and long-time friends said to me, "Janet, you haven't changed a bit."

Daddy's frank objections underscored my own inner turmoil. I had no idea what to expect, or even what I wanted from college. All I knew was that I had to have a life unlike Mama's, whose discontent was palpable and often vocal. I would not wind up with a husband, children, and unending housework, either at home, or in somebody else's house to earn a few dollars. I wanted no part of that life. As a child, reading books and writing stories had been as much fun for me as playing games with the other kids. I was so taken with books that, at age twelve or thirteen, before I started high school, I decided to go visit a book publisher. The Bobbs-Merrill biography series for children was a favorite of mine, and I had noticed that the books' publisher was located in Indianapolis. I told Mama I'd like to visit them. I wanted to see how books were made because I might work there when I got older. She liked that idea and told me how to get there on the bus. Alone, I took the forty to fifty minute ride to the company. I was exhilarated as I approached the building and saw the BOBBS-MERRILL sign. I opened the door and walked in. About thirty feet from the entrance a neatly dressed white woman was seated behind a desk facing the door. I walked up to her, smiling with anticipation.

"What do you want?" The receptionist snarled at me.

I was not fazed. "I want to see how books are made. I think I'd like to work here when I grow up."

She gave me an incredulous glare then stood up, and in a forceful voice said, "Get out! Get out! Negroes don't work here."

"What?" For a moment I was confused by her outburst.

"Get out of here!" Now she was yelling and pointing at the door I had just entered.

When she made a move to come from behind her desk, I quickly turned around and left. For a long time I wandered, disoriented, while her words sank in. Negroes could not work for book publishers. On the bus ride home I gave in to tears. I was bereft. Working with books was all I ever wanted to do. I knew there were lots of things Negroes weren't allowed to do, but I hadn't even thought that books and publishing were among them. *I AM A NEGRO. ALWAYS WILL BE. SO, THERE'S NOTHING I CAN DO ABOUT IT. THAT'S THAT.* I swallowed hard, took a deep breath, and pushed my dream of becoming a writer or editor deep down inside.

My father may have been disparaging and me confused, but Mama was ecstatic that I was going to college. She was having the time of her life reading the IU catalog and exclaiming over the courses offered. She actually wanted to go with me to sign up for classes, but I wasn't having it. When I brought my books and notebooks home, Mama examined each one carefully and stroked them lovingly. It felt like I was going to college *for her*.

After being disabused of my publishing dream, I had no idea what I wanted to do. An educated Negro woman's best chance for professional employment was teaching school, but I never liked the well-traveled road. Nevertheless, the point of going to college was so I could get a job that did not require an apron or an iron. Consequently, there I was in my first semester at the Indiana University Extension, signing up for Introduction to Teaching. I also enrolled in Freshman Literature, Introductory Psychology, Music Appreciation, and a geography class. I also included the first of the three required composition courses, a total of fifteen hours. The Extension was on Delaware Street in downtown Indianapolis, a dozen blocks from my library job. On a typical day I reluctantly climbed out of bed around 6:30 a.m. to be at the library by 8 o'clock. I worked all morning, quickly ate the lunch I brought from home, then caught a bus to the Extension. I could have walked, but by riding the bus, I got in another thirty minutes of work. On some days I had classes until 9 p.m. If I got hungry, I grabbed a pecan roll or a Baby Ruth candy bar from the café on the first floor. Other students gathered there to chat and drink coffee, but I didn't have time for that. Besides, the place's grungy look and unappetizing smell killed any desire I may have had to sit down to eat.

Between classes I worked in the Extension's administration office several hours a week. The part-time job was required by my work-study scholarship and defrayed the cost of tuition. My library salary covered other expenses—books, social activities, and bus fare. I studied whenever and wherever I could, sometimes, if things were slow, at my desk at work. I did not however, allow classes, work, and studying get in the way of dating, parties, and Attucks basketball games. I was seventeen years old and my social life was as important to me as school. Mama excused me from household chores, but I still went to church with the family every Sunday. At the end of the semester I got my first university grades. I had a D in geography, a C in psych, and B's in everything else. I remember very little about what happened in these classes. But so far as I can tell, these many years later, I got A's and B's in classes that fed my interest in story telling, and the history of people and places. Some teachers tapped into those interests, but many did not. I generally got C's in the classes that I found boring, but didn't require much of me, and D's in classes that bored me, but required more attention than I was willing to give. I was pleased with my first college grades, because, as promised, the classes were much more difficult than high school had been.

In the second semester I continued with composition, freshman literature, and geography, and also took American history, and history of western civilization. That turned out to be more reading than I could handle, so I withdrew from western civ. I improved my grade in geography to a C, but the literature and comp grades dropped to C, and there was only one B, in American history. That summer, I earned a B in the last of the comp courses, and got a C in American government. Without much effort I had made mostly A's and B's in high school, but at the end of my first year at IU, I was clinging to a C average. Still, I had completed thirty-one hours and was a bona fide college sophomore.

Hindsight indicates that another year at the Extension would have benefited me, but I couldn't wait to get to campus. I had visited Rozzie and envied her real college life—in a dorm on campus. The beauty of Indiana University's Bloomington setting—wooded, undulating hills graced with elegant limestone buildings—also seduced me. Most tantalizing was the freedom of the students. Every night just before the girls were locked in at 10:30, the outside of their dormitories were thick with necking couples. I had never seen such a massive and open display of affection. I was shocked and stirred by it. I had only seen my parents kiss one time. Daddy was on his way out of town and we were all at the door seeing him off. I asked Mama to kiss Daddy goodbye and she pecked his cheek. That was it. Touching was all but taboo in our family. Mama was suspicious of affection shown to anybody over the age of three. I had necked plenty, but always furtively and in the dark. Once I saw that unabashed necking was the order of the day, I was determined to get to Bloomington as soon as possible.

Mama was as eager for the campus experience as I was—undoubtedly not for the same reason—if I could swing it financially. On campus I wouldn't have my work-study scholarship, but I had saved most of my earnings the previous summer, and I would hold on to every penny earned in the coming summer. Mama promised to help out whenever she could.

On a bright warm day in September 1955 we loaded the car, and Mama, Daddy and I made the one-hour drive to Bloomington. We found the dorm and I went inside to get my room assignment from the resident assistant (RA). My roommate hadn't yet arrived so I had first dibs on everything. We were given the corner room at the end of the hall, next to the emergency exit. All but about three square feet of the small room was taken up with iron-framed bunk beds, two small desks, two four-drawer chests, two chairs, and two closets. The desks, chests, and chairs were blond wood. The makeshift closets were three-sided wooden boxes painted white with a dowel inside for the clothes and a metal rod in front with a curtain to hide the clothes from view. Daddy hung my clothes in the closet on the wall opposite the bed. Mama unpacked my sheets, pillow, and bedspread and made up the bottom bunk. I filled the drawers of the chest next to my closet with my underclothes, towels, extra bed linen, and put my toiletries on top. I set my radio and clock on the desk in front of the window that overlooked the campus; the other window faced the gravel driveway at the back of the building. I had also brought an iron that I put on the closet shelf. There was a telephone on the wall just inside the door, easily accessible from the bed, especially the top bunk. Daddy wrote down the number.

I now lived in Cedar Hall.

Four of the fifty-three women living in Cedar Hall were Negroes. I didn't know my roommate or the other two Negroes. There were five Negroes on campus from Manual High School, but we were scattered in different dorms. From my class were Faye Wilkey and Esther Quarles, who lived in Maple Hall, and Helen Baker in the scholarship dorm, Pine Hall—all in Trees Center. Except for Cedar, the Trees dorms each held 140 women. Rozzie had also lived in Trees, in Walnut Hall, but she didn't return for a second year. My cousin Webster Brewer, who was a year ahead of us at Manual, lived in the Kappa Alpha Psi fraternity house, called the Kappa Kastle.

Cedar Hall, former army barracks and my home on Indiana University's campus. Used by permission Indiana University Archives

Trees Center was also the site of a grass-covered valley with sloping sides that romancing couples used as a trysting place. Two years before I arrived, IU's famous Institute for Sex Research, led by Dr. Alfred Kinsey, had published their second study, *Sexual Behavior in the Human Female.* In tribute to Kinsey's groundbreaking work, students dubbed the place where they conducted their own sexual surveys, Kinsey Hollow. Kinsey Hollow was about the size of a football field and we joked that you had to be careful walking through there after dark or you might step on a friend. It's still there, adjacent to Smithwood, now named Read Center. It doesn't seem as deep as it did fifty years ago, but perhaps it was filled in with soil from the excavation for the new School of Education building. That building, opened in 1992, occupies the space where the Trees Center barracks once stood. I doubt that today's students use Kinsey Hollow the way we did. After all they are regarded as adults, rather than being treated as potential juvenile delinquents the way we were.

The nineteen well-used barracks that made up the residential halls of Trees Center were moved to the campus from Bunker Hill Air Force Base near Peru, Indiana in 1946. IU had become overcrowded with returning World War II veterans and needed additional housing immediately. The two-story wooden barracks were painted white and projected to be used no longer than five years. Nineteen years later, at the end of the school year in 1965, the last one was finally demolished. University literature described Trees as residences "for students on close budgets." Those of us in Cedar Hall had budgets that were even more restrained. Cedar was a cooperative dorm; our reduced housing fee did not cover maid services, bed linen, or a meal plan. We shared a communal bathroom with several showers, but only one bathtub. We also kept our own rooms tidy, had a rotating schedule for keeping the common areas clean, and brought bedclothes from home. Our most engrossing challenge was getting enough to eat because we were perpetually short of cash.

We devised all kinds of ways to obtain food, sometimes resorting to a hope that the evening date would spring for a hamburger or pizza. For a while I dated an air force veteran in school on the GI Bill, who was always willing and able to feed me. Babysitting for a professor's children was another way to get something to eat. I also managed to keep my stomach full the semester I worked as a waitress serving banquets at the Union Building. Servers were forbidden to eat the leftover food, but that simply made us quick and clever thieves. Occasionally, a friend who lived in one of the other dorms lent me a meal ticket if she was going out of town for the weekend or was just not interested in getting up for breakfast. Eating in a university dining hall meant you had to dress appropriately—no flip-flops, shorts, or halter-tops, and no pants on Sunday.

Cooking in our rooms was absolutely prohibited, but when the RA wasn't around, some girls warmed up Campbell's soup or Chef Boyardee spaghetti and meatballs on electric hot plates. The same hot plates were also used to heat straightening combs when we didn't have money for a beautician, or our edges or kitchens needed a touch-up before a big date.

Mama sometimes baked my favorite dessert—yellow cake with chocolate icing—and mailed it to me. I always shared it with the other Negro girls so they would remember me when they had food.

For emergencies we all stockpiled our staples—sardines, potted meat, Vienna sausages, and crackers. A real treat when I had money, or a date with money, was going to Fergie's Big Boy at Third and Jordan and feasting on a hamburger with everything. It was thick, sloppy, and delicious, requiring both hands and a wide-open mouth. After a while I found out about the Chatterbox, a restaurant on Third, half a block west of Fergie's, and across the street from the School of Education. At the Chatterbox you could get a breakfast of oatmeal, toast, and milk for thirty-five cents, and for fifty cents, a meal of meatloaf, potatoes, vegetable, and a drink. The Chatterbox sold meal cards for five dollars, and punched out the amount spent until it was used up. By using the card sparingly, I could make it last nearly a month.

Cedar Hall was a stone's throw from the dazzling new 1,060-room Smithwood Hall. Smithwood was a sumptuous seven-floor brick-and-limestone building with four wings that formed an X. Residents there enjoyed a sun deck on the roof, recreation rooms in the basement, and three hot meals a day. The building opened in 1954 and affluent coeds lived there. I wasn't surprised that several black girls resided in Smithwood, but I was unprepared for Cedar Hall being full of white girls, at least one of whom was a Jew. Didn't all white people, in particular Jews, have money? Interactions with the white girls in Cedar followed the same pattern as in my neighborhood and at Manual High School; we were cordial, and chatted from time to time, but we didn't socialize together or become friends.

Being on campus wasn't as uniformly wonderful as I had hoped. The sheer size of IU nearly overwhelmed me. There were close to 12,000 students, about 350 of whom were Negro. Except for the girls in my dorm, I saw other black students only in the Student Union's Commons and on weekends. There were none in my classes. Nor did I have any black professors. Richard Johnson was the first, and so far as I knew the only, tenure-track black faculty. He had joined the School of Music in 1951. I was in yet another fly-in-the-buttermilk situation.

I was shocked to find that my chemistry class met in an auditorium that seated two hundred or more students. Just as surprising was that the teaching assistant (TA) who corrected my exams seemed not to have heard the same lectures I did. I had loved chemistry in high school, but I never grasped what was required of me in this college class. The TA was surly and clearly uninterested in my problems. I didn't know where else to turn for help. I wound up with five hours of D in chemistry. I was equally out of it in the introductory psychology lab, a class that met at 7:30 in the morning. Since I had taken the intro psych lecture course at the Extension, I expected the lab to be familiar, but I was totally lost. The disheveled, unshaven TA seemed as annoyed at the hour of the class as I was, and sometimes he didn't show up at all. In the lab we were training white rats to do something, I don't remember what. My rat was retarded and never learned a thing. Another D. I failed to keep up with the reading assignments in English history and got a D in that class as well. After about fifteen minutes, I walked out of my French final exam; I saw no reason to continue sitting there staring at the questions. That was an F. From then on I took Spanish. (To dispel any gathering notion that I am as retarded as my rat, please note that as a graduate student I took two years of French and earned A's and B's.) I had three D's and an F to show for my first semester on campus. I didn't think it was possible for me to make such horrible grades. I was distraught and not sure how to make things better. My parents couldn't help me with this.

Years later when I read his autobiography, I was surprised to learn that James Comer, who was a diligent pre-med upperclassman when I came to campus, had also struggled when he first arrived. "I was reeling with confusion and fear by the end of the first month. ...I was the only black student in a [chemistry] class of 350. The burden of proving black intelligence rested on my very slim shoulders. I would freeze, unable to respond even when I knew the answer. But often I didn't know it; I simply was not functioning well." Jim learned to function well, however. He graduated from the Howard University College of Medicine and became associate dean of Yale University's School of Medicine. He is perhaps best known for the Comer School Development Program, designed to improve the educational experience of poor minority students.

From this distance, I can see that I was a budding free spirit who had been locked inside a box of Baptist fundamentalism in India-no-place for eighteen years. In my first solo foray, I was more interested in getting to know people from places where I had never been, and dating guys who talked about things I hadn't contemplated, than I was in sitting in classes and studying. For years I had hankered to be away from my parents' omnipresent supervision. It seemed that every Negro in Indianapolis either knew Smith Cheatham personally, or by reputation, and they expected a certain behavior from his daughter. Like a good girl, I comported myself so as not to betray or embarrass my parents. A major benefit of that restraint, however, was that, unlike a number of my friends, I did not become a teenaged mother, or get shoved into an early marriage. I had witnessed a tragic case of teen pregnancy that I've never forgotten. One of Rosie's friends, whom I'll call Lily, got pregnant at fourteen by a boy not much older. When her family found out it was too late for an abortion, so they sent her to relatives in another city to give birth. (Abortions weren't legal then, but the older we got, the more we heard about how to, or which doctors would, get rid of a baby.) Lily wanted to keep her child, but her mother insisted she give him up for adoption. All the joy was gone from Lily after she returned from giving birth and then losing her son. Before her twenty-fifth birthday, she was diagnosed with uterine cancer and not long afterwards had a hysterectomy. The son Lily was forced to give away was the only child she ever had. As young women, Rosie and I laughed that we were fortunate Mama and Daddy had us terrified of sex. We were not so much terrorized as determined not to shame our parents. Now I know that, like much of our generation, we were remnants of the prudish sexual hypocrisy of the Victorian era. Kathlyn, a divorced, older Cedar Hall resident, ridiculed my sexual virginity, and I began to question whether I should be proud of not having allowed a boy to go all the way.

Being the responsible elder daughter of Annie and Smith Cheatham was exacting. For reasons that she never explained, Mama had higher expectations for her daughters than for her sons. Perhaps she wanted her girls to have what she couldn't. Or, she may simply have been following the customary Negro practice of assuming that sons could fend for themselves, but daughters had to be educated to avoid domestic work and being at the mercy of lascivious employers. Rosie and I were told not to bring home a grade lower than a B, yet Mama was pleased when my brothers made Cs. I also had to be a good daughter to compensate for James's having disappointed my parents by becoming a teenage father, and not completing high school until he passed the GED test in the army. So long as I was taking classes at the Extension and working part-time, my routine was essentially the same as it had been in high school, and I maintained regular study habits. On campus, nobody knew my parents so I relaxed and had a good time, *a real good time*. At every opportunity I honed my bid whist skills. In the Commons between classes I was always ready for a quick game, and sometimes in the dorm we became so involved in a game that we played until the wee hours.

After those dismal first semester grades, somebody suggested that I sign up for Reading and Study for Self-Improvement. I got a B in that facile class, but otherwise I continued to be ineffectual. I had been in honors English at Manual, but the professors in my literature classes at IU casually referenced terms and books I'd never heard of. It was clear my classmates knew things I didn't, and I had no idea how to catch up with them. At the Extension, my instructors were helpful when I had questions, but on campus, I ran into professors and teaching assistants who seemed personally affronted if I asked for aid. I went to see Dr. Robert Mitchner, the only professor who taught English Grammar for Teachers, a required class. I wanted to ask him how I could improve my mid-term grade. I arrived on time for my appointment in his office and told him why I was there. He simply said, "I can't help you," then turned his attention to the top of his desk. I stood there awkwardly for a minute, trying to think of a better way to phrase my question. When I asked for his help again, he didn't look up, and didn't say another word. I felt like dog shit that he had just scraped off his shoe. He gave me a D, which at least insured I wouldn't have to take it again.

There were periods when things went well, and in Mama's scrapbook under the caption, "Treasured Letter," was a description of one of those times.

October 10, 1956
Dear Marmee,

I received your letter today. I don't think I was sad at all Sunday. In fact after you left, I talked to Morris [my boyfriend of the moment] and he wanted to know why I was so happy.

I went to the concert [IU Philharmonic Orchestra on Sunday, October 7] *alone. I don't like to go to concerts with*

*anybody because people talk too much. It was <u>very good</u>.
There were several people there that I knew.*

*Good news: I got back a paper that I wrote for my
Chaucer course and I had an "A-." It really made me happy.
I have been appointed chairman of a discussion group in my
Psychology class. I'm the only Ned* [current slang for Negro]
*in the class. I had a test in Spanish Monday, but I haven't
gotten it back yet.*

*I baby sat last night for a short while made a $1.00. I
work tomorrow and Friday.* [I had a job as a banquet waitress at the Union Building.]

*I really am doing just fine. I wrote to Grandma. I got a
letter from Marie B*[eanum, one of my Michigan cousins]
today. One from Lucille [Southerland, a friend in India-
napolis] *the other day.*

*I paid my rent, and I still have about $6.00. I also
bought some crackers and soap and stamps and another
book that I needed for American Lit.*

Have Rosie and Reggie had any tests yet?

*Everybody be good. How is the new TV? Is it a combi-
nation, radio, record player etc? I would like to see it, but I
don't know when I'll get the chance.*

Tell Popsy I said "Hiiii!"

> *Love,*
> *Big Sis, Your eldest daughter,*
> *Janet*

The other piece is for Rosie. [Most of my letters were written to
Mama because she wrote me every week, but sometimes I enclosed a
page for another family member.]

My plan had been to major in English with a minor in history,
but the way things were going, I began to doubt that I was college
material. Some of the Negro students' parents and grandparents were
educated and they had been groomed for college all their lives. One,
Ralph Waldo Emerson Jones Jr., was the son of a *college president*,
Grambling in Louisiana. Cora Smith (Breckenridge), who remains a
friend, was a member of Pleiades, an honorary for excellence above

the normal world, and also selected for Mortar Board, a national honorary for senior women who are outstanding in scholarship, leadership, and service. Cora continued that service as a member of the national board of directors of the NAACP, and as the first black elected to the Indiana University Board of Trustees. Paul Carter Harrison, a sophisticated New Yorker, partied hard and still did well in his studies. He is now a distinguished author and playwright in his hometown. We referred to Gloria Randle (Scott) as "the brain," and justifiably so. Gloria was the first black student to graduate with a degree in zoology in 1959. She too was a member of Pleiades and later earned law and doctorate degrees. Gloria went on to become national president of Girl Scouts of America, and also served as president of Bennett College in Greensboro, North Carolina.

My good friend Raphael (we pronounced it RayFEEL) Hardrick is the son of one of Indiana's most talented artists, John Wesley Hardrick. The elder Hardrick's award-winning paintings were recognized and exhibited nationally. Raphael was a brilliant student, but couldn't get into IU's medical school because they had filled their Negro quota. The rumor was that IU would take only two blacks a year. Rather than wait for a "Negro" slot to open, Raphael went to Germany and completed medical school there. He never returned to live in the U.S. Jim Comer was admitted to IU's med school, but chose to go to Howard, a historically black university in Washington, D.C. Jim said being at IU was like "playing your home games on the opponents' court. Instead of cheers you get jeers—and worse. ... I just wanted to be a student, not a black student who had to prove something every step of the way. I wanted to feel that school was my place—home court." Frankie (Felicia) Weathers was another black student from my era who settled in Europe. Frankie had a magnificent voice and became a successful classical singer.

There were plenty of others like me who were the first in their families to go beyond high school, like my cousin and fellow Manual alum Webster Brewer. But Webster was focused. He went to law school and became a judge in Marion County Superior Court in Indianapolis. I was in awe of all these students and felt like something was wrong with me.

Twenty-three years later, my nephew, Michael Cheatham, enrolled at IU. I talked to him about the challenges he would face, but more important, he was a part of Groups. The Groups Student Support Services Program, which is still functioning, helps students from underrepresented populations make the transition from high school to college life. The program also teaches them the skills they need to succeed in the classroom. In addition, when Michael arrived on campus in 1978, there was a Black Culture Center, where Caramel Russell welcomed and counseled black students. Michael credits Carolyn Calloway-Thomas, his advisor and Speech Communications professor, for his success at IU. Calloway-Thomas, who is black, mentored him and pushed him to excel. After graduating, Michael spent several years as an executive with a major hotel chain, and currently is president and owner of Inspired Solutions and Associates.

Considering that I did not have the kind of reception and nurturing that Michael did, and given my confusion, I marvel that I somehow managed to accumulate credits toward my degree.

Chapter 13

Evading the Dragon

The large monster …always comes to trample on our
dreams of becoming great without sacrifice…. We all want
to be heroes, but we just don't want to fight the dragon.
And that is understandable. Dragons have bad breath.

~ Wynton Marsalis, artistic director,
Jazz at Lincoln Center

The *racial* climate in Bloomington felt more threatening than in
Indianapolis. Bloomington is fifty miles south of Indianapolis and
that much closer to the Mason-Dixon Line. That location is exacer-
bated by the fact that the road between Bloomington and Indianapolis runs through Martinsville. At that time Martinsville had a reputation as a sunset town, meaning that Negroes might be welcome to
work there, but would be subject to arrest, or worse, if caught in the
town after dark. Traveling between Bloomington and Indianapolis,
we were wary and apprehensive until Martinsville was behind us.

When I got to Bloomington in 1955, Herman B Wells, president
of Indiana University, was being lauded for having desegregated the
school; however, it still was not a congenial environment for us. At
the time I thought it was because there were so few Negroes around,
but in writing this book, I decided to check out what was going on at
IU in the years before I arrived. I already knew that a branch of the
NAACP was started on campus in 1945, and that aroused my curiosity. If President Wells had seen the discrimination against Negroes
and ended it, why had students felt the need for an aggressive organization like the NAACP?

I learned that the reality of desegregating the campus was more
complex than the surviving myths indicate. As often happens when
stories are told about breakthroughs in the Struggle, the contribu-

tions of Negroes are omitted. Like other whites credited with being our benefactors—most notably Abraham Lincoln, and lately Alan Lomax—Wells was, as one might expect, pulled and prodded along that path by Negroes. Our desire to be accorded the same respect that others take for granted is, understandably, more important to us than to anybody else. Wells adroitly walked the tightrope between relentless pressure from blacks to be fully included in the life of IU, and demands by whites that Negroes be kept away from them. He did this balancing act for fifteen years before university dormitories were fully desegregated in 1952, three years before I arrived on campus.

For decades Negroes had been leaning on IU's administration to desegregate university dormitories, but a mass meeting called by Negro students on January 31, 1945 seems to have been a galvanizing moment. I wondered what had incited that meeting and found a possible cause. Eleven days earlier on campus a taxi had run down three black students who were crossing Indiana Avenue at Seventh Street. The taxi driver, Joseph Smith, killed Fred Holland of Indianapolis and Anna Katherine Lewis from Evansville. Patsy Crenshaw, also from Indianapolis, was hospitalized with an injury to her leg. Fortunately, a fourth student in the group, Wendell Parker, another Indianapolis resident, escaped without harm. Suddenly two of the 109 Negro students were gone. That must have been quite a blow! I remember how I felt when Corinne, a young black woman in my Chaucer class, was killed in an automobile accident en route to Bloomington after a holiday break. I didn't know her well, but I was shocked and upset by her death because there were so few of us on campus, and I rarely had a class with another black student. The unexpected deaths in 1945, right on campus, of two of their number had to rattle that small group of Negro students.

The mass meeting called by students eleven days after these deaths focused on the whites-only policy of the university dormitories. I was surprised that the report of the meeting didn't mention the student deaths. On the day the impromptu meeting was called, the front page of the campus newspaper had an article headlined, "Grand Jury Fails to Reach Decision in Taxi Accident." That article left the impression that the white taxi driver might be exonerated. I would have been outraged at that, and I imagine some of the students felt similarly and decided they had to do *something!* They called a mass meeting. No doubt there were some in the meeting insisting that they wait and see how the matter would be resolved. However, with a room full of students clamoring for action, they found an issue that everybody agreed needed immediate attention—the university's denial of campus housing to Negro students. That night they decided to form a branch of the NAACP with a first order of business to get Negroes admitted to university dormitories.

Smith, the taxi driver, claimed to have been going twenty-five miles an hour, although eyewitnesses said he was speeding. His passenger, Leonard Bourke, a white man, fled the scene. Later when police picked him up, he was unable—or possibly unwilling—to give an account of what happened. A grand jury finally indicted Smith for involuntary manslaughter. His punishment was a five-hundred-dollar fine. I could find no record of how students responded to the dispensation of the case.

Postwar housing was inadequate for all IU students, but Negroes felt especially aggrieved because they were barred from living on campus at all. Finding suitable housing had persistently been a monumental challenge for Negro students. In 1914 Elder W. Diggs, a founder of Kappa Alpha Psi fraternity, had to live in a converted stable. Before black students were finally welcomed on a first come, first served basis in un-segregated university housing, Samuel Dargan provided places for many of them to live. Dargan was the Negro curator of the IU law library who owned several properties adjacent to campus. There were also a few black families in Bloomington who rented rooms to colored students, but these services were insufficient and, in some cases, inadequate. For one thing, Dargan's houses had no dining facilities, and Negroes were not allowed to eat in Bloomington restaurants. Marie Love (Johnson) described her living quarters in one of Dargan's properties, Elms House, on the corner of Ninth and Dunn. "I had two roommates and our room was a passageway to another room that two other students had to get to, and to the bathroom."

But at least Marie Love had someplace to stay. Clara Willis of French Lick had to leave IU because she had no place to live. When I remember how my mother and I had laid out my wardrobe, scrimped together money to buy an iron and a typewriter, boxed up food staples, plus the general excitement of my whole family when I was leaving for campus, my heart ached for Clara Willis. After undoubtedly similar preparations and excitement, Clara arrived on campus to receive the devastating news that there was no housing for her. Like me, before she left home, Clara had been assured of housing, but "the officer who gave her this information by mail did not know she was a Negro."

In 1940, five years before the campus NAACP was started, President Wells received a report expressing concern that if IU didn't remedy discrimination on campus, the university "will be faced with the action of the Assn. of Advancement of Colored People [*sic*]. It is moving from campus to campus as rapidly as they can get to it...." The report said IU was vulnerable on several points: "1. Housing for girls. 2. The use of swimming pools. 3. The practice house experience for girls taking Home Economics. 4. Practice teaching for colored students. 5. Cafeteria facilities. 6. Military training."

Two of the six listed issues had already been addressed. Earlier that year Wells had ordered the reserved signs that segregated the cafeteria removed, and the report said, "there have been a few of them eat there without any difficulty." In addition, the military "has taken one man ... and has no objection to taking others." Evasive tactics were recommended for the other items on the list, including housing for girls, which was described as "very bad." A Negro parent distraught about the circumstances of his daughter's housing had lodged complaints with the university, the mayor, and the chief of police. "As a result," the report concluded, "Mrs. [Kate Hevner] Mueller [dean of women] felt she would have to use the same rules relative to housing colored girls that she uses on white girls."

Obviously, they continued with two different sets of rules because segregated housing for women did not end for another twelve years.

In 1942, two years after this report, Mueller wrote to Wells, "Circumstances have been forcing on us a new policy in regard to our colored women students." Mueller had worked out a plan to use White Hall at 137 Forest Place, on campus just south of the administration building, to house twenty colored girls. Mueller admitted her plan had disadvantages: "1) The girls would probably patronize the Union Building cafeteria much more than formerly; 2) it would be an opening wedge into the campus which it would be difficult for us later to dislodge, and 3) it might eventually attract even more colored students to our campus." Considering these flaws, Mueller concluded that they should continue "keeping our hands off all their affairs." She hoped the university's neglect wouldn't be noticed.

Meanwhile, Wells had to turn his attention to the other side of the tightrope. In September of that year, Harley and Edith Skirvin, a white Bloomington couple, objected to three houses the university had leased for colored students in the square block between Ninth and Tenth and Dunn and Grant streets. The irate citizens said, "If the university cannot refuse admission to the Negro students, it must and should house them on its own property." To reinforce their complaint, the couple had forty-five of their neighbors join them in a petition to the board of trustees. Wells met with the disgruntled citizens and firmly told them, "There is no legal, ethical or economic justification for [your] demand."

The hands-off policy that Mueller hoped wouldn't be noticed was, of course, apparent to Negroes. Black students, desperate for help, asked the Indianapolis branch of the NAACP to intercede in the housing crisis after they were forced to sleep in chairs, on floors, or return home for lack of housing. The NAACP, led by their president, Priscilla Dean Lewis, took the issue to Governor Henry Schricker. Schricker contacted Herman Wells, who had been president for seven years. Disingenuously, Wells said there was no *race* issue involved because many white students had also been denied admittance to university housing. The NAACP pressed Schricker for a solution; he, in turn, pressed Wells, and the *Indianapolis Recorder* kept the Negro community up to date on the strife at the state's largest tax-supported university. Something had to be done.

Despite its disadvantages, Wells dusted off Mueller's proposal of a year and half earlier and put it into operation. The white students who were living in White Hall were asked to leave and twenty black women moved in. In September 1944 these women became the first Negroes to live on campus at Indiana University. The ironic name of the hall was not changed. Opening a house on campus to twenty black women shattered precedent, but it didn't do much to alleviate the residential crunch. Four months later housing was still at the top of the agenda when IU's students organized a campus branch of the NAACP. Over six hundred students, more than ten percent of IU's total enrollment of 5,691 joined the NAACP. At the time, there were just over one hundred colored students at IU.

In perusing the documents about Negro housing at IU, I kept running across the name of Daddy's associate, Faburn E. DeFrantz, executive secretary of the colored YMCA. In September 1945, eight months after the campus NAACP was established, DeFrantz, his son Robert DeFrantz; Robert Starms, field secretary of the NAACP; Walter Bailey, who had been president of the Negro Student Council when he was at IU; and Joseph H. Ward, an activist physician—all from Indianapolis—visited Wells in Bloomington to discuss the housing situation. Wells informed Governor Ralph Gates of the meeting and offered to work with him to resolve the problem. Wells also told the governor that the issue "just as I thought it was in the beginning," was that the group really wanted the total removal of the University's prohibition against Negroes in the dorms. Later that month, Wells told the board of trustees that the general dormitories should be opened to Negro students. However, Wells had to overcome resistance on the board, so two more years elapsed before the process began. Ora L. Wildermuth, a board member from Gary, said, "I am and shall always remain absolutely and utterly opposed to social intermingling of the colored race with the white." The intramural center on campus is named for Wildermuth.

In the fall of 1947, apparently without fanfare, black males were admitted to IU's dormitories. It took five more years of lobbying to get Negro women into the dorms. The faculty advisor to the campus branch of the NAACP alerted IU in January 1948, that the national NAACP was prepared to file suit because the university "still falls short of equality in its treatment of Negro students." At the top of the list of shortfalls was Negro women living in segregated housing. Despite this warning, Wells submitted a plan to the board of trustees seven months later to *increase* segregated housing for Negro women by acquiring Lincoln House on Forest Place near the Union Building. At the time white women occupied Lincoln House, but they were moved out. Wells said the house would be "refurbished comparable to our best equipped dormitory," an indication that the other off-campus dorms for black women: the aforementioned Elms House, and Hayes House on East Tenth, were not comparable. Wells knew that increasing segregated housing, no matter how elegant the accommodations, was not a good idea. Near the end of his proposal he stated, "We have received additional evidence tending to support the point of view that this new arrangement will not satisfy the [Negroes]. Instead it may increase the agitation." He was undoubtedly referring to a memo alerting him that "a delegation of leading Negro citizens ... called upon Governor Gates concerning the housing of Negro women students on campus."

Willard B. Ransom, president of the Indiana State Conference of the NAACP, immediately wrote to Wells expressing his displeasure. Frank M. Summers, an IU alum living in East St. Louis, Illinois, returned the contract that assigned his daughter Katherine to live in Lincoln House. He told them to keep his deposit "until such time as integrated accommodations are available." A year later, Wells wrote the university's lawyer about yet another session with "the anti-segregation group" who threatened to make "an immediate appeal to higher authority." Wells closed his letter by saying, "Having dealt with these people now for a good many years I think I am competent to judge the situation, and I am convinced that we must take affirmative action...or lose control of the situation with the certainty that the total interests of everyone will be injured—theirs and ours alike." The following semester, in the fall of 1950, a few black faces appear in the yearbook photos of women's dormitories. In 1952, three years before I arrived on campus, Lincoln House was closed and all of IU's students were officially welcome to live wherever they chose on campus.

It took a while for me to figure out why there was more resistance to having black and white women living together in the dorms than there was to integrating the men. Then it hit me: conventional American sentiment demands the protection of fragile white womanhood. This mythology, used to justify many Southern lynchings, is such a persistent part of the American psyche that it remains entrenched in the twenty-first century, decades after the women's liberation movement. That's why a missing white female roils the media waters in an orgy of concern, while a missing Latina or black woman barely ripples the surface.

As a fifth generation Hoosier, President Wells knew Indiana's landscape well. He explained, "In taking the steps required to remove those reprehensible, discriminatory rules, we tried to make a move if possible when the issue was not being violently discussed pro and con on the campus." And he acknowledged in his autobiography that the "NAACP and prominent black alumni" maintained "constant pressure for change." It's not surprising that Wells had to grow into his role and move cautiously. He ascended to the presidency in 1937, when he was thirty-five years old, and *racism* was a warm, fuzzy blanket for most whites. Those reprehensible rules Wells referred to were the natural order of things in Indiana. Not long before he became IU's president, the state was flaunting its allegiance to the Ku Klux Klan.

Fast-forward fifty years to IU in 2003. I was quite surprised, but proud, when my alma mater selected its first African American, Adam Herbert, to be the university's seventeenth president. Confounding my expectations even more was that, at the time, Cora Breckenridge was the only black on the nine-member board of trustees. My elation lasted almost two years. Apparently in the minds of some, even in twenty-first century Indiana, the Klan image of the dumb, lazy, dangerous Negro is alive and well. In an eerie forecast of the disrespect accorded President Barack Obama by the U.S. Congress, some faculty members were criticizing Dr. Herbert publicly before he could settle comfortably into his new position. Three months prior to his second anniversary, a group from the Alliance of Distinguished and Titled Professors questioned his competency to lead the institution. At the end of his first two years, the local newspaper ran a long article examining his brief tenure with a big bold headline, "A Question of Leadership." A few months later President Herbert turned down a selection committee's recommendation for a new chancellor asking them to reopen the search. A cadre of white professors, some of whom were undoubtedly in the group who had earlier questioned Dr. Herbert's competency, were outraged at this exercise of the president's authority.

These professors mounted an all-out campaign to discredit the new university president. I was stunned by the strident and public nature of the attack. One of the professors boldly proclaimed his disdain for Dr. Herbert, "The guy is doing a really bad job, but if we get a good chancellor in to work with him, then the guy has two and a half years left to limp through his presidency." I immediately concluded that the professors felt at liberty to *publicly* disrespect the university's president because he was black; however, I did inquire to see if perhaps this behavior was typical of IU faculty. I spoke to two high ranking officials—one white, Dr. Ken Gros Louis, interim senior vice president and chancellor, and one black, Dr. Charlie Nelms, vice president for institutional development and student affairs. Combined, Drs. Gros Louis and Nelms have more than sixty years of service to Indiana University. In separate interviews, each of them assured me he had never before witnessed faculty members publicly assailing an IU president.

The Black Faculty Council also believed that the ferocity of the complaints was attributable to this country's traditional lack of respect for African Americans. The attacking professors denied any *racist* intent, and I doubt that it was a *conscious* act of *racism*. More likely it was a visceral response to their first encounter with an African American in a position of authority over them. I agree with writer Malcolm Gladwell that, "people are ignorant of the things that affect their actions, yet they rarely *feel* ignorant." Scientist Albert Einstein goes a little further in saying essentially the same thing, "A large part of our attitude toward things is conditioned by opinions and emotions which we unconsciously absorb as children from our environment. In other words, it is *tradition*—besides inherited aptitudes and qualities—which makes us what we are." [emphasis added]

It was also revealing that the complaining professors did not include any colleagues of color in their coterie. Not even David Baker. Baker, an African American, is a distinguished professor, one of the most admired, and certainly one of the longest serving faculty members at IU. At the Black Faculty Council's press conference, Baker said, "This is the first time in my memory [nearly forty years at IU] I've seen the president publicly called to task in this manner by members of the faculty." At least one white faculty member was willing to acknowledge that *race* played a role in the debacle. Michael Wilkerson wrote in a newspaper column, "Whites had a hard time explaining why, during the often unpopular tenure of Myles Brand [the president who preceded Herbert], there had been no public protests…. Those faculty who have dared address race directly have begun to walk a path that is both seldom trod and too long avoided. Let's follow them; it's the only way into the light."

Dr. Herbert apparently decided life was too short to endure being under siege by his own faculty. Three years after his arrival in a letter to the Board of Trustees in 2006, he summarized his accomplishments, then added, "I feel an obligation to the University to give the Board of Trustees as much advance notice as possible that I do not wish to serve the university as president beyond the period of my current contract which ends July 2008."

When I arrived in Bloomington as a sophomore in 1955, we could go wherever we wanted on campus, but the Struggle was still on in the rest of the town. We weren't welcome in the student hangouts near campus. They either directly refused to serve us or pretended not to see us. Nick's English Hut on Kirkwood Avenue not far from the campus's main entrance at Indiana and Kirkwood, refused service to two students I knew: DeWitt Jackson, a senior from Indianapolis, and Laurence D. Scott, a freshman from Lebanon. Both Jackson and Scott were members of the campus NAACP. The owner of Nick's was quoted, "We'll close the place before we serve Negroes." Fifty customers walked out in support of the two black students. A barbershop, also on Kirkwood, wouldn't cut black hair. I joined other members of the NAACP to picket the shop. To avoid *racist* encounters insofar as possible, we Negro students stayed close to campus, except for regular excursions to the colored Elks Lodge, across from a cemetery on West Seventh Street. The Elks had begun construction of a new building but only completed the basement, which they opened as a bar, with a jukebox and room to dance. Since we entered by descending stairs to an underground space, we referred to it as the Hole. We went to the Hole when we wanted to relax, eat, drink, and dance.

Although in 1940 Wells had removed the rope around the Negro area in the Student Union's Commons, and the "reserved" signs from the tables, fifteen years later most black students continued to sit in that space. This time however, it was by choice, which makes all the difference. The first time I went into the Commons, I was delighted to see a group of black students and immediately joined them. Having been smothered in whites all day, I welcomed the effortlessness of being with my people. Besides, we didn't go to the Commons between classes to test the limits of white acceptance; we went to eat, relax, gossip with friends, or play a few hands of bid whist. I heard that students from Africa had refused to sit in the "reserved" section. If questioned, I suppose they explained that, despite appearances, they were not descended from the Africans who had been enslaved. Their British accent would, I imagine, put to rest any concerns that a homegrown Negro had forgotten his place.

My roommate that first year on campus was Phyllis Dickerson from Gary. Phyllis was also a sophomore and had moved into Cedar when her grades dropped too low to continue living in Pine Hall, the scholarship dorm. The university assigned roommates and never put whites and Negroes together. Phyllis was very bright, but her mind never seemed to be in the same place as her body. She was about five feet tall and wore thick glasses. I recall Phyllis telling me that her life began when she got her first pair of eyeglasses in elementary school. Until then she had assumed everybody saw things in an ill-defined blur because that was all she had ever experienced. I liked Phyllis, but she was too sedate for me. We managed to co-exist amiably, but didn't become friends. To my surprise and everybody else's as well, Phyllis out did us all when she landed a husband. She left school to marry one of the U.S. Air Force guys studying languages at IU.

The stated or understood mission of every coed seemed to be finding a husband. Young women who were going steady or pinned were envied. Those who were engaged, and had a diamond ring to prove it, were drooled over. Although husband-children-picket fence had never been a fantasy of mine, I wanted to fit in. I became an active participant in the gaggling and giggling over who was pinned, engaged, or about to be. I remember being part of an admiring circle surrounding Joyce Sterling when she showed off her engagement ring.

I had turned down a marriage proposal shortly after graduating from high school. Randy, nineteen years old, and home on leave after a few months in the army, asked me to marry him. We had dated maybe three times, so I chuckled and responded, "You're joking."

"I'm *not* joking. I'm ready to get married." Randy's feelings were hurt.

"Randy, I'm seventeen, a long way from being ready to get married." That's the same answer I should have given six years later when Holsey Hickman proposed, but by then suppressing my natural impulses had become a way of life.

Within Indiana University, so far as our social life was concerned, we Negroes had our own separate black college. All three hundred or so of us either knew each other personally, or knew about one another, because we attended the same functions. With five active black sororal and fraternal organizations, there was always something going on, and the black Greeks competed with one another to host the best happenings.

Kappa Alpha Psi, a black fraternity, has the distinction of being the only national fraternal organization founded at Indiana University. The fraternity was incorporated in 1911 with the name Kappa Alpha Nu. The name was changed in 1915 because some white students persisted in referring to them as Kappa Alpha Nig. The Kappas' first chapter house was leased by one of their founders, Elder Watson Diggs. As was still the case thirty years later, dormitory space was not available to Negroes, and accommodations for them in Bloomington were scarce. Diggs rented the five-room house at 721 Hunter Street in 1914 and shared it with his fraternity brothers. My one memory of being inside a Kappa Kastle, as their houses were called, was attending a pajama party at 425 North Dunn where everyone was dressed for bed. Some of the young women wore alluring negligees that made me feel frumpy in my up-to-the-neck pajamas over my underclothes.

In my first year on campus, Alpha Kappa Alpha sorority had a dance to welcome pledges, a Christmas party, and a moonlight picnic at McCormick's Creek State Park. The picnic was described in the yearbook: "Couples spent the evening roasting marshmallows and dancing." Sure they did. That same year, Delta Sigma Theta sorority had a Mardi Gras dance, Alpha Phi Alpha fraternity hosted a Spring Formal, and Kappa Alpha Psi fraternity had a Monte Carlo Casino. I remember going to the Winter Formal held in the Student Union and hosted by all of the black Greek organizations, including Omega Psi Phi fraternity. Plowing ahead with my campaign to have a fulsome social life, I officially became a coed by honoring the campus tradition of being kissed at midnight in the Well House for the twelve chimes of the nearby Student Building clock. Of course, this was only possible on a Friday or Saturday night when girls were not locked up until 12:30 a.m. I also pledged Alpha Kappa Alpha. I found the pledging process degrading: we were instructed to wait on the big sisters—polish her shoes, pick up her cleaning, or whatever else she might order us to do. I was once put on social lockdown because a big sister was interested in my boyfriend. I disliked everything about it but didn't have the courage to withdraw. When the semester ended my grades weren't good enough for me to cross the burning sands and become a full-fledged soror. I was invited to try again, but I'd had enough. Even if I'd made acceptable grades, where was I going to get four hundred dollars for the initiation fee?

Money was a perpetual problem for many of us, but playing sports helped a number of the male students pay for their education. At the beginning of my second year on campus, we celebrated two of those student-athletes who had won gold medals in the 1956 summer Olympic games. Milt Campbell, from Plainfield, New Jersey, and a member of IU's football team, was recognized as the world's best athlete when he won the decathlon. At the previous Olympics, when he was just eighteen, Campbell had won the silver medal in the decathlon. Greg Bell of Terre Haute won his gold for the long jump.

Even though black athletes competed in several other sports on campus, IU did not want black basketball players. Indiana University had been playing intercollegiate basketball since 1901, but didn't recruit their first Negro player until 1947. And it wouldn't have happened then except for outside pressure. I was surprised to find out that there was actually a black, Preston Eagleson, on the football team from 1893 to 1895. He was the first African American to play sports at IU. Another black, George Thompson was a noted track athlete in 1905, but when he traveled with his teammates, they had to use subterfuge in order for them all to stay in the same hotel. Thompson's teammates told suspicious desk clerks at whites-only hotels that Thompson was Hawaiian or Cuban. So long as the hotel employees believed that Thompson was not an American Negro, he could stay in the same hotel as whites.

I don't know how long it would have taken before blacks were allowed to play basketball at IU had it not been for Faburn DeFrantz bringing yet another group of black leaders to see President Wells in the spring of 1947. The group wanted a commitment from Wells that if Bill Garrett were admitted to IU, and made the team, he would be allowed to play. Garrett was a sensational athlete, who had just led Shelbyville High School to the state championship, and been named Indiana's Mr. Basketball. After his meeting with DeFrantz's group, which included some IU alumni, Wells spoke to Zora Clevenger, the athletic director. Clevenger informed Wells, apparently for the first time, "The basketball coaches [in the Big Ten Conference] have an understanding [not to recruit black players] and, if we were to violate that understanding, we'd probably have a hard time getting a schedule...." Wells said he "was astonished to learn that [IU] didn't recruit black basketball players." Clevenger said he'd talk to Branch McCracken, the basketball coach, and, "if he wants to do it, I'll back him."

McCracken liked the idea of adding a fabulous player like Garrett to his team, but he hesitated because he felt he'd be ostracized by his fellow Big Ten coaches. Wells told him, "If there's any conference backlash against it, I'll take the responsibility for handling it." At the time, Wells was heading the Big Ten presidents' organization. Until recently, lore had it that in 1948 Bill Garrett was the first Negro to play basketball at a Big Ten school. However, the University of Iowa reports that Richard Culberson, a black man, played for the Hawkeyes in their 1944-45 and 1945-46 seasons. Apparently the Iowa coach wasn't concerned about ostracism. Garrett was definitely the first black man to play for the Hurryin' Hoosiers', and he was their leading scorer all three years he was on the team. (In those days, freshmen weren't allowed to play varsity ball.) He also earned all-Big Ten and all-America honors.

So far as my studies were concerned, nothing changed the second year. I continued to struggle, escaping my feelings of academic inadequacy with an intense social life—partying, and dating intelligent and talented black guys. I went out with athletes, pre med students, and young men from exotic places like Boston and New Jersey. It was a pleasure to date without Mama's running commentary about which guy would make a good husband, or who was just breath and britches. My mother loved coming to campus, so whenever she and Daddy had a free Sunday afternoon, they drove down for a visit. Perhaps hoping that I would be in my room studying, she decided to surprise me one Sunday by not calling first. Mama got surprised because I wasn't in my room, and she didn't know where else to look. They drove around campus hoping to spot me. Every time they saw Negroes, they stopped and asked if they knew where I was. Nobody did. After two frustrating hours, they went home. Apparently they didn't believe that could happen again, but it did. After a second futile surprise trip, Mama called to plan their visits, but she never let me hear the end of the times they couldn't find me.

I was on academic probation, and when I wasn't able to bring my average up by the end of my third semester on campus, the university

For six months in 1962 both my brothers were stationed in Korea. James (standing) was in Seoul and Reggie in Tageu.

invited me to leave. I should have been chastened, but instead I was hurt and angry. Fortunately, the state library welcomed me back to work a few months early. I needed the money, because in addition to my awful grades, I was broke. And that's what Mama told everybody: "Janet had to come home to work and make enough money to go back and finish her education." To avoid her keen disappointment and unending questions about the real reason I was back home, I volunteered to stay with my sister-in-law, Dolores, whom we call Dodie.

Dodie's husband, my brother James, is six feet two, slender, and quite intelligent, but when he was discharged from the army, he could only find jobs that required heavy lifting. He first worked at a steel foundry, where the heat was so intense workers took a break every fifteen minutes. James lasted for three days. Then he spent a couple of years busting his hump handling heavy mailbags at the post office. James had not been particularly fond of army life, but he knew from experience that the army did not care about credentials or color. If you could do a job, they let you do it. In the military he could have a desk job. He concluded that was a better deal than the backbreaking menial labor available to him as a civilian, so he joined up again. When that term ended, he was offered a reenlistment bonus and re-upped, deciding at that point to make it his career. In the army James was an instructor in financial management, and although he was posted to both Korea and Vietnam, he was never involved in combat.

Unfortunately, the armed service's family allotment was so small that when Dodie left work for the birth of their first child, Kevin, she couldn't afford the rent on their apartment. My parents arranged for her to move into Lockefield Gardens where rent was based on income.

Lockefield was one of this country's first federally funded public housing projects, built specifically for Negroes, and located in the heart of the black neighborhood on the west side of Indianapolis. In 1938 when Lockefield opened, "Those who moved in...received affordable housing that far exceeded the quality of private accommodations in the surrounding neighborhood." Daddy must have called in a favor because "at the end of 1956 over 694 families were on [Lockefield's] waiting list." Dodie's name had certainly not been on the list, but she moved there in 1957. Like Mama, Dodie believes danger lurks everywhere, especially in unfamiliar places. She would not stay in Lockefield alone, so I went to live with her, sleeping on a rollaway bed in the living room. When she returned to her job at Ft. Harrison's army finance center, Dodie moved back to her familiar south side neighborhood in Barrington Manor.

While I lived with Dodie, I worked full-time and took classes at the Extension. By the end of the year I had completed nine hours without further damaging my grade point average. In January 1958, I returned to campus and Cedar Hall. This time my roommate was my Manual classmate Helen Baker. Mildred Morgan (Ball) from Gary lived just down the hall. The three of us became fast friends and often laughed together that we shared the same body type—we were all around five feet four, with ample hips and minimal breasts. But the similarities ended there. Mildred was an accomplished athlete and a physical education major. She had the take-charge personality of a woman who has been reared by a man; her mother died when she was five years old, leaving her dad the

My roommate and running buddy, Helen Ester Baker.

lone parent of eight children. Mildred attended Hampton University before coming to IU and had an aristocrat's penchant for well-made, expensive clothing. Like me, Helen was an English major. Helen's reticence made her appear delicate, but she was actually quite resolute and goal oriented. Both she and Mildred were skilled modern dancers. While she was an undergraduate, the IU Dance Department tapped Mildred to take over classes when a teacher went on maternity leave. Helen's parents had insisted that she turn down an opportunity to join a touring company when she was fifteen.

Nancy Streets, Miss Indiana University, 1959. Used by permission Indiana University Archives

We were all attractive young women: Mildred was light-skinned with long thick hair, and Helen was an acknowledged beauty with what in those benighted times we called good hair—meaning it was straight like most white folks' hair. When *Ebony* magazine came to campus looking for beautiful Negro coeds to photograph, they selected only high yellows, except for tan Helen. No doubt Nancy Streets was one of the beauties *Ebony* photographed. If they didn't find her on that foray, they definitely caught her later. Nancy was on the cover of *Jet*, another Johnson Publication's magazine, as the first Negro to win the title of Miss Indiana University.

It was 1959 and the judges may not have known Nancy was black because you couldn't tell by looking. Perhaps the jubilant Negroes and the *Jet* cover tipped them off, but it was too late; the winner had been announced. However, the university yearbook still had time to snub her. The *Arbutus* refused to include Nancy in their annual spread of campus beauty queens. Several IU alumni wrote vitriolic letters to President Wells expressing their shame and dismay that he had allowed a colored girl to be chosen queen. Wells' response to these letters was a masterpiece of circumspection. He expressed his gratitude to hear from the writer, then his sorrow that "an event at Indiana University has failed to please you." In each reply Wells explained that the "contest was not an official undertaking of the University," and that the majority of the judges "had no connection with the University." These facts, he said, "of course, have no bearing on whether the girl in question should have been chosen." He closed with the hope that "you will always write to me when you learn of events and situations which displease or please you at Indiana University."

Mildred, Helen, and I were not at all interested in our differing skin colors and hair textures. We bonded because we were all independent women from working class families who were preparing, we hoped, for stimulating careers. We commiserated with and comforted one another because we were in school under our own power, financially strapped, and operating within a *racist* environment. We all had professors who expected and even hoped we'd fail. We also parsed our relationships with the guys we dated. We were family to one another for more than thirty years, gradually drifting apart as our paths diverged.

Through Helen, I met her cousin David Baker, a graduate student in music. I was in awe of Dave because he was older, and he was a celebrated musician who knew famous people. Dave is now Distinguished Professor of Music and Chairman of the Jazz Department at IU, as well as conductor and musical director of the Smithsonian Jazz Masterworks Orchestra.

Marie Turner was another close friend I made on campus. Because both of her older sisters had college degrees, Marie had expected to attend college. She grew up on the northwest side of Indianapolis, but we hadn't run into each other at home. Although I was less disciplined than Marie, we spent a lot of time together. Both of us were English majors who loved literature, and fancied ourselves intellectuals-in-the-making. Most of the Negroes I knew were Baptists, Methodists, and occasional Roman Catholics, but Marie was an Episcopalian, or as she put it, an English Catholic. From Marie I learned there was a black Episcopal church in Indianapolis, St. Philip's on West Street, now Martin Luther King Jr. Street. Marie was dating

Bill Raspberry, who she said was studying to be an Episcopal priest. I suppose she met him at her church because Bill didn't grow up in Indianapolis. I met him when he came to campus to see Marie, but he attended Indiana Central College, now the University of Indianapolis. Obviously Bill changed his mind about the priesthood because he became a journalist. I remember that he worked at the *Indianapolis Recorder* for a while before he left town. The next I heard of him, he was working for the *Washington Post*, where he was a long-time columnist. In 1994, Bill won the Pulitzer Prize for Distinguished Commentary, and in 1997 the *Washingtonian* named him one of the top fifty most influential journalists in the national press corps. Bill died in 2012.

My year away from campus did nothing to vitalize me; my focus when I returned was as diffuse as it had been earlier. I enrolled in more literature and history classes and picked up my social life where I had left off. I had neither passion for a particular career nor a drive to make money. To remain on campus, it was critical that I make a 2.0, C average. I made a 1.75 and was sent packing again in June 1958, the year my class graduated. Of the six Negro Manualites at IU with me, four of us graduated but only two finished in four years.

My going to IU had whetted Mama's desire for one of her children to graduate from college, and I was, perhaps, her only hope. James had settled on the U.S. Army. Reggie was working at Sears, Roebuck & Company, where he started as a janitor but eventually became a top salesperson with stock options. Neither he nor my sister had any apparent interest in additional education. Mama refused to accept my banishment from campus, and unknown to me, wrote a letter to IU's Dean of Arts and Sciences. The letter said in part, "We are sure 'financial' worries and trying to work part-time have caused some of her grades to be low. This year she wouldn't have financial worries if she can be readmitted.... A relative of hers who is in sympathy with her in her effort to try to graduate has promised to pay all of her expenses." I discovered this letter years later in Mama's scrapbook. I was not surprised because Mama did not accept defeat easily, and she was an inveterate letter writer. We always had a portable typewriter and it got plenty of use. Mama wrote letters to everybody—the U. S. president, members of Congress, editors of newspapers, the mayor, and of course family members. She pasted the carbon copies of her formal letters and their replies in her scrapbook. Reading her copy of that letter to the dean was a painful reminder of the anguish I caused her, and of how she yearned for me to graduate from college. I have no idea who the sympathetic relative was with the means to finance my education. My guess is that Mama persuaded Rosie (or thought she'd be able to) to use a part of the money she was saving for her wedding. The dean replied, but Mama's letter hadn't swayed him, so the beneficent relative was never identified.

I've examined my incongruous behavior of those years and concluded that I was stalled by subconscious questions: If I got the degree, who would I be? And what would I do? Teach school? I didn't want to do that. More important, would I still be welcome, or content, at home?

Chapter 14

Walking in My Sleep

I have a strong suspicion...that much that passes for constant love is a golded-up moment walking in its sleep.

~ Zora Neale Hurston
in *Dust Tracks on a Road*

After my second ejection from campus Rosie and I drove to Bloomington on Saturday, September 26, 1959 to attend a concert by Ahmad Jamal, the innovative jazz pianist. He was the season's first performer in the IMU (Indiana Memorial Union) Pop Concert Series. I liked Jamal a lot and owned his album *But Not For Me*, that included the hit "Poinciana." A couple of years earlier I had driven to Chicago with friends to hear him at the Pershing Hotel. During the intermission of the IMU concert, Gordon Mickey introduced himself to Rosie. She preferred tall men, so Gordon's six feet seven inches immediately got her attention. Gordon was a member of IU's basketball team, in school on an athletic scholarship. I guess it was love at first sight because until they married three years later, they burned up the road between Indianapolis and Bloomington.

Rosie had majored in business in high school and was a skilled secretary who took dictation in shorthand and typed 120 words a minute. While she was acquiring her secretarial skills, she was consistently on the honor roll. Thirty points were sufficient to make the honor roll; however in 1956 her senior year, Rosie topped the list as the only student with forty-two honor points. With this kind of record to commend her, and Daddy's connections to get her considered, in 1957she was hired as a secretary in the Indianapolis Public Schools' central office. It was the first time a Negro had ever worked there. My younger sister was ecstatic to be joining me and the few other Negroes who had office jobs in downtown Indianapolis. Unlike me, however, Rosie was in step with other young women our age and knew exactly what she wanted: make enough money to dress fashionably for a busy social life, find a suitable man to marry, and have a spectacular wedding. Rosie had founded and was president of the Calypsos, a social club. The Calypsos sponsored a number of social events throughout the year, including an annual and elaborate Orchid Fantasy. At age twenty, when she plucked a college man right out from under the IU coeds, her life was right on track.

It was not surprising that Rosie and I had different aspirations. About the only interests we shared were similar tastes in music and our love of basketball. Otherwise, as young women, our paths rarely crossed: we were usually not attracted to the same people and ran in different circles. From her teen years on, Rosie had been involved in girls' social clubs, and I've never had much interest in joining anything unless it had a specific purpose, like a professional organization. Because Rosie had been a good student, Mama talked to her about going to college, but Rosie made it clear she wasn't interested, and that was the end of it. After she had been married five or six years, and while Gordon was in graduate school at IU, Rosie suddenly changed her mind. She told me that several of the women she met at IU, like her, were uneducated while their husbands' were obtaining graduate degrees. That disturbed Rosie. She decided it wasn't a good idea for a professional man to have an uneducated wife. She obtained the first of her three degrees at IU in 1970, the year before Gordon earned his doctorate. Aside from Rosie's early lack of interest in attending college, Mama found her lifestyle completely satisfying.

I, on the other hand, felt like a misfit. All my Indianapolis friends were engaged or married; some already had a couple of children. I didn't want to get married, but I had no idea what to do with myself. I couldn't take pride in my college studies, because three years of college without a degree didn't mean much for a Negro. My shame over having failed at IU was deepened by Mama's palpable disappointment. I continued to work at the library, feeling rudderless, but sure of one thing: I needed to complete my degree, no matter how long it took. The IU Extension didn't grant degrees, but no matter how low my average was, I could take classes there, and that's what I did. I also continued my interest in public affairs. In April 1959 the national convocation of the United Negro College Fund had met in Indianapolis. On a Sunday afternoon I went to their public closing session to hear Senator John Kennedy of Massachusetts. I was impressed with him, but had no idea that he would one day be the country's president.

A few months later, I was attending a party at the FAC (Federation of Associated Clubs) building on North Capital Avenue. I saw Mason Bryant, a guy I knew, talking to Holsey Hickman. I recognized Holsey because he had played basketball for Attucks High School. He wasn't the team's best player, but whenever he came into a game, the girls swooned. We thought he was so good looking, with a killer physique—six foot one, broad shoulders, slim torso, and shapely muscular legs. I asked Mason to introduce me. In addition to his good looks, I found Holsey's sonorous voice and deliberate demeanor seductive. We immediately began going out.

I was flattered that Holsey Hickman was interested in me, a south side girl. Not only was he fine, but he lived in Indianapolis's best black neighborhood on the north side. His family had been educated for generations: his late great-grandfather, W. W. Hyde, was a lawyer in Indianapolis. Several of Holsey's family members were teachers, including his great aunt, Fannie Hyde Sykes, who taught elementary school. I found out that my parents knew Mrs. Sykes because her husband, Herman, belonged to Daddy's lodge, and the two couples had met at lodge functions. Daddy also knew Harry Hickman, Holsey's father. Harry was a meat cutter who handled purchases at a neighborhood grocery that bought Daddy's chitlins. Holsey's parents were divorced.

When Holsey came to pick me up for a date, he always took time to chat with Mama and Daddy. My parents learned that, along with his impressive family, he also belonged to church, and that made his star rise even higher. One of Mama's evening rituals was making a cup of instant coffee and drinking it alone at the kitchen table because nobody else in the house drank coffee. When Holsey was there, he always joined her and she was delighted by that. After we married, I discovered that he didn't like coffee.

When we met, Holsey was twenty-five and I was twenty-two, and we were both part-time students living with our parents. Immediately following his high school graduation, Holsey spent four years in the air force. After his discharge, he used the GI Bill to enroll at Butler University. Butler is a well-regarded private school located a few blocks from where Holsey lived. I had been there to attend the high school basketball tournaments that were held in the fieldhouse. The tree-lined streets of the neighborhood adjacent to the university were a coveted destination for Indianapolis's upwardly mobile Negroes. The homes there were generally larger, sturdier, and always more expensive than the ones in my neighborhood. Holsey was taking accounting courses at Butler and hoped to become a CPA. He earned money by helping his former stepfather paint houses, and lived with his mother, Doris Stokes, and his fifteen-year-old brother Michael Stokes. Doris was a short, curvy, attractive woman who seemed to enjoy her life. She earned a living singing in nightclubs accompanying herself on the organ. Doris worked all the time, so I assume she was talented. I asked a couple of times, but Holsey never took me to hear her perform. I sensed that he would have preferred a mother more like mine. I liked Doris's sophistication and effervescent personality and we became friends.

Holsey asked me not to call his mother by her first name. "I call your mother Mrs. Cheatham."

"You can call my mother by her first name if you want. That's between you and her." Holsey didn't dare. Mama usually introduced herself as "Mrs. Smith H. Cheatham"—not exactly an invitation to familiarity.

I also became good friends with Holsey's brother, Michael. He was a slender, handsome young man; mature for his age, intelligent, and well read. Over the years, Michael and I talked about everything, including his being gay. With Michael I indulged my desire to know more about homosexuality. I asked him everything. Growing up I had occasionally heard the terms sissy, fag, and queer, used disparagingly about effeminate men, but in our house there was no talk, disparaging or otherwise, about homosexuals. Many of the musicians playing for and directing Negro church choirs were known to be gay, but I never heard anybody denigrate them. Of course, back then openly talking about sex of any kind was just not done. As a consequence, my only attitude about homosexuality was curiosity about how a person could be attracted to someone of the same sex. Michael and I talked about that, and I learned that his attraction to men was as natural for him it was for me. In addition, and to my surprise, I discovered that the dynamics of same-sex entanglements are much the same as hetero-sexual ones. I had thought there might be fewer disagreements when two people of the same sex were in a relationship.

Michael also told me about the parties in Indianapolis that were attended by both gay men and lesbians. He outed several people I thought of as "straight," who were in fact closeted gays. Michael said he often saw my cousin, Ronald, at these parties. Family members had observed Ronald hanging out with guys who were openly gay for years, but nobody talked about it. I had heard James refer to Ronald as a sissy, but I didn't take that seriously because Ronald always had a girlfriend. Apparently, he was bisexual. Ronald married, had eight children, and was devoted to his family until his death. Knowing Michael, and reading James Baldwin's *Giovanni's Room*, helped me understand that being homosexual is simply an aspect of who you are, just as being female is a part of what defines me.

When I brought up Michael's sexual orientation to Holsey, he denied it, so we didn't talk about it. Holsey was ten years older than Michael and their relationship was often contentious. Michael said, "Holsey tries to be my daddy." Holsey considered himself the man of the house, and felt compelled to advise not only Michael, but his mother as well. Michael and I remained close until his death at age thirty. His flight to Washington, D. C. crashed into a mountain during a winter storm in November 1975.

Holsey also had another brother, Harold Owsley "Dickie" Hickman, who lived in Indianapolis, but only occasionally attended family functions. Every family seems to have a rascal who bucks inherited traditions, and I think Dickie was that person for the Owsleys. I liked Dickie's irreverence and sense of humor.

My family had its own tensions. Along with me, Rosie and Reggie, both twenty, were still at home, and the same household rules applied as when we were teenagers. We had to be home every night at a reasonable hour, and be on time for Sunday school, no matter how late we were out the night before. That rankled. The tug-of-war Rosie and I had over sharing a room was still going on, except that now it was between two women. Worst of all, she'd sneak and wear my clothes. I didn't want her touching my clothes, let alone wearing them. When I took out a new sweater I'd bought and found sweat stains in the armpits, I wanted to wring her neck, but instead I settled

In front of the new house on St. Peter Street around 1963. (l-r) brother-in-law, Gordon Mickey; my third nephew Michael standing in front of his dad, James; Daddy; Reggie; and in front of him, my second nephew Kevin, another of James's sons.

for screaming threats at her. That resulted in yet another loud, nasty argument. Needless to say, my parents were sick of us.

We had recently moved into a newly built home at 1041 Saint Peter Street, six blocks from our old house. The new one was ranch style, made of real bricks, with three actual bedrooms that thankfully all had doors. Mama had often expressed her desire to live in a house that had not been previously occupied. It was one of her three big dreams. The other two involved us: she wanted one of her daughters to have a big wedding, and at least one of her children to graduate from college. Anticipating (and hoping) that her grown children would soon be gone, Mama made a den of the smallest bedroom, so Reggie had to pull out the sofa bed every night. He felt left out because he didn't have his own room. To state it plainly, there were too many adults in one small house. We moved into the new place in 1959, and each subsequent year one of us left. I departed in 1960. Reggie, a step ahead of being drafted, left for the army and Korea in 1961. Rosie was the last to leave when she married in June 1962.

Mama channeled her disappointment over my school collapse into complaints about my not being married. So far as she was concerned, there was no reason for me to remain single since I was no longer a full-time student. She called me an old maid and nagged me regularly. In the 1950s most women were married by age nineteen, and had their first child at twenty. I was twenty-two.

"A woman your age needs to be married."

"Mama, I don't want to get married."

"Well, you can't keep layin' around with all kinds of men. *Nobody* will want you."

"Good lord, Mama! What are you talking about? You make me sound like a prostitute."

"All I know is that somebody different is steppin' up here to take you out every week."

With this conversation, or its equivalent, Mama leaned on me to find a husband. She was not concerned about Rosie, because Rosie was younger, and it was clear that her relationship with Gordon was serious. When Holsey and I continued to see each other, Mama stepped up her campaign to marry me off.

Meanwhile, Holsey and I were having a good time. In April 1960 we attended a dance at the Indiana Roof Ballroom, where Ray Charles and his band performed. I couldn't wait to see Ray Charles in person; he was my favorite. I like everything Brother Ray did, from the rollicking exaltation of "I Got a Woman," to the sorrow and lamentation of "Your Cheatin' Heart" or "Drown in My Own Tears." The dance cost five dollars per couple, and was sponsored by Alpha Kappa Alpha Sorority. Everybody was going. Gordon and his roommate, Walt Bellamy, drove up from Bloomington to escort Rosie and her best friend, Brenda Dickey. Bellamy and Gordon were teammates at IU. Bellamy's outstanding college basketball play led to an all-star career in the NBA, and induction into the Hall of Fame. The six of us had a ball partying together, jitterbugging to hits like "What'd I Say" and "Let the Good Times Roll," and holding each other close as we swayed to "Georgia on My Mind." Rosie, Brenda, and I savored that night for a long time.

Holsey's sister, Patsy Sharpe, her husband, Alvin, and their three daughters lived in an apartment on the second floor of Doris's house. Patsy looked like her mother, and like her, she was usually smiling and pleasant. I always enjoyed visiting them. Apparently Patsy also thought Holsey and I were right for each other because she joined the lobbying for us to marry. It's almost as if I let my mind go limp and floated along with what was expected of me. I have tried to recollect when and where Holsey proposed marriage, but there is no trace of it in my memory bank, and he doesn't remember either. I guess I repressed it because I didn't have the courage to turn him down. I do recall Holsey and my father sitting at our dining room table when Holsey asked him for my "hand in marriage." But Holsey would not have talked to Daddy unless he and I had already agreed. The dining area in our home was separated from the living room only by the furniture arrangement, so I heard Daddy's response.

"If that's what you and Janet want to do, it's alright with me. The only way I'd get involved would be if you mistreated her. Her mother and I have been married for thirty-two years, and I have never laid the weight of my hand on her in anger. As long as you don't abuse Janet, you're alright with me."

Daddy's reply reminded me of something Mama had told me years earlier. She said that Grandpa, Daddy's father, had a reputation for regularly beating Grandma until their sons put a stop to it. Knowing this, before they married Mama made a point of telling Daddy she would not have a husband who hit her. Daddy promised he would never hit her and kept his word.

After his conversation with Daddy, Holsey and I were caught up in the wedding preparations whirl. I should have been excited, but instead I was nervous. *WHAT IN HELL AM I DOING? WHY AM I DOING THIS? THIS IS NOT WHAT I WANT.* I believe Holsey was also apprehensive because Patsy had to intervene so I would have my engagement diamond before the bridal shower. My misgivings were reinforced one day while Holsey and I talked on the telephone. In the background I heard Doris say something; I couldn't tell what. Holsey turned from talking to me and yelled fiercely at his mother. I was stunned. As the customs of the day demanded, our courtship was polite and genteel. We were together only when we were carefully dressed to go out. We had our private and hidden moments of heavy petting and quick sexual encounters, but at no time did we spend more than six or so hours together. I didn't know that Holsey ever got upset, so the anger I heard in his voice scared me. My parents had made a point of not having heated arguments in our presence, and I had never heard Daddy yell at Mama like that. Mama didn't approve of emotional outbursts, so I had long ago learned to contain my emotions—affection as well as anger. Holsey's flare of temper shook me to my core and I couldn't stop thinking about it. What if he yelled at me like that? I definitely decided that we shouldn't get married.

"Mama, I don't feel right about marrying Holsey..."

"Girl, what are you talking about?"

"I was talking to Holsey on the phone, and he..."

Mama shrieked. "I don't want to hear it!" She was not going to entertain even the *notion* of my not getting married. "We've already ordered the invitations!" Her tone was incredulous.

"Well, they haven't gone out. It's not too late to cancel the wedding."

"Get out of my face. I don't want to hear it."

I saw no reason why we couldn't call it off. There were only a few people to notify. I had no desire for the kind of wedding extravaganza Rosie was planning. Mine was to be a modest church ceremony with two attendants—Rosie and Patsy. I was paying for nearly everything, so the decision should have been mine. However, even though I was an adult, I didn't dare disobey my parents. Plus, Mama was so emphatic about everything. In my wavering state her certainty was somehow reassuring.

Still, I went to see Doris, my future mother-in-law. She had been divorced twice and had no intention of marrying again. Maybe Doris would understand my fears. I told her about my reluctance to get married. She listened to what I had to say, then assured me that pre-wedding jitters were to be expected.

"I know you're nervous. And Holsey is too. But you're so good for him. Everything will be fine. You'll see."

I didn't think to ask, "What about what's good for me?"

We were married August 27, 1960, about a year after we met. A hundred or so people attended the wedding in the chapel of New Bethel Baptist Church at 1541 Martindale Avenue (now Andrew J. Brown Avenue). The sanctuary of the church was large enough to hold a thousand people, so I decided to use the chapel, which seated about two hundred. I had "outgrown" what I considered the backward fundamentalism of the family church in Lovetown. I joined New Bethel because the pastor was educated and pitched his sermons

Holsey and I just after being pronounced husband and wife.

as much to the intellect as to the emotions. A punch-and-wedding-cake reception was held in the church function room immediately after the ceremony. Two weeks later, a photo of Holsey and me cutting the cake, and an account of the wedding were in the *Recorder*. I smiled at the fancy description of my dress. The "wedding gown was ballerina length, white lace over taffeta with a panel in the back, trimmed in sequins and pearls." Rosie and Patsy wore "French lime bell shaped satin dresses with matching shoes and hats." The article included a line that after a honeymoon at Lake Idlewild in Michigan, the couple would be at home to friends at 2005 ½ Highland Place.

Holsey got a room for us in a downtown hotel for our wedding night. But I was not comfortable; he seemed like a stranger. I couldn't take off my clothes in front of him so I changed into my filmy, yellow nightgown in the bathroom. If we had gone to a hotel a day earlier, we could have been arrested. Before the wedding I had risked my reputation as a "decent" woman by having sex with him. Suddenly, we were licensed to "do it," and everybody knew we were doing it. It was difficult for me to make that instant emotional leap from regarding sex as illicit and secret to seeing it as blessed and celebrated.

We honeymooned at the lakefront home owned by Holsey's family in Idlewild, Michigan. Idlewild, one of several vibrant and popular black summer resorts, is in the western part of the state near the Lake Michigan port and white resort of Ludington. Middle-class Negroes, so they could have "relaxation without humiliation," had developed their own resorts in several areas of the country, including American Beach near Jacksonville, Florida; Highland Beach near Baltimore; Sag Harbor on Long Island; and Oak Bluffs on Martha's Vineyard. Here in

Indiana, Negroes built a resort on Fox Lake. Fox Lake is in the northeast corner of Indiana, a mile southwest of Angola. A group of white businessmen bought the property along the south side of the 142-acre lake in 1924 and sold lots to black families. In 1928, Carl and Mamie Wilson were the first Negroes to build on their property. Eventually several cottages, a clubhouse, and a hotel were built at the lake, and that led to the establishment of the still existing Fox Lake Property Owners' Association.

In the early 1950s, when Reggie, Rosie, and I were teens, Mama decided one summer that we should spend a week at Fox Lake. My parents rented a small and somewhat rustic cottage from Charles Harry, a zoology teacher at Attucks. Daddy knew Mr. Harry because they both volunteered at the YMCA. (Years later, I met Mr. Harry's son, Charles IV, when we were both students at IU.) We kids had a great time at the beach, playing in the water and going on boat rides. We also attended the clubhouse dances where we met young people from all around the Midwest. It didn't seem like much of a vacation for Mama because she still had homemaking duties, like preparing meals. We couldn't afford for all five of us to eat out. Mama loved Fox Lake, though, and she and Daddy went back several times over the years. Without all of us along, they were able to stay at the Mar-Fran Hotel, where Mama could actually get some rest.

Idlewild was established in 1915, and socializing and carousing were such serious undertakings there, that people referred to it as a place where the men were idle, and the women were wild. Several other family members were vacationing at the lake while we honeymooned, including Willa Owsley, Holsey's grandmother. One afternoon she knocked hard on the door of our room and yelled, "Come on outa there. You're honeymooning too much." I had gotten over my embarrassment.

Mrs. Owsley apparently also selected the small one-bedroom apartment where we would live. The apartment was one of several in a large, very old house that Mrs. Owsley owned. The house, on Highland Avenue near Twenty-first Street, was in what is euphemistically termed a declining neighborhood. It was painted dark green, and four-foot-tall hedges enclosed the front yard. Our apartment was at the rear of the first floor. Inside, Holsey had put new linoleum tile down on the uneven floor. The two small closets were inadequate for even one person, and the bedroom smelled moldy. A narrow aisle in the cramped kitchen separated the sink and counter from the stove and refrigerator. A small area behind the kitchen was just large enough for a table and four chairs. At least the kitchen and eating area were bright with lots of windows that let in the light. It occurred to me that the space had probably originally been a back porch. I was keenly disappointed in our living quarters. My parents had finally moved our family out of a closetless, decaying house like this, and now I was moving back into one. I had expected that in marrying Holsey Hickman I would take a step forward, not backward. I told myself that with both of us working—Holsey sorting mail at the post office and me as a clerk-typist at the state library—we would shortly be able to do better.

Mrs. Owsley had also come with us to buy the furnishings for our home. I was surprised enough that she was along, but I was truly startled when she began directing us on what to buy and how much money to spend. Holsey appeared to be trying to please her, but I insisted on my own tastes rather than hers. I concluded that either she was paying for everything, or Holsey was borrowing money from her for the purchases. A couple of weeks earlier he had shown me a bankbook with a balance of $1,000 that he said was to be used for an apartment and furniture, so I was baffled by this turn of events. Later, I decided he had probably gambled away that money, then turned to his grandmother for help.

Although Holsey and I were hot for each other, neither of us was prepared for marriage. We had capitulated to social expectations and, in particular, to the pressure of our respective mothers. My ideas about being married were gleaned from observing my parents, and a lifetime of listening to Mama's complaints about Daddy's shortcomings. I have no idea how young I was when Mama began confiding her dissatisfaction to me. She told me, "All men play around."

"Not Daddy?"

"Yes. Your daddy plays. But I hold my head up high and refuse to let it bother me. He comes home every night. And I know where his money goes."

I wasn't sure that I believed her, but it was distressing to hear Mama say that my daddy was not a good person. And, worse, that no woman could expect any man to be faithful. I recall once going through a list of couples who appeared devoted to one another. For each couple I asked, "Does Mr. _____ cheat on his wife?" There was only one man that Mama conceded *might* be faithful. Mama couldn't shake my confidence in Daddy; however, she laid a subconscious burden on my young psyche in equal parts sadness and distrust. I labored with the weight of it until my nephews, and later my son, became adults. These males, whom I diapered and loved from birth, were the first men I was able to see as vulnerable and honorable. After my siblings and I had grown up, I periodically shared the conversations Mama and I had. That was when I found out that Mama had not talked to them about many of the things she told me. No doubt being the first-born daughter made me her confidant.

Mama made it clear that she remained married to provide a home for her children. As a child, I believed that her marriage and children were the cause of Mama's sorrow. Now I'm not sure which came first, Mama's querulousness or the marriage. I promised myself that I would have a happier life than she did. I spent years searching for that happiness before discovering that first I had to be happy with myself.

Many couples believe that staying together for the sake of the children is the right and noble thing to do. What these parents don't recognize is that children absorb every bit of the unresolved conflict in a discontented household. Children from "ideal" families can become emotional cripples wracked with guilt because they don't recognize the genesis of their inability to sustain committed, intimate relationships. At least people whose parents split up have a clue. Or, as is sometimes the case, they are more careful in choosing a partner and work harder to sustain the relationship. With my three siblings and me, only Rosie was never divorced.

My first year of marriage was more traumatic than any other comparable period of my life. Like many young women of the time, I was sleepwalking in a fog of idyllic marital expectations. A year later, I was deeply wounded, but wide-awake, my presumptions having been smashed one by one. A few weeks into my marriage I had the first brutal wake-up call.

One Friday Holsey had not come home from work at the usual time. By 11 p.m. I was frantic. What could have happened? I felt that Holsey must be hurt or dead, because I could not imagine him voluntarily putting me through this. Then I had another thought:

"He's been in an accident and the police called his mother because they don't know he's married." But Doris was at work. What could I do? In those pre-call-waiting days, if I used the telephone, Holsey, the police, or a hospital would get a busy signal, and I'd miss the call. For hours, I was nuts with worry. At 2:30 a.m., when I knew Doris would be home, I called her. She was not concerned.

"Oh, Honey, don't worry. I'm sure he's fine. He just got caught up in something. Go to bed. He'll be home soon."

How could she be so nonchalant? But if his mother wasn't anxious, maybe there was nothing to worry about. I went to bed, but now I was becoming angry and couldn't sleep. If he wasn't hurt, then where the hell was he? At 6 a.m. I heard Holsey's key in the lock. He walked into the bedroom and, just as Doris promised, he was unharmed. So, he had *chosen* to stay out all night. I pretended to be asleep, but I was in shock. We had not been married two months and he had betrayed me already. I felt like somebody had driven a long wooden stake into my head that was slowly piercing my body, splintering along the way. At the same time, rage was rising in my stomach, and questions raced through my mind. Where had he been? And with whom? How could he possibly explain this atrocity? I lay there trying to decide what to do. Holsey got into bed and reached for me. His hand on me had the same effect as a sharp pin on a tightly blown-up balloon. I exploded out of bed screaming, "Don't touch me! Where the hell have you been?"

He didn't say a word. Not, "I'm sorry," not "The car broke down." Nothing. I demanded that he answer me, but he didn't open his mouth. His refusal to speak fed my fury. *WHO DO YOU THINK YOU ARE? YOU CAN'T TREAT ME LIKE THIS!* I darted to the kitchen, snatched the broom, and rushed back. He was still lying in bed. Lifting the broom over my head, I swung it and hit him as hard as I could. I got about three licks in before he rolled out of bed and grabbed me, pinning my arms to my sides. His restraining me reinforced my feeling of impotence. *HE DIDN'T LOVE ME. HE WOULD NOT HAVE LEFT ME ALONE IN AGONY ALL NIGHT IF HE LOVED ME. I KNEW I SHOULDN'T HAVE GOTTEN MARRIED.* I refused to cry, but I felt thoroughly defeated. I couldn't get loose, but I continued to ask where he'd been. He never told me. Holsey kept me pinned until I stopped struggling, and he never said a word.

I couldn't fathom Holsey. He was usually considerate and attentive, periodically bringing me flowers for no particular reason. Suddenly, he stays out all night, and makes no attempt to justify his behavior. No matter when I asked, he refused to talk about that night, and I saw no sign of contrition. Without fawning, Holsey was his usual self, behaving as though nothing had happened. I decided that the all-nighter was an aberration that he wouldn't repeat. Two weeks later, he didn't come home again. This was unbelievable! Obviously, he felt he could do as he pleased. I was too humiliated to tell anybody that my new marriage had failed. Instead, I swirled the anguish around in my head trying to figure out what I was doing to make him treat me like I didn't matter. I kept our apartment clean, cooked decent meals, and didn't refuse him sex. Still, almost every payday Holsey stayed out all night. He would not admit it, but I was told that he was gambling. That gossip made sense when I considered that he often returned with little money, and once, and only once, he came home around 9 p.m. and gave me one hundred dollars cash. I suppose he won that night. This was a real windfall for a couple whose combined salaries were about four hundred dollars a month. The problem was, I never knew how much, or how little, money we would have. We often raced to pay utilities before they were disconnected. I was not accustomed to living with that kind of uncertainty; it was debilitating, and I wanted out of the madness. But I had to make this marriage work since I had disappointed everybody by messing up at school. Finally, I talked to Mama and Rosie about what was going on.

"Well, at least he doesn't get drunk and beat you. Everybody has a cross to bear. This is yours." Mama was dismissive.

Rosie was sympathetic. "What are you going to do? Do you think he has a girlfriend?"

"I heard that he gambles. But what difference does it make? The point is he comes home *when he feels like it.* And he doesn't respect me enough to pick up the phone to say he won't be home. There I sit like a damned fool trying to keep his food warm! The worst part is, most of the time he comes home broke!"

"You know some women meet their husbands at work on payday to make sure they get the money."

I didn't think Holsey would go for that even if I had the nerve to try it.

My second wake-up call was even more devastating. I had been married eight months and was five months pregnant, in maternity clothes. The pregnancy was not planned, but in those pre-pill days, women commonly got pregnant in the first year of marriage. The impending birth of our first child had not changed Holsey's routine. It was another payday, 11 p.m., and I hadn't heard from him. He'd probably come home broke again, and I was just sick of it. I was also pissed at being stuck in the house alone on a Friday night. I was not going to spend the rest of my life with a man I couldn't count on. I was going home.

I called home. My brother answered the phone.

"Reggie, come get me. I'm coming home."

"Okay." Reggie didn't ask any questions.

Daddy could sleep through an explosion, but Mama heard every sigh. When the phone rang, she possibly thought it was one of Reggie's friends, but when she heard him preparing to leave the house, she wanted to know where he was going.

"To pick up Janet."

"Pick up Janet for what?"

"She said she's coming home."

"You wait just a minute. Let me to talk to her."

Mama called me. "What did you tell Reggie to come get you for?"

"Holsey hasn't come home again, and I'm tired of it. I'm not putting up with this anymore."

"Well, you can't come here."

It took several beats before I *heard* what she said. "I can't come home?" My question was a whisper because I was having trouble breathing.

"No! You cannot come here. *That's* your home. The place for a woman who's expecting is with her husband." Mama sounded annoyed that I even *thought* I could come home.

I nearly collapsed. I believed what Robert Frost said in his poem, "Home is the place where, when you have to go there, /They have to take you in."

It had not occurred to me that there would *ever* be a time when I couldn't go home. IF I DON'T HAVE A HOME, WHERE CAN I GO? I AM TOTALLY, UTTERLY, ALONE. COMPLETELY ABANDONED. AND I'M

TRAPPED BECAUSE I'M PREGNANT. HOLSEY AND MAMA HAD PRETEND-
ED TO LOVE ME TO GET WHAT THEY WANTED. BUT THE REAL DEAL IS,
I'M ON MY OWN. IF MY MOTHER AND MY HUSBAND DON'T LOVE ME;
WHO CAN? NOBODY WILL EVER TRICK ME LIKE THIS AGAIN. My heart
tightened.

Life for my mother was about sacrifice and making do. She often
repeated the phrase, "Hope for the best, but expect the worst." If she
had moments of joy and a few days of happiness here and there, it
was more than she anticipated. She described marriage as a way of
making a home for yourself, and sex as something you endured in
order to have children. Later, when I read about her childhood in
her diaries—the early loss of her mother, and the lack of games, fun,
and books—I better understood her outlook. I, on the other hand,
had two nurturing parents, family vacations, picnics, parties, and a
library card—a bountiful childhood. I had expected my marriage to
be equally sanguine. I became angry, depressed, and frustrated. In
that state of consternation, I gave birth prematurely. Our son Paul
was born on May 27, 1961, six weeks early, and immediately put in
an incubator. Not only did I leave the hospital without a baby, but
Holsey forgot to bring the bag I had packed. There I was, relieved to
no longer be pregnant, but having to wear maternity clothes anyway.
I hated that.

Being a mother was not a storybook experience either. The usual
family visits to see the new baby didn't occur because Paul remained
in the hospital for two weeks. Mama had an air of triumph now that
I was a mother. She believed that rearing a child would temper me,
settle me down. Daddy was disappointed that he didn't get a grand-
daughter because he already had three grandsons.

I pumped my breasts to keep the milk flowing because I was
determined to nurse my baby. However, when we brought Paul home,
he was too weak to suckle or even to hold my nipple in his mouth.
He had been taking a bottle in the hospital, so that's what I had to do
as well. None of the physician's recommendations to stop the milk
worked, so the few clothes I could get into were either wet where my
breasts were dripping, or stiff where the milk had dried. Mrs. Owsley
showed me how to bind my breasts, and that old-fashioned remedy
finally did the job.

What I remember most about this period is that I was exhausted all of the time despite the fact that Paul slept a lot and rarely cried. When I wasn't caring for the baby, I was preparing meals, cleaning house, sterilizing bottles, mixing Similac formula, and filling bottles. These tasks were made more onerous by the fact that we were in a financial crisis. I wasn't working, so my paychecks had stopped, and Holsey was still gambling his away. One occasion I remember well is that the only food in the house was one can of Similac, and we were flat broke. Daddy knocked at the door. From time to time when he visited his married children, he'd bring packages of meat—ham, bacon, or pork chops—from his job at Stumpf Brothers. He usually went straight to the refrigerator and put the meat inside. This time I grabbed the packages at the door. I didn't want Daddy to see that vacant refrigerator. He would have been appalled, and rightly so, since Holsey worked everyday at a better-paying job than he had. I saw no reason to upset Daddy when there was nothing to be done about it. I was an adult, and this was my problem. Somehow I'd have to learn to deal with it. I had nowhere to go.

Chapter 15

Paying the Price

People pay for what they do and, still more, for what they have allowed themselves to become. And they pay for it very simply: by the lives they lead.

~ James Baldwin, from *No Name in the Street*

When Paul was seven weeks old Grandma died. The whole family was jarred by her unexpected death. She went to bed one night and didn't get up the next morning. I imagine she decided she'd seen enough and there was really no reason to wake up and see it all again. She and Grandpa had been married sixty-one years. Grandma was around seventy-seven years old. Her life expectancy when she was born in the 1880s, was half that amount. A lean, wiry woman, Grandma was in no way infirm. I knew Daddy was deeply shaken because, for the first and only time, I saw him shed tears. In disbelief, he kept repeating, "Mother was never sick."

I was inspired by the way Grandma died, and hope that I leave this earth the same way. Even so, I couldn't believe she was dead. She was my kind of woman. Grandma was known to have preferred work in the field to housework. When we visited my grandparents, it wasn't unusual to find Grandpa in the kitchen preparing meals because, he said, he got tired of waiting for Grandma to cook. My favorite thing to eat at their house was hot water cornbread fried in a black iron skillet. Mama sometimes made cornbread in a skillet, but it was thick with a consistency more like cake. Their cornbread was flat and crunchy. Grandma and Grandpa moved from Tennessee to Indianapolis before I was born and were always a part of my life. After I married, I lived fairly close to them—they were on West Twelfth Street, and we lived on Highland between West Twentieth and West

Twenty-first streets. I passed their street whenever I went downtown or to my parents' house, and it was easy to stop in for a few minutes to say hello. I couldn't imagine that Grandma would no longer be there. It was also my first experience with death in the immediate family. I was six or seven when Aunt Christy, Daddy's older sister, died, and I don't really remember it. Seeing Daddy, whose strength I thought had no limits, struggling to accept his mother's death, was as wrenching as losing Grandma.

Holsey and I dropped Paul off at Doris's so she could care for him while we went to Grandma's funeral. When we returned, Doris opened the door before Holsey could unlock it. As soon as we stepped inside, Doris blurted, "Paul slept the whole time you were gone. I woke him up to feed him, but he wouldn't eat. You might want to take him to the doctor." Doris was always careful not to be intrusive.

I reassured Doris. "He always sleeps a lot and doesn't really eat much." What did I know? It was 1961, twenty-eight years before *What to Expect the First Year* was published.

Doris was trying to quell her anxiety, while still insisting that we take Paul to a doctor right away. It was a Saturday evening, so we knew our pediatrician wouldn't be available. Although I didn't feel any real concern, Holsey and I took Paul to the emergency room at Riley Hospital for Children. I held my sleeping baby for an hour or more until a nurse took Paul to an examining room and put him on a table. There we waited another couple of hours for a doctor to look at Paul. When the doctor arrived, I was staggered by what he did. After a quick glance at Paul, he actually performed that television cliché of pulling Paul's eyelid back and shining a light in his pupil. Abruptly, Paul became a priority and the hospital staff rushed him away. Their only words to us were, "We're going to admit him." Then I became alarmed.

Again we waited for what seemed an extremely long time. Finally, when we were allowed to see Paul, I gasped. Our little son was encased in a clear plastic oxygen tent. All we could do was look at him as if he were an animal in a glass cage; we were firmly told not to touch. Everyday, after Holsey went to work, I went to the hospital for all twenty-one days Paul was there. I just sat looking at him under that plastic tent, in agony that I could not hold and comfort him. One day I arrived at the hospital to find that Paul had been removed from the oxygen tent and placed in a steam room. Nobody had said a word about this change beforehand. Now, I was told, I could hold him. Outside the pediatric steam room, I put on a mask and gown, then went inside, sat in a rocker, cuddled Paul and fed him. In the steam room, he made a remarkable recovery. He ate heartily, gained weight, and was more lively and robust than he had ever been. I could tell we'd be taking him home soon.

Every time Holsey and I asked what was wrong with Paul, the doctors said they didn't know. A week or so into the steam room treatment, I arrived and was told that Paul wasn't there. I was directed to a crib in the corner of an open area. Paul didn't look like the same child I had seen the day before. He was listless, unkempt, and his diaper was soaked.

I grabbed the first nurse I saw and yelled at her. "What the hell's going on? Why isn't he in the steam room? He was getting better!"

She responded cavalierly, "He can't spend his life in a steam room."

Her words were like a punch in the face. My mind blurred. I felt faint. They had cast him aside. Then a thought thudded into my brain: *Paul is going to die.* I insisted that Paul be cleaned up, then I held him and tried to feed him, but he was not interested in eating. That same night, around midnight, we got a call asking us to come to the hospital immediately. As we walked toward the ward where I had seen Paul earlier, a doctor met us in the hallway. He said Paul had died of histoplasmosis. Despite their insistence they had no idea what was wrong with our son, suddenly he was able to tell us the precise cause of his death.

I closed down, became numb. This couldn't be real. I shed no tears. Made no sounds of grief. I don't remember our families gathering around to comfort us, although I'm certain they did. My folks were still reeling from Grandma's death just weeks earlier, but she was nearly eighty years old. For a baby to die was a rare occurrence in my family, and I recall that everybody seemed shocked. Several family members had not even seen Paul because he spent so much of his short life in the hospital. Despite that, nobody was expecting him to *die.* My cousin Ronald and his wife Loretta had a daughter, Kimberly Jeannine, born ten weeks before Paul, and she was doing fine. James and Dodie's second child, Michael, had even been born *prematurely* the year before, and he was thriving!

The next thing I remember clearly after being told that Paul had died, is that Holsey and I were in People's Funeral Home meeting with B. J. Jackson, the director—probably discussing how we would pay for the burial. From the corner of my eye, I saw a man walking through the office holding Paul in his arms, but Paul wasn't a stiff corpse; his arms and legs were dangling. *He's not dead!* I rose to take my baby, but Holsey grabbed my arm holding me back. Jackson jumped up and closed the door, then apologized for the embalmer's abominable faux pas.

The next day, I was trying to find something to wear to Paul's funeral service, but none of my clothes were suitable. I knew that family members wore black at funerals, but my one black item was a bare-shouldered party dress. I called my mother. "Mama, I can't go because I don't have anything to wear." Mama and Rosie came right over and looked through my clothes. They said it would be okay to wear my dark blue suit.

After a brief service at the funeral home, Paul was buried at Crown Hill Cemetery. When they lowered his coffin into the grave I couldn't bear the sight of my child being put into that hole to be covered by a mound of dirt. I felt my body sagging. Holsey pulled me up and held onto me until the ceremony was completed. It was August 26, 1961, the day before the first anniversary of our marriage. Mama gave us some money and told us to have a nice dinner the next day to mark the occasion.

While Paul was in the hospital, Mama had sought to reassure me by describing a dream she had. "I saw you and Holsey struggling in deep water, but you both made your way out. So, everything's going to be all right." Some months after Paul died, she told me the rest of the dream. "Paul was in the water with you and Holsey, but he never got out. I knew then he was going to die, but I didn't want to upset you. It could be a blessing. If he was going to be sickly, it would be awful hard on you to see him suffer. You can always have other children."

I remember Holsey's aunt, Betty Jo Owsley, came to visit us and brought a snapshot she had taken of Paul in his bassinet. It was the only picture we had of him. I will always be grateful that Betty Jo also brought us a copy of *The Little Prince*. The book pointed out that what is truly important is invisible to the eye. That comforted me then and provided succor on many other occasions. As my consciousness slowly returned, I realized that Paul had lived for twelve weeks and was home with us for only seven of those weeks. I had worn the same dark brown plaid cotton dress to the hospital every day Paul was there. I threw the dress away. Holsey asked me why I never wore the robe he gave me to celebrate Paul's birth. Until he asked, I was oblivious to the fact that I wasn't using it. I gave it away.

Not long after Paul died, a man who identified himself as Dr. Nestor from the Marion County Board of Health, came to our house early one Saturday morning. At the time the infant mortality rate per 1,000 live births —children who died before their first birthday—in Indiana was an alarming 22.5 percent for whites and a tragic 40 percent for nonwhites. By 1998 those figures for Indianapolis had dropped, but the 14 percent rate for blacks was still nearly double the 7.5 percent for whites. Nestor said he was trying to determine how Paul had contracted histoplasmosis and he asked permission to collect dirt from the house. He seemed surprised and disappointed when he stepped inside, saying, "I won't be able to find much here." By shaking the throw rug in front of the door, he got a little. He told us that histoplasmosis is a fungus that enters the body through the lungs and suggested that Holsey and I be tested for it. He left quickly and didn't tell us anything else. I wanted to know more, specifically, how Paul had gotten it. I went to the library and did my own research and found that the *Histoplasma* organism thrives in moderate temperatures and moist environments. The spores are airborne and the disease produces an illness similar to tuberculosis. Histoplasmosis is not contagious and ordinarily not fatal, except in people whose health is already compromised—as in a premature baby like Paul. Holsey and I had skin tests—very much like the one given for tuberculosis. Like eighty percent of the people living in the valleys of the Mississippi, Ohio, and Missouri Rivers, our tests were positive for *Histoplasma,* but our lives were not in danger and no treatment was required.

I could accept Paul's death only by convincing myself that it was fortuitous. After all, our marriage was too unstable for us to be raising a child. Holsey thought we should have another baby right away. But getting pregnant had helped me figure out my ovulation cycle. I now knew when I was likely to be fertile. I made a private vow to abstain from sex during my fertile days, and that way not get pregnant again until our life together seemed a lot more promising. For now, we were broke and broken. I needed to get back to work. I called the library and told them I was ready to return, and began pulling my work wardrobe together. I went to the shallow closet in which I had stored the boxes that held my high-heeled shoes. The shoes had been in the closet since April because I stopped wearing heels in my sixth month of pregnancy. I pulled out the boxes, opened them, then recoiled in horror. All the shoes had mold on them! The closet was in our bedroom, about three feet from where Paul's bassinet had stood. My god! The fungus that had killed our son was in that room! There was a dank cellar underneath our bedroom and although I hadn't been down there, I could smell the moldy dampness. I had never liked that apartment; now I had good reason to get the hell out. I showed the shoes to Holsey and told him we had to move.

"We can't afford to move. Mama is giving us a break on the rent here. We'd have to pay a lot more anywhere else." Holsey called his grandmother, Mama.

"A *break*? Forty-five dollars a month for this place is not a *break*."

Holsey ignored the insult to his grandmother's house. "Anyway, I look after this property for Mama so we have to stay here."

"Holsey, you saw my shoes. We can't stay here." I was beside myself, but I couldn't bring myself to say that I believed the mold in our bedroom had killed Paul. I decided that no matter what Holsey said, I was getting out of that raggedy-ass place. I can see now that this was my first step toward taking charge of my life. My frustrations with Holsey, my anger and unexpressed grief over Paul's short life, were channeled into finding a home that was more to my liking.

I went back to work the second week in September, and when I got paid, I looked for a nicer place to live. I found a one-bedroom apartment, with hardwood floors, on the second floor of a well-kept building, in a decidedly better neighborhood. Plus, it was only fifty dollars a month. This was perfect! I gave the manager a twenty-dollar deposit, and asked him to hold it until my husband could see the place. Holsey went to inspect the apartment as soon as I told him about it. When he came back he handed me the check I had given the building manager. Holsey had told him we decided not to move.

I was so angry with Holsey that I wanted to slap him as hard as I could on both sides of his face until my arm got tired. I settled for emphatically telling him, "Well, we may not move into that apartment, but we are *not* staying here."

Holsey responded just as determinedly, "I told you we *can't* move. I'm taking care of this property for Mama."

Apparently Holsey told his grandmother that I was being headstrong about moving. One evening while he was talking to her on the phone, she asked to speak to me. When Mrs. Owsley told somebody what to do, she didn't countenance dissent. She spoke to me in a hard voice that indicated she was about to set me straight.

"Janet, Holsey tells me you want to move."

"I *am* moving."

"No child. You're not. I've got Holsey looking after that property for me."

WHAT MAKES YOU THINK YOU CAN TELL ME WHAT TO DO? "Well, maybe Holsey can't move, but *I* can."

She seemed startled and also pissed. Her tone became angry. "You don't just move out without giving notice."

"Okay. Here's my notice. I'll be gone by December first." It was then near the end of October.

Mrs. Owsley was shocked into silence. I gave the phone back to Holsey.

I don't know what did it, perhaps my doing the unheard of—talking back to his grandmother. Whatever it was, Holsey finally understood that I meant to move, so he found a place for us himself. It was half of a duplex, or in Hoosier parlance, a double, that rented for sixty-five dollars a month. The house was on Forty-second Street, across from the rolling green expanse of the unused section of Crown Hill Cemetery. The attractive house was relatively new, had a small open front yard, and was painted white with turquoise trim. The spacious living room was carpeted. A comfortable kitchen was large enough to include a dining area. In addition to a hall closet, a closet nearly filled a whole wall of the bedroom and there was a linen closet in the bathroom. And there was no basement. The house was in the upscale, and proudly integrated Butler-Tarkington neighborhood, where most of Holsey's family lived. I loved it! I was more than a little impressed that Holsey had defied his grandmother because I knew that wasn't easily done in his family.

Years later I realized that Holsey and I never discussed what we expected from each other in our marriage. Neither of us really knew who we were as individuals, let alone what we wanted or needed in a spouse. And we didn't know each other. Like most of our generation, we jumped into the marriage, each with different ideas of how things should be. The pitiful thing about being ignorant is that you don't know how uninformed or misinformed you are. Consequently, you speak what little you know with conviction and an authority that you hope will persuade others to your point of view. Whenever Holsey did anything in a way that differed from the way things were done in my family—in particular, unlike how my father operated—I let him know he was wrong. Holsey was equally adamant that his family rituals were the proper way to go. We probably would have worked through these differences, but my biggest stumbling block was accepting the proper role of a wife.

My mother gave me two rules for a successful marriage: one, let the man think he's in charge, and two, always do your part.

The implication of the first rule is that the woman actually runs things while the man believes he does. I never came close to mastering that one. Holsey gave orders like he either thought I was his child, or he was in the military. One of the things he worked on was my not knowing my place as a woman. He said I embarrassed him when we were with our friends. Most of our socializing was with Holsey's pals. His close friend Kenneth "Jughead" Wilson and his girlfriend, Anna Cowherd; Roger and Pearl Lyons, who were a little older and married with three children; and Don and Phyllis Thomas, married with one child. Holsey, Jughead and Don had played basketball together at Attucks, and Don was then Bill Garrett's assistant coach. Phyllis had been in my brother James's class at School 19. When we got together, usually at somebody's house, the women would gather in the kitchen and talk about giving birth, clothes, cooking, or the men. Since those topics didn't interest me, I joined the men, who were talking politics and sports. Holsey would look at me and nod his head in the direction of the kitchen—he didn't want to make a scene—but I stayed put. When we got home he pointed out that it was rude of me not to help out in the kitchen. I was so brainwashed I didn't say a word about the men not helping out. When we had people over, I asked the women to allow me to serve them. I explained that I preferred to be waited on when I was their guest. Otherwise, I said, we females never got a night off. When that didn't work, I'd say that my kitchen was too small for all those helping hands, but my efforts to disrupt the gender separation were in vain. The women always wound up in the kitchen. I am still uneasy when women come into my kitchen to help me clean up. I prefer to visit with my guests and clean up after they leave. I used to feel compelled to join in when a woman started clearing my table and cleaning my kitchen. Now I just tell them to stop.

Holsey also found it necessary to monitor my eating. Not long after we married, he had said, "You know, Janet, you could lose some weight, because I prefer thin women."

I shot back, "Well, I wasn't thin when you met me, so you never should have asked me out." But inside I was like one of those toy metal tops that we played with as children. A perfectly still top could be sent wildly spinning when the plunger was shoved down. Holsey's off-hand remark sent me spinning in anguish. *MY HUSBAND DOESN'T LOVE ME AND DOESN'T LIKE THE WAY I LOOK. I GUESS HE MARRIED ME BECAUSE PATTY WOULDN'T HAVE HIM.* Patty was a very slim young woman from black Indianapolis's upper crust—her father was a dentist—whom Holsey had dated before we met.

When I got pregnant, Holsey seemed to panic at the possibility that I would get fat, and literally took food away from me when he decided I'd had enough. That, of course, just forced me to eat when he wasn't looking. His buddy Roger saw him snatch a ham sandwich out of my hand just before I took a bite. He was appalled.

"Holsey, man, you need to quit that! Let the woman eat; she's expecting."

Holsey was not moved, "Man, I'm not having a fat wife. The more weight she gains now, the bigger she'll be after the baby is born."

I was trying to be a good wife and do what was "right." I had never seen my parents have heated disagreements, so most of the time I went along with Holsey to avoid an argument. But I wasn't happy about it. I had waited a long time to be free of my parents' regulations; now Holsey was restricting me more than they'd ever thought about doing.

According to Mama's second rule, the wife's part was keeping a clean house, cooking the meals, and doing the laundry. (For reasons of his own, Holsey did his own socks and underwear, and that was fine with me.) Holsey also believed that household work was my domain. And I was good at it; after all, I'd had lots of training, first at home with Mama, then at the Teetors with Aunt Viola, and in home economics classes in high school. Both of us had full-time jobs and worked everyday. Holsey finished at 3 p.m. and my job ended at 5 p.m. When I got home he was already there, feet up, reading the newspaper. I rushed in the house and quickly began preparing dinner. After we ate, he returned to the living room to watch television while I cleaned up the kitchen. That was our daily routine. I was doing "my part," but I resented mightily his being able to relax while I was scurrying from the minute I walked in the door, sitting down only to eat. One night I was exhausted after cleaning the kitchen, so I told Holsey I was going to bed.

"I hope you're not going to bed and leave this paper all over the floor." Holsey was referring to the newspaper he had just read. I suppose he was too worn out from turning the pages to pick it up himself.

I screamed, "Who the fuck do you think I am, your goddamn maid? You pick up the fuckin' paper. You put it there!" Holsey was stupefied. He didn't know what had come over me. We never cursed, and he was accustomed to my picking up after him. I was sick of waiting on him. At least if I were working for the Teetors, I'd be getting paid. I helped him pay the bills. Why couldn't he share the household chores? Instead of asking this pertinent question, I stomped off to bed in a rage. After that Holsey folded the paper and put it on a table, but nothing else changed.

I began working at the Indiana State Library in 1952 as a fifteen-year-old library page. Since then I'd had a number of different work assignments and by 1960, the year I married, I was the only black working in the administrative offices on the fourth floor. The glass doors to the director's suite opened into my office. I was the receptionist/switchboard operator. When people came to see Harold Brigham, the library's director, I was the first to greet them. A wooden door separated Mr. Brigham's office from mine. Inside his spacious office were his secretary's desk and a large conference table. I can see now that Brigham's secretary, Esther Williams, was my mentor. She was a tall, elegant, beautifully dressed, divorced woman with two grown children. When I worked as the receptionist, we talked about all kinds of things, both personal and professional. Initially, I thought she was engaging in the usual white curiosity about Negro life, that is, "How on earth do you manage to keep smiling when whites are doing everything possible to make your life miserable?" However, Mrs. Williams treated me as a peer and shared confidences with me about her own life. And she didn't draw the line at social interaction; she and a few other white members of the library staff attended my wedding.

Esther Williams was one of the few people who didn't think that having another baby right away was the best antidote for Paul's loss. Instead, she encouraged me to finish school before I had any more children. Not long after I returned to work following Paul's death, I was offered a position as a professional librarian. I was astonished. I had neither a degree nor any training in library science. Although she never said so, I believe Mrs. Williams may have suggested the move to Mr. Brigham. It was she who pointed out to me that another woman without a degree had worked for many years as a librarian. It felt like a miracle. I was now a *professional*. And I would have a career working with books! Everybody was proud of me—Mama, Daddy, Holsey, Doris, Mrs. Williams; even Mrs. Owsley started talking to me again. The promotion was contingent on my taking classes in library science and completing my degree. I had worked in the library for seven years but never made the connection that I could be a librarian, possibly because I didn't know any black librarians.

In January 1962, a month after Holsey and I settled in our new home and five months after Paul's death, I enrolled in my first library science class at the Extension. I had not taken a class for more than a year, since shortly after we married. I took one library science class each semester for the next three semesters and made all A's. That exhausted the library classes offered at the Extension. To continue with my library studies, I needed to return to campus. The State Library offered me a grant to study at IU in Bloomington for the summer of 1963. The A's had repaired my cumulative average, so I was allowed back on campus. The grant would pay for everything—tuition, room and board, books, and supplies. In one summer I could take the nine hours I needed to complete a minor in library science. I figured out that after completing the summer work, all I would need for my degree was one semester of course work and practice teaching. Incredibly, I was close to graduating from college. For the first time I believed it would actually happen.

I was so excited. I couldn't wait to tell Holsey. After Paul died, I had tried to sell him on the idea of both us going back to school. I hoped that in the wake of the trauma we could transform the marriage and make a fresh start. I wrote to IU requesting information on married housing. Holsey looked at the material and said we couldn't afford to do it. So, I got material from Ball State, which was less expensive than IU. He wouldn't even look at the brochures. Well, this time money was not an issue.

I told Holsey my wonderful news, "I have a grant to study at IU this summer!"

He did not share my glee. "What do you mean, study at IU? Where?"

"On campus. In Bloomington. The library is paying for everything!"

"You can't just drop everything and go away to school!"

"Holsey, you don't understand. The library is *paying for everything,* tuition, room and board, everything! And they'll hold my job until I come back."

"That doesn't make any difference. You're a married woman. You can't just up and leave. You've got responsibilities." Undoubtedly, he was referring to cooking, cleaning, and picking up after him. Although he took his own responsibilities very lightly, Holsey was vigilant about keeping me accountable.

"Holsey, the library would not have promoted me if I hadn't promised to take the library science courses. I *have* to go. I've taken all the courses offered at the Extension."

"What about me? What about our marriage?"

"I'll be fifty miles away, not on the other side of the world!"

"Will you still get paid?"

"No, but my job will be waiting when I come back."

"We can't get by without your salary, we just bought a new car. Why won't you get paid?"

"Why would they pay me? I won't be working."

"Well that settles it. You can't go. I can't pay all these bills by myself."

I was learning that the deliberation I had found so seductive in Holsey came from fear and insecurity. I had thought it was born of contemplation. This was probably a perfect manipulate-him-into-thinking-it's-his-idea situation, but I still hadn't figured out how to do that. Holsey couldn't see a way to work this out. And I couldn't see letting this crucial juncture slip away. I didn't refute him, but the conflict between what I wanted and what he would have me do strengthened my will rather than weakened it.

On a Sunday morning after this exchange, Holsey and I were in services at our church, Mount Zion Baptist at West Thirty-fifth and Graceland. After his sermon, and before he opened the doors of the church—the plea for new members to join—Reverend Andrews, the pastor, had something else he wanted to do. He said, "Someone here has received the call to preach, but he hasn't answered that call. Now is the time to answer the call." A hush of anticipation settled over the congregation. A few moments passed and nobody moved. Reverend Andrews continued, "When God calls you, you better answer." Then, Holsey stood up and walked to the front of the church.

WHAT? WHERE HAD THAT COME FROM? I was in shock. I had seen absolutely no indication that God was talking to Holsey, and certainly no hint that Holsey was listening to God. Holsey was still gambling and staying out all night. *HE CAN'T POSSIBLY BE SERIOUS. I GUESS HE THINKS PREACHING IS A SURER WAY OF MAKING AN EASY BUCK THAN GAMBLING. OH MY GOD, THIS MEANS I'LL BE A PREACHER'S WIFE!* I started to cry. The people in church thought I was shedding tears of joy, or maybe that the Holy Spirit had moved me.

From that day on Holsey sat in the pulpit with the other men who'd been called. In many Baptist churches, soon after a man receives the call, he is ordained and eligible to pastor his own church. Reverend R. T. Andrews, an educated man himself, would not ordain ministers until they had graduated from a seminary. Reverend Andrews did, however, give them opportunities to preach. He usually assigned Holsey to the 8 a.m. service, meaning we had to get up as early as on a Monday morning. Making bad matters worse, Holsey spent those Sunday mornings barking at me about every little thing. We would be raging at each other as we prepared to leave for church. I was pissed over being robbed of my Sunday sleep-in, and Holsey was scared and nervous. Then, after having these fierce arguments, I was supposed to sit up front gazing lovingly at my husband while he sermonized on how to live a Christian life. It was hell!

Holsey's new vocation motivated him to quit smoking, drinking, and gambling. At least there were some redeeming features to this fantastic undertaking. Unfortunately, he didn't stop with altering his behavior; he decided to correct mine as well.

"Janet, you need to stop playing whist with your friends. Word might get back to Reverend Andrews. You have to quit smoking too."

"You must be joking. I wasn't called to preach! I'll play cards whenever I feel like it." I continued to smoke as well. Holsey tried to monitor where I smoked, in an effort to keep church folk from catching his wayward wife. The discord we'd had over his gambling away his paycheck was replaced by his self-righteous insistence that I behave like a proper minister's wife, whatever that meant. I had no faith in his call, anyway. I saw it as an effort to divert attention from my career to his. I also think he hoped a minister's wife would not leave her spousal duties to go away to school. If so, he was seriously deluded. The only thing that would stop me from going to Bloomington would be if I died before I could leave. I had fumbled school before, but I was not about to blow this opportunity.

Chapter 16

Moving Forward

The way forward is with a broken heart.

~ Alice Walker

In the summer of 1963 I returned to IU's Bloomington campus. This time I didn't have to scramble for food money or help clean the dorm. I was living in the affluent students' dorm, which I called Smithwood, although it had been renamed Read Center in 1961. This time I knew what my professional goal was: to be a certified librarian. This time I was keenly interested in the courses that would help me achieve that goal. In the eight years since I had first taken classes on IU's campus, the enrollment had increased from twelve to nineteen thousand students. And, to my surprise, there were black students everywhere. Some things had not changed; IU still assigned roommates so that their skin colors matched. My roommate, Nellie, explained why there were so many black students on campus. Nellie was a home economics teacher from Alabama and one of hundreds of black graduate students attending Indiana University courtesy of their state governments. She said all-white, state-supported Southern universities refused to enroll Negroes. By paying those students to attend school elsewhere they felt they could avoid lawsuits. I presume this option was not available to whites.

I certainly remembered the uproar from whites when blacks had tried to desegregate Southern universities, but I had no idea the universities were *paying* blacks not to attend their schools. Autherine Lucy (Foster) was refused admission to graduate school at the University of Alabama until the NAACP took the case to court. She won her legal challenge and was the first black to enroll there in 1956. But when white students rioted, the university expelled her. James Meredith was another black student who needed a court decree when he decided to enroll at the University of Mississippi. Meredith graduated in 1963, but only after three thousand whites had protested his enrollment. More than twenty thousand U.S. troops had to be called in to restore order at Ole Miss. In the melee, two people were killed and one hundred sixty injured.

With receptions like those, I could easily understand why many Southern black students decided to take the money and run. Most of the black graduate students at IU were educators whose bachelor's degrees were from black colleges that didn't offer graduate work. Herman B Wells, who had retired from the presidency in 1962, had welcomed the South's educational refugees to IU. Indiana University was known as the "mother of college presidents" when Wells became the seventy-first IU alum to become a college president in 1938. More recently, IU has become known as the mother of black college presidents, possibly as a result of the large numbers from the South who completed their graduate studies there. Former presidents William H. Harris at Paine; Leroy Keith, Morehouse; Gloria Randall Scott, Bennett; John Turner, Knoxville; and the late Walter Washington, Alcorn State were among the African American college presidents who graduated from IU.

It was a real treat to see so many black faces on campus, and that summer I made spending money typing papers for several of them. I also helped my roommate write a couple of papers. Nellie was astonished that I wasn't a graduate student, saying, "Janet, as smart as you are I can't believe you don't have a degree." Nellie and most of the Southern students were at IU without their spouses and many of them behaved as if they were vacationing at a resort. They were serious about having a good time. I was invited to their social activities but wasn't particularly interested. I had work to do.

I did attend my first opera that summer, Verdi's *Aida,* performed in Memorial Stadium on Tenth Street, site of IU's football games. It was Indiana University's first outdoor opera, with a cast of nearly four hundred and a chorus of one hundred forty-three voices. Fourteen thousand people saw the four performances. Like many other black students, I was there primarily to see the sister who was sharing the title role. Susan Cobb, a black graduate student in the School of Music, starred in two of the opera's performances, possibly a first for IU.

It was a spectacular production and I enjoyed the show enough that I have since seen other operas, but I still prefer Ray Charles.

The year I returned to campus was the one-hundredth anniversary of the Emancipation Proclamation. Commemorative activities were taking place all over America. Indiana got into the act with the publication of a ninety-eight-page history of Negroes by Emma Lou Thornbrough. Following Daddy's example of purchasing books on Negroes wherever they could be found, I bought a copy. Not long before, when I was the switchboard operator/receptionist at the state library, I had purchased another of Thornbrough's books, *The Negro in Indiana Before 1900*. Gayle Thornbrough, Emma Lou's sister, worked at the Indiana Historical Bureau, which shared an office suite with the library director. Gayle had talked to me about her sister, a professor of history at Butler University, and showed me the book.

Leading up to 1963, Negroes had a slogan, "Free by '63." We felt it was ridiculous that one hundred years after the historic presidential proclamation, we still didn't have the same liberties as other Americans. In an effort to secure that freedom, demonstrations had been going on all year. I followed the news reports of the revved up Civil Rights Movement closely and was intensely proud that our people were refusing to put up with segregation any longer. In April, Martin Luther King Jr. was jailed in Birmingham for violating an injunction against demonstrations. In May, as a response to King's incarceration, thousands of demonstrators took to Birmingham's streets. They were resolved not to accept that city's virulent *racism* any longer.

Bull Connor, the Commissioner of *Public Safety*, for all the world to see, played out the white fear that without the advantage of the caste system, they could not compete with blacks. I wanted to personally take a baseball bat to Connor when I saw the television footage of him brutally assaulting the protestors with police dogs and water cannons. I couldn't be there with them—I wasn't up to taking that kind of punishment without striking back anyway—but I believe their determination inspired me to act in my own best interests when I had tough decisions to make. IU must have been inspired as well; that year their golf club accepted its first black member, Forrest Jones. Jones, an Indianapolis teacher, had been on IU's golf team when he was a student.

I was glad that Negroes were forcing the issue; direct action was the only thing left. We had tried for so long to cajole and litigate whites into a change of behavior, and it wasn't happening. Malcolm X also intrigued me. He said he was nonviolent with those who were nonviolent with him. That made sense. I, and most of America, first became aware of Malcolm on the 1959 CBS telecast, *The Hate That Hate Produced*. Malcolm was more straightforward with white folks than any black leader I'd ever heard. I liked that, and apparently other blacks did as well. "In Los Angeles alone, five hundred people joined the [Nation of Islam] the week after" the program was aired. But while Malcolm's candor gave a number of us a boost, most Americans were frightened by what he had to say. Inadvertently, Malcolm enhanced King's appeal. Before Malcolm became nationally known, many whites thought Martin Luther King Jr. was dangerous; afterwards, King began to look good.

Not surprisingly, the more demanding blacks became, the more white resistance escalated. I remember the summer of 1963 as particularly volatile. In June Governor George Wallace was determined to keep the University of Alabama the last *officially* segregated state system in the country. He had run for governor on the slogan, "segregation now, segregation tomorra', segregation forever." I despised him, and jeered at him as he became the national symbol of segregation by making good on his promise to "stand in the schoolhouse door" to stop Negroes from being admitted. But Nellie was afraid that Wallace's open defiance of desegregation would goad Alabama whites into more violence.

That night President Kennedy spoke to the country, and in clear, forceful language, publicly supported our Struggle. He said, "We preach freedom around the world, and we mean it, …but are we to say to the world, and much more importantly, to each other that this is a land of the free except for the Negroes?" Wow! We had never heard a United States president say anything like that. I was even more encouraged when the president spoke to the fact that *racism* was "not a sectional issue." He said, "Difficulties over segregation and discrimination exist in every city, in every state of the Union." He also promised to ask Congress to enact legislation so that every wrong has a remedy. "Unless the Congress acts, [Negroes'] only remedy is the street."

Way to go President Kennedy!

The next day we were yanked out of our hopeful expectations. A cowardly *racist* in Mississippi had responded to the president's speech by shooting Medgar Evers in the back. Evers, the NAACP's field secretary in that state, was killed as he prepared to enter his home. Myrlie Evers, his wife, and their three children heard his car, then the shots, and ran outside to find his bloody body. I was livid, and also aghast at how vicious and determined these *racists* were to maintain the illusion of white supremacy. I suppose that's why they burn crosses, the symbol of Christianity, to indicate that their acts are destructive of everything Jesus taught. When we watched this news on television, the Southern students were hurt and angry, but not as shocked as I was. They nodded their heads knowingly; this was exactly what they expected. Evers's assassin, Byron de la Beckwith, got away with murder for over thirty years, but was finally convicted in 1994.

The violent, brutal images in support of *racism* that summer, in particular the Birmingham public safety officers—police and firefighters—attacking peaceful, unarmed children, women, and men were shown repeatedly on television sets, not only in this country, but also around the world. The conduct of these vicious *racists* may have been ignored, as it had been in the past; however, the Cold War was on. The United States needed to save face in its competition with the Soviet Union to be the world's moral leader and preeminent power. On June 19, a week after the horror of Evers's assassination, President Kennedy sent Congress the promised civil rights bill. He asked Congress to "look into their hearts and help end racial violence, disunity, and national shame." The bill promised federal protection to African Americans so that we could shop, eat out, vote, and attend school wherever we wanted without being attacked. The *Recorder* called it the "most sweeping civil rights bill since reconstruction."

Later I learned that on May 24, prior to the president's speech to the nation, U. S. Attorney General Robert Kennedy had met with a group of prominent blacks in New York City. The Attorney General asked James Baldwin to arrange the meeting because he wanted ideas on how the *race* problem could be resolved. Among those at the meeting were entertainers Harry Belafonte, Ossie Davis, Ruby Dee, and Lena Horne. Dr. Kenneth Clark, psychologist and author, and playwright Lorraine Hansberry, who wrote *Raisin in the Sun*, were also present. "The [three hour] meeting was a reflection of ...

how deeply concerned American blacks were about the continuation of racism in America." Like many whites then and now, the attorney general was not expecting the indignation and urgency of black feelings about the persistence of *racism*. One of the people at the meeting said that Kennedy's shock "over the sentiments expressed [was] reflective of how the Administration underestimates the explosive ingredients inherent in the continued existence of racial discrimination and segregation."

We blacks on campus barely talked about anything except the intense struggle going on to end *racial* discrimination. We argued endlessly about whether or not Congress would pass the civil rights bill. Some of us felt they had to, but others didn't believe Congress cared what happened to us. Several black leaders decided to do more than speculate. To show support for Kennedy's bill, as well as to put pressure on Congress to pass it, they planned a March on Washington. A massive march sounded impressive to me, but Nellie and several others were not so sure. They thought it would wind up in a violent free-for-all with marchers injured, arrested, and possibly killed. Some folk even said all those black folk gathered in one place would make easy pickings for a *racist* sniper.

Bayard Rustin was the executive director of the planned demonstration, and it was to be led by A. Philip Randolph, Martin Luther King Jr. and other civil rights luminaries. Rustin was a longtime movement organizer who had advised King during the Montgomery Bus Boycott in 1955. Randolph was the founder and president of the Brotherhood of Sleeping Car Porters, the first black labor union organized in 1925. King was president of the Southern Christian Leadership Conference (SCLC). Randolph had aborted a planned March on Washington in 1941 after President Franklin Roosevelt issued the Fair Employment Practices Act. The executive order banned *racial* discrimination in defense industries and created the Fair Employment Practices Commission (FEPC) to investigate violations of the order.

As captivated as I was by these dramatic events, I had to turn away and face the upheavals in my own life. In mid-August of this "hot summer" I returned to Indianapolis feeling triumphant. I had completed my library science studies and made straight A's! I expected Holsey to be as happy as I was. He wasn't much interested.

"Janet, I'll be leaving for Nashville in a couple of weeks."

"Nashville…? What are you going to Nashville for?"

"Reverend Andrews pulled some strings to get me into the American Baptist Theological School there."

I was stunned into complete silence!

"I'm taking the car so I'll have transportation when I get there." Holsey continued to tell me about this startling change in our lives.

"How long will you be gone? What about your job? Who's going to pay on the car?" I found my voice in a rush of questions.

"Well, you'll be making more money when you go back to the library…."

Then, I got it. This was payback! Holsey expected that while he was gone, I would maintain the household, and make payments on the car. He said he'd have a part-time job, but he didn't say anything about sending any money back.

I was completely taken aback but didn't say anything more; we rarely talked about what was on our minds. My thoughts, however, were in overdrive: *WHAT A HYPOCRITE! HE DIDN'T WANT ME TO TAKE SIX-WEEKS OFF MY JOB TO GO TO SCHOOL FIFTY MILES AWAY, FOR FREE. NOW, HE'S GOING TO QUIT HIS JOB AND PAY TO STUDY FOR A YEAR, TWO HUNDRED MILES AWAY? HE CAN'T SERIOUSLY BELIEVE I'M GOING TO CARRY THIS LOAD BY MYSELF. WHAT KIND OF FOOL DOES HE THINK I AM?* I should not have been surprised, but I was. As I continued to turn Holsey's plans over in my mind, anger evolved into relief. I realized that, in fact, Holsey had given me a way out. I had desperately wanted to stay at IU and finish my degree, but because Holsey had objected to my being away in the first place, I knew he would never agree to a whole school year. Trying to be a dutiful wife, I returned home to my husband. Now that he was leaving, we could put this marriage out of its misery.

A few days later after I'd had time to think about Holsey's new venture, I told him what I'd decided, "Holsey, I've decided to go back to school too."

"Wait a minute, Janet. Both of us can't leave…"

"Then it makes more sense for me to go. I can be done by June."

"But I've made all the arrangements. Plus, Reverend Andrews pulled some strings to get me in… And, somebody's got to take care of the bills."

I exploded, "Oh, and that somebody should be me? I *know* you don't think I'm going to be up here paying on that car while you're driving it down there! I tell you what. Take the damn car. Go to Nashville. And you can have this house, and everything in it. I am *done*." While Holsey did whatever he pleased, I had become an emotional contortionist trying to accept his all-night romps, his gambling, his lack of support for me, and his sudden unexplained decision to become a preacher. I wasn't happy about our marriage before he decided to leave for the seminary. It would be a rank capitulation to his ego if I put off completing my education so he could pursue some ill-considered idea of studying for the ministry. Holsey had been audacious right from the start, but this was the last straw. If being a wife meant always deferring to your husband's wishes, then I didn't want to be one, ever. I would get my degree and go on about my business *alone*.

The 1963 March on Washington was scheduled for August 28. As if signaling the end of one era and the beginning of another, one of my family's heroes, W. E. B. DuBois, died in Ghana the day before the march. He had lived for nearly a century, having been born in 1868, three years after the Civil War ended. We had long admired Dr. Du Bois and faithfully read the *Crisis*, the NAACP journal he founded. Mama was a particular fan of Dr. DuBois, often referring to him as "a highly educated man." Before I was old enough to go with him, Daddy had heard DuBois speak at one of the YMCA's Monster Meetings. Anybody would be proud to have lived the kind of long and useful life he had.

I was distracted from the history-making March. While those 250,000 or more Americans were gathering at and marching on the nation's capitol, Holsey and I were moving our things out of the little double on Forty-second Street. I didn't want anything we had acquired during our marriage, but Mama insisted that I "get something." I took the bedroom and living room furniture. Rosie and Gordon, who had been married a year, needed furniture for the two empty bedrooms in their three-bedroom house, so I stored it there. Holsey kept the kitchen furnishings, including the appliances.

In September 1963, Holsey drove to Nashville and I got a ride to IU. Our marriage, begun under a cloud, had become thunderous. Like many storms, however, it didn't last long and when it was over, everything was clear. In the three years Holsey and I were together, I lost my naïveté and took the first steps to becoming myself. At the time, I assumed Holsey's electing to study in Nashville was payback for my summer in Bloomington. In retrospect, however, I've thought perhaps his decision to leave was his sly way of ending the marriage. When I filed for divorce the following January, Holsey vigorously objected, but he didn't express remorse for anything that had happened.

Several years later, at a family gathering, I talked about how devastated I was when, at a very low point, Mama had turned her back on me. Daddy hadn't heard the story. He couldn't believe Mama had refused to let me come home.

"I wish *I* had known you called. I would have come got you and you could have stayed here as long as you wanted to." Daddy looked at Mama as if he dared her to dispute him.

Mama didn't flinch. "That's why I didn't tell you. She was infamilyway. She needed to be with her husband."

"A lot of good it did." Daddy's wry comment ended the discussion.

Now I consider Mama's rude kick out of the nest, Paul's death, and Holsey's disregard for my feelings and aspirations as propitious. These were traumatic and painful ruptures, but they helped free me. I ran from the pain without realizing that my anguish would travel with me. However, in my determination to get away, I opened up to possibilities beyond the confines of the world I knew.

My return to school was unplanned, so I had to scramble. I knew I could get a job—and I did, at the School of Education Audio-Visual Center—to cover housing and food, but I needed tuition money immediately. Tuition was $11.00 a credit hour, and I meant to take a full load, fifteen or sixteen hours. Gordon, who graduated from IU the year before, was teaching in the Indianapolis Public Schools, and Rosie was still employed in the IPS central office. They were the only family members likely to have any extra money, so I asked Rosie if they would lend me tuition money. I could have asked Daddy; he was famous for somehow coming up with whatever we needed, whether it was cash or connections, but I figured it would be less of a financial burden for Rosie and Gordon. Our family bonds sometimes seemed fragile as a result of growing up with little intimacy and affection, but in times of distress we could definitely count on one another. One or both of my brothers were the first people I called when I was pulling out of a marriage, and Rosie and I were close despite our different interests. We had always talked to each other about things Mama wouldn't discuss—monthly periods, boys, necking, sex, contraception. They were happy to help me and I was deeply grateful.

Uncle Oliver, Daddy's brother, had a day off work and drove me to Bloomington to look for housing. We passed a ROOM FOR RENT sign near campus and, although I doubted they would rent to Negroes, I decided to check into it anyway. I called the landlady, whose name I no longer remember. I'll refer to her as Mrs. Ryan. She met me at the rooming house and didn't appear disturbed by my skin color. Mrs. Ryan asked if I was a student, told me men were not allowed in the house overnight, and that rent was due promptly on the first of each month. It was extremely rare for a rooming house so close to IU's main entrance at Kirkwood and Indiana to rent to nonwhites, but Ryan seemed just the type to buck convention. She was a tall, laconic blonde with a cynical veneer that I imagined came from having to make her own way in a difficult world. A space at that prime location was possibly available only because of her policy to rent to anyone who abided by her rules, regardless of skin color.

Once I got settled in my new digs and into the idea that Holsey and I were indeed finished, I began to relax. It was like waking up to the sun after several long dark days. I was eager for fresh experiences and living off campus was a start. I couldn't have lived off campus when I first came to Bloomington eight years earlier. Women had to be married or twenty-five years old to live in housing that was not university-approved. Not only that, but even approved off campus housing for Negro students was extremely limited, and usually a distance away. I could hardly believe I had space in a house three blocks from campus. The two-story frame house at 413 East Fourth Street had a porch and a small front yard. Entering the house you stepped into a large foyer that functioned as a sitting room. The stairs to the second floor were on the left. A sofa, two chairs, and a television console were squeezed into the foyer. The television received only one local channel so it was rarely used. There were three bedrooms on the second floor, and the living-dining areas on the first floor were also used as bedrooms.

On the right side of the foyer was a door that led to two rooms. The larger of the two rooms was the only one in the house with two beds. I took the only unoccupied bed left in the house, the one against the far wall. Sunee, a librarian from Thailand, had taken the bed near the door. North of this room was an anteroom occupied by Zhen, a graduate student in music. The only separation between the two rooms was a wide archway and a sheet that Zhen had tacked up to obtain some privacy. A swinging door on the south side of our room opened into the kitchen. Two white women—Beverly and Linda— and Ling, a Chinese woman from Hong Kong, occupied the three second-floor bedrooms. Even if I'd had a choice, I would have taken a first-floor bed because the private rooms upstairs were more expensive. There was a bathroom on each floor, and the six of us shared the sitting room and kitchen.

Zhen was a quiet, serious young woman from Taiwan who played the clarinet. She dressed sedately and her hair, the blackest I had ever seen, hung to her waist. Sunee, my roommate, was forty-two, older than the rest of us, who were all in our twenties. Sunee's husband and children remained at home while she was attending graduate school at IU. Sunee was a happy person, smiling and friendly, with short curly hair and tan skin. My new roommates marveled at my height. Both of them were three or four inches shorter than my five feet, five inches. I thought of myself as short because everybody in my immediate family is taller, but Zhen and Sunee helped me see that I am actually tall.

I was more surprised that Sunee and Zhen didn't think of me as a Negro. It took a while for me to recognize that when they referred to "the American," they were talking about me. I corrected them, explaining that Negroes were not really Americans. I told them we didn't have the privileges of American citizenship—equal opportunities for jobs, good schools, living anywhere we wanted. I said, "The only time we're considered as Americans is when the country needs bodies for a war."

It reminded me of a story I'd heard about how proud Negroes were when radio announcers referred to boxer Joe Louis as "the American" during his second fight with Max Schmeling in 1938. When Schmeling won their first bout in 1936, Nazis were ecstatic; one German writer said, "France, England, and white North America cannot thank Schmeling enough for this victory, for he checked the

arrogance of the Negro and clearly demonstrated to them the superiority of white intelligence." When that statement was made, Nazi
noses were particularly out of joint because Jesse Owens, a Negro,
had won four gold medals at the Olympic games in Berlin earlier that
year. They saw Schmeling's victory as their revenge. By the time the
second Louis-Schmeling fight was held, two years later, the word was
out that Germans were forcing Jews into concentration camps. President Franklin Roosevelt told Louis, "Joe, we need muscles like yours
to beat Germany." In the second fight Louis became a symbol of the
countries that wanted to defeat Hitler and the Nazis; consequently, he
could be called an American. My explanations made little difference
to Sunee and Zhen. They still regarded me primarily as an American,
which I came to accept, but it didn't feel right.

According to Sunee, Ling, who lived upstairs, was from a wealthy
Hong Kong family. That explained Ling's air of brash sophistication.
She was an inch or so shorter than I, dressed fashionably, and had
stylishly cut and permed hair. In appearance Ling and Zhen were
complete opposites, but they were friends and visited each other
regularly, speaking Chinese, so I had no idea what they talked about.
My housemates taught me that the cultures and food of China and
Thailand had some similarities; and that although both Zhen and
Ling were Chinese, technically neither of them lived in China. Hong
Kong was under British control, and Taiwan, although at that time
internationally recognized as China, was actually an island off the
coast of the mainland.

Beverly and Linda were white Americans. Linda was a little
taller than I, slender with short bottle blonde hair. When she was in
the house, she stayed in her room. I don't recall that we ever talked.
After a while Beverly and I became friendly and picked up a running
conversation whenever we had time. Beverly was about five foot eight
with thick, shoulder-length brown hair and pockmarked skin. She
was easily fifty pounds overweight. She prided herself on being a free
thinker who didn't conform to expected behavior. I was fascinated
by her eccentricities and enjoyed talking to her. One day she asked a
question I never expected to hear.

"Do you have sex on the first date?"

"Of course not. Nobody does that."

"I do. I always have sex on the first date."

"Why on earth would you do that?" THIS WOMAN IS REALLY CRAZY.

"If a guy only wants me for sex, we can get that out of the way. Once he's had sex, if he's not interested in me as a person, he'll move on. If he is interested in me, he doesn't have to spend time trying to get me in bed because we've already done it. We can get to know one another."

I had no response for her revolutionary idea.

Beverly also surprised me by talking about being fat. In my experience only thin women drawing attention to their figures talked about being fat.

"I lost seventy pounds because everybody said my life would be better if I were thin. I was skinny for a year. Nothing changed. Now I eat what I want, drink beer, and enjoy myself."

We also talked about *race* and *racism*, another first for me. Negroes talked about *racism* ad infinitum among ourselves, but it was an unwritten, unspoken rule that in the presence of whites we didn't mention it. Most whites were markedly uneasy discussing *race*. And since discomfited whites could make our lives even more difficult, around them we pretended *racism* didn't exist. Beverly believed that poor whites were as oppressed as blacks. I totally disagreed and regaled her with stories about *racial* discrimination.

Beverly responded, "You say you're the first in your family to go to college. Well, nobody in my family had ever graduated from *high school*. I was the first!" Her voice rose as she made her point. "Somebody helped you get a scholarship. I had to work *four years* before I had the money to come to IU."

"Okay, but once you have a degree, you can get any job you're qualified for. I can't. The poorest, most ignorant white person can go places Sidney Poitier can't." (Poitier had recently won the Academy Award for Best Actor.) "White people can do anything they want."

"*Some* white people. Not *my* people." Beverly was frustrated that I couldn't see that being white in and of itself did not automatically confer a life of privilege. To prove her point, she borrowed a car and took me to see where she grew up. We drove southwest of Bloomington and stopped at a shambles of a settlement. Several filthy white children, in clothes that looked like the rags Mama used for cleaning, stopped playing to stare at us. Their homes were little more than rickety sheds lined up along a river. There was obviously no plumbing. Beverly said the children rarely went to school because they were teased and called river rats.

I was astonished. My relatives in the rural South lived better than this. They didn't have indoor plumbing, but they owned land and had substantial homes. I sympathized with Beverly, but privately I knew that any one of those raggedy kids could grow up, kill a black man, and get away with it.

Linda and Beverly never used the kitchen, but the rest of us sometimes prepared meals there. Sunee and Zhen cooked regularly using ingredients shipped to them from New York, Chicago, or overseas. Sunee enjoyed cooking and often prepared meals for herself, Ling, and Zhen. One day I watched as she prepared a dish. She identified the unfamiliar items she was using—pale yellow bamboo shoots, wormy looking bean sprouts, dried mushrooms, squares of bean curd, and thin transparent rice noodles.

"Here, Janet, taste it." As she stirred the ingredients, Sunee offered me some.

"No thanks. I don't want any." The dish smelled really good, but I'd never had any of that stuff and it didn't appeal to me. Those dried, black mushrooms looked especially gross. And whoever heard of eating bamboo?

"Just try a little." Sunee insisted.

"Okay, just a little bit." I liked Sunee and didn't want to offend her. "My god, this is delicious!"

I couldn't believe how good it was! I asked for more and ate so much it was embarrassing, but Sunee was pleased. That was an important lesson: new experiences should be *examined* before you make a decision about them. Sunee also read palms. After studying my palms, she told me I'd marry three times and have a long life. I hope her life span prediction is as accurate as the one about marriages.

Chapter 17

Altering My Images

No amount of persuasion can change a [wo]man's reaction to what [she] knows. But what [she] knows can be changed, and the most direct manner is to alter the images within [her] mind.

~ Dennis Kimbro in
Think and Grow Rich: A Black Choice

The global flavor of the rooming house multiplied. Zhen dated a young man from India, Ling was involved with a guy from England, and I had a friend, Ricky Singh, from Guyana, or what the English called British Guiana. (The tradition of 413 East Fourth continues. The house is now the site of Masala Wok, a restaurant serving Indian and Chinese food.) Ricky was one of a group of forty businessmen from developing nations studying American management concepts at IU's business school. When he saw me sitting alone in the Commons at the Union Building, he approached me with a line unlike anything I had ever heard.

"You're a mestizo, aren't you?"

I looked up to see a handsome, perfectly proportioned, and impeccably dressed miniature man. At least he looked miniature to me, accustomed as I was in my family to men nearly six feet tall or over. Ricky stood about five feet two inches and had brown skin and straight black hair. He spoke with an accent that I came to identify as West Indian. "Mestizo? What's that?"

"Of mixed race."

I laughed. "No. All my people are Negro."

"That can't be true. My wife is Negro and she doesn't look anything like you." He sat down, pulled out his wallet, and showed me a picture of his wife and four children. "Look." His wife's skin was much darker than mine, but I was more blown away by the fact that a woman who looked to be my age had four children.

I smiled. "In this country you're either Negro or white. If you *ever* had an ancestor with a *drop* of African blood, you're a Negro. It doesn't matter what you look like."

"Really? It's not like that in South America and the Caribbean."

"Where are you from?"

"Guyana. You've probably never heard of it. It's on the northeastern coast of South America. My people came to Guyana from India to cut sugar cane."

"And your wife's people are from Africa?"

"The Europeans brought her people over as slaves. "

"So we have that in common. But you're right. I don't know anything about Guyana. How big is it? Are all the people Indian and African?" I was surprised to find out there were black people somewhere other than the U. S. and Africa.

Ricky clearly enjoyed talking about his homeland. "Guyana is a small country, about the size of one of your larger states, but," he quickly added, "not as big as Texas. It's tropical. Mostly forest. But we export bauxite and sugar cane."

"What's bauxite?"

"The raw material that makes aluminum."

"How many people live there?"

"About half a million; half East Indian, a third African, maybe ten percent Amerindian—that's the native people—and the rest are European, Chinese, and mestizo."

"Are your children considered mestizo?"

"Yes, but *race* isn't so important in South America as it is in North America. Brazil has a whole range of color and class distinctions, but even there..."

I interrupted him, "You say *race* isn't important, but are Negroes *equal* to whites?"

"Sometimes. Sometimes higher. Your status depends on your education and income, not on skin color." Ricky explained.

After meeting Ricky I started noticing news reports about Guyana. I read an article about Cheddi Jagan, their prime minister, and had more questions. Jagan looked suspiciously white to me. "What is your prime minister? Mixed? Or white? And why is he a communist?"

"Cheddi Jagan's people, like mine, came from India, and he's not a communist. He just prefers a Marxist approach to the distribution of resources. Whenever your government doesn't like somebody, they call him a communist."

Ricky became animated. He was upset by what was happening in his country. "They don't like Jagan, and the British and Americans are pitting Guyanese of African descent against those of Indian descent. We never had that kind of ethnic tension in Guyana. I'm Indian and my wife is African. Nobody cared that we got married."

"Well, this country thrives on *racism*. If America is involved, *race* will definitely be an issue."

"By the way, Forbes Burnham, the leader of the opposition party, is Negro. If his party had won the election, he'd be prime minister."

"You're kidding." A black prime minister somewhere other than Africa. Now, that was something!

Ricky suggested some news sources that would broaden my *Indianapolis Star* perception of the world. I learned that Jagan was democratically elected by the Guyanese to lead them from home rule to full independence. Britain had expected Burnham to win the election, and when he didn't, they reneged on their promise to grant sovereignty to Guyana. Together with the United States, Britain covertly undermined Jagan's regime, sufficiently destabilizing the country so that he lost to Burnham a few months after Ricky and I met. Ricky was expecting that outcome, but he was still unhappy about it. When Ricky left IU to return home, I promised to visit him in Guyana one day. We kept in touch by mail for a couple of years.

Just as my worldview was expanding, President Kennedy was assassinated. Kennedy was the first president I was old enough to vote for, although I felt deceived when I realized that my vote had not counted. With the antiquated winner-take-all electoral college system, I was effectively disfranchised when Indiana went for Richard Nixon. When the announcement came that Kennedy had been shot, I was in the School of Education library. Somebody brought in a radio and everything stopped while we listened to the news reports. About thirty minutes later I couldn't believe it when the news reporter said that Kennedy was dead! Tragically, we had become accustomed to civil rights activists being killed in the South, but how could somebody kill the president of the United States? Things like that just didn't happen. Plus, he was surrounded by Secret Service agents. I should have known that a president who stood up for us wouldn't be allowed to live. Now, Lyndon Johnson, a Southerner, would be president. Damn!

In the days following Kennedy's murder, that unused television in the rooming house was on continuously. On this occasion WTTV the local station was carrying the same images as all the networks. For the next several days we who lived there packed into the foyer with our friends. We were mesmerized by the unfolding events—the ascendance of Lyndon Johnson to the presidency and the solemn, ceremonious funeral attended by heads of state from around the world. Zhen's boyfriend remarked that Americans were astonishingly restrained. If India's leader were killed, he said, the streets would be crowded with people wailing and tearing at their hair.

Living off-campus was not the only change from my earlier sojourn at IU. In 1955, except for classes, I could have been enrolled in a black college because my social life was exclusively Negro. Now I was interacting with people from a variety of cultures. Also, I had previously been enrolled in the College of Arts & Sciences, majoring in English with a minor in history. For my final campus tour, I switched to the School of Education. English remained my major, but now my minor was library science, which at the time was a division of the ed school.

A nice surprise that semester was getting to know my cousin Michael Hunt, Aunt Ovella's eldest son. Michael was about five years younger than I, so when we had visited Michigan, he was too young for me to pay attention to. At IU he was studying Russian and Arabic in the U.S. Air Force Language Program. (In the 1950s the languages in the Air Force program were primarily eastern European like Bulgarian, Hungarian, and Polish.) I discovered that Michael was a very bright young man and we had fun hanging out together.

To be certified as a secondary language arts teacher I was taking Principles of Secondary Education and Methods of Teaching High School English. The classes were tedious beyond belief, but I met Jessie Reiss, a venturous young woman from New York City, who encouraged my own sense of adventure. Jessie was also preparing to teach high school English and was in both classes. She was twenty-four, two years younger than I, but in addition to our shared classes, we were both ending short failed marriages. At first I thought Jessie was a lot smarter than I. But I noticed that she struggled with her classes and spent more hours studying than I did. Finally, I understood what the difference was. Jessie was much better *informed* than I, and had opinions on subjects I'd never even thought about, like the labor movement. Not only

Jessie Reiss in Israel, 1965-66.

had Jessie grown up in the diverse and stimulating environment of New York, but her parents were better educated and more widely read than mine. It occurred to me that Jessie, with her broad exposure to information, had taken the same standardized tests that I had. That was when I began to have some insight into how uneven the playing field is. At the end of the semester when her husband moved out, Jessie and I became roommates. She needed help with the rent, and at Jessie's apartment I would have my own room.

Jessie was a Jew, five foot three, attractive, with brown hair that she could sit on, and that she lightened to honey blonde. She grew up in Queens with her parents and a younger sister. Jessie believed in exploring new places and trying things she'd never done. After she completed school, she spent two years in Israel on a kibbutz. When she learned that my traveling had been limited to nearby states, Jessie insisted that I visit her family during spring break. She even finagled a bus pass from a friend so that I didn't have to pay to get there. What a precious and unexpected gift! I was going to New York, the city of all cities!

Jessie's parents and sister welcomed me like a member of the family; I felt completely at home. Mrs. Reiss gave me a subway map and pointed out the closest stop. With the map to guide me, I rode the subway around the city, baptizing myself in the sights and sounds of the Big Apple. I marveled at Wall Street, was smitten by Greenwich Village, and ambled comfortably through Harlem, stopping to gawk when I happened upon the famed Abyssinian Baptist Church. I even took the ferry to Staten Island to see an IU rugby team play a game.

The highlight of the trip was a Passover seder. I knew about Passover from church, but had no idea what a seder was. I went with the Reiss family to a relative's much larger apartment where about twenty people had gathered for the historic ritual. Mrs. Reiss sat next to me translating the Haggadah from the Hebrew so that I could follow the ceremony, but the best part was the food. I thought the gefilte fish was tasteless, but the other new dishes—potato kugel, kasha, and roast duck—were absolutely delicious. I particularly liked the four cups of wine that were a required part of the meal. I was tipsy by the time I finished eating.

Jessie was set to do student teaching in Indianapolis shortly after I returned from New York. She asked if I thought my parents would rent her a room for the six weeks. I knew Daddy would love having a new set of ears for his stories. Mama, however, did not trust whites and would need to be convinced. I told her how warmly Jessie's family had welcomed me, and brought Jessie to meet them. Jessie greeted them with hugs and asked if she could call them Mama and Poppa. That did it. Jessie stayed in my old bedroom for the duration of her assignment.

Jessie's hobby was cooking and while she was at my parents' house, she decided to do something special for Mother's Day. She planned a big dinner for the family—my parents, my siblings and their spouses, and the grandchildren. That meal was a subject of family conversations for years. Jessie made a spicy meatloaf that she covered with pastry in which she wrote MOM on top. She also served bell peppers stuffed with rice, and for dessert, an applesauce cake. These were new recipes for us; our meatloaf had always been naked. My Negro family was also impressed that a white woman spent the day in the kitchen preparing a meal for them. Jessie enjoyed her time with my family as well. She said the next time she heard comedian-activist Dick Gregory, she understood more of his humor. We kept in touch for years.

I had done my student teaching earlier in the semester. This was 1964, fifteen years since the Indianapolis Public Schools (IPS) had begun the desegregation of the student bodies of the schools. A few black teachers had been scattered throughout predominately white elementary schools shortly after deseg began. And in 1955, when two white male teachers were assigned to Attucks, the *Recorder* announced that, "all Indianapolis high schools now have mixed teaching staffs." Not wanting to overwhelm white teachers and students, the "mix" usually meant a lone black teacher in a predominately white high school. And, of course, every black teacher selected to teach in a "white" high school had to have impeccable credentials and years of experience. Negroes spoke in reverential tones about the selected teachers and the schools to which they had been assigned. One by one, the best Attucks High School teachers and department heads were picked off to integrate the faculties of Shortridge, Tech, Howe, and other "white" high schools. The chosen ones took pride in representing the *race* as the "only Negro" teacher in these schools. It was in this atmosphere that I was to do my student teaching. Nine years after the *Brown* ruling, eight years since the successful end of the Montgomery Bus Boycott, and on the heels of the March on Washington, it seemed to me mighty late in the game for us to be *thrilled* that a few black teachers were being allowed into "white" high schools.

I was already disgruntled about having to jump through the student-teaching hoop for a license I had no intention of using. But I wanted my degree and this was the means to that end. Going back into the Indianapolis Public Schools also reminded me of the agonizing days at Manual. In anticipation of another round with IPS, I adjusted the chip I carried about the Manual experience, pushing it a little closer to the edge of my shoulder.

To sign up for my student teaching assignment, I was given a four-by-six card to fill out. On this card was a space for my name, subject area, and blank spaces numbered one and two, where I was to indicate a first and second choice of the high school where I wanted to be assigned. I selected Manual as my first choice, primarily because I didn't have a car. I would stay with my parents and get a ride with Daddy, who drove past Manual on his way to work. (At this point, Daddy was near retirement and no longer going to work in the middle of the night.) For my second choice I wrote Tech, another high school not far from where my parents lived. I've been unable to remember or track down the name of the professor managing the assignments, so I've dubbed him Dr. Olsen. He called me into his office.

"You have to change one of your choices. Negro student teachers in Indianapolis go to Crispus Attucks."

"Are you saying that in fact I don't have a choice?"

Dr. Olsen looked at me quizzically for a moment. "Do you want to leave it this way and see what happens?"

I responded firmly, "I most certainly do. I'm not doing my student teaching at Attucks." I had no problems with Attucks High School, but I was not going to cooperate with IPS's *racist* policies.

Dr. Olsen sent the form to IPS. When it was returned, he handed me the card. A number three had been written in followed by Crispus Attucks. In the comment space was a note saying I had been assigned to my third choice. In 1940, IU had been under fire for their *racism* in practice teaching assignments, now here was IPS twenty-four years later, still operating under that despicable policy.

I was outraged and told Olsen, "They're not getting away with this!"

"If you want to fight this, I'll help you. Their own rules say that no teacher is to have more than one student per year, and you're the third student assigned to this teacher this year. Sometimes Attucks teachers have had two students *at the same time.*"

"I definitely want to fight it."

"I'll contact the Civil Rights Commission." Although he had given me no indication of his interest, Dr. Olsen, who was white, seemed to have been waiting for this opportunity.

I later learned that in 1960 Gloria Randle Scott, who was studying at Indiana Central College (now the University of Indianapolis), was also told she had to do her student teaching at Attucks. Gloria protested the assignment. She was living near Manual and explained that it would be a hardship to trek across town to Attucks. When IPS discovered there was a black biology teacher at Manual they allowed Gloria to do her student teaching there.

A powerless Indiana Civil Rights Commission (CRC) had been created three years earlier in 1961. Two years later, Governor Matthew Welsh gave the commission some teeth, including the power to issue cease and desist orders when a school or training center was discriminating against students. Harold Hatcher, a white Quaker, was appointed director of the CRC. Hatcher had previously worked for Indianapolis's American Friends Service Committee, gently persuading companies to open skilled and white-collar jobs to Negroes in places where blacks either had never worked or had been employed only in menial positions. He was initially mandated to use the same diplomatic approach at the CRC. Hatcher carefully screened the Negro applicants, and would not send them for interviews unless they were overqualified for the positions. Indianapolis sorely needed an assertive organization to monitor and document black employment, but the people who ran the city and kept Negroes under control resisted the establishment of an Urban League until 1965. In comparison, neighboring cities had Urban Leagues much earlier—Detroit in 1916, Chicago in 1917, and Gary in 1946.

I'd had a prior encounter with Hatcher in 1961 when I heard that the Civil Rights Commission helped blacks find better jobs. After Paul died, and before I returned to work at the State Library, I decided to check with the CRC. Perhaps they could steer me to a better-paying job than clerk-typist. After all, I did have three years of college.

Hatcher nearly salivated when he saw my application. I was just the kind of Negro he was looking for: accustomed to working with whites, overqualified for the jobs he had available, and experienced. Hatcher first asked me to interview for a job as a supermarket cashier. I declined. That seemed to me a decided step down from working at the library.

Hatcher was not pleased. "What do you mean, you're not interested? This supermarket has never had a Negro cashier, and I've convinced them to take a look at a few people. We can't make any progress if you aren't willing to be interviewed."

"Do you have anything else?"

"You need to understand that these companies are doing us a favor. I do have a bank that's interviewing for tellers, but I can't send you for an interview unless you improve your attitude."

I don't recall what I did to assure Hatcher of my humility, but I went to the bank interview. My hope of earning more money working in a bank were dashed when I learned that tellers were paid less than I had earned at the library. Adding injury to the meager salary, Hatcher told me that he had turned down the bank's offer to hire both the black women they'd interviewed. Of course, Hatcher recommended the other woman and, without a hint of irony told me, "It's not a good idea to hire two Negroes at a time. They might not get along with each other. I told the bank to see how one Negro worked out before they hired a second one." After that experience, I was glad to return to work at the library, and I wanted nothing more to do with Hatcher. I had little faith he would be helpful with the student teaching situation.

While Dr. Olsen contacted the CRC, I decided to do what I could on my own. I called Richard Blough, chairman of the English department at Manual High School. When I was in his English class, he seemed to be a decent, fair person, and I had been a good student. He might be willing to have me student teach at Manual. I was right.

"Janet Cheatham! Of course, I remember you!" Blough was happy to hear from me. "We'd love to have you do your student teaching here. There's nothing we like better than having our graduates come back as teachers. Stop by my office with your forms and we can set this up right away."

Two days later when I got to Blough's office, everything had changed. He couldn't have been more distant and stiff if I had been a talking dog. "I'm sorry Janet, but we don't have space for a student teacher this semester."

"I don't understand. On Tuesday you said you'd be glad to have me."

"I thought we had room, but we don't. Excuse me, I have a meeting." Blough fled the scene and left me standing there, thoroughly pissed off that I had allowed myself to be rejected by Manual once again. I suspect that either Manual's principal, or perhaps IPS officials, had informed Blough that Negro student teachers were allowed only at Attucks. Besides, according to their perverted way of thinking, they would need a Negro teacher to supervise me, and they didn't have one. It was IPS; what should I have expected?

To my surprise, when I returned to campus, Dr. Olsen informed me that Hatcher had actually come through. As a result of the intervention of the Civil Rights Commission, I was assigned to Harry E. Wood High School for my student teaching.

Wood High School, at 525 South Meridian Street, was in a sprawling four-story red brick building built in 1895 and well past its best years. Ironically, it was the same building originally occupied by Manual High School. Before the new Manual was built on Madison Avenue, I had walked the halls of this decrepit building for three years. I was reminded of the nauseating odors from the nearby Kingan's meat packing plant that permeated the area. Shortly after the new Manual opened in September 1953, the facility on Meridian Street was chris-

Harry E. Wood High School, formerly Manual High School.
Courtesy of Gordon K. Durnil

tened the Harry E. Wood Vocational Training School. Appropriately, the school was named for a man who had taught jewelry making and manual training at Manual, then went on to become Director of Manual and Vocational Training for the entire school system.

I have no doubt the assignment to Wood was meant to punish me because I had dared question the *racist* policy of the school system. Not only did IPS ignore the schools I had requested, but the assignment was to a school that, in the status hierarchy of Indianapolis high schools, was at or near the bottom. And in case the school itself didn't sufficiently communicate their contempt for me, they placed me with a teacher who spent the morning with a group of learning-disabled students. (It has since occurred to me that perhaps he was the only faculty member who would accept a dissident black student teacher.) I had no experience or training in special education and I don't think the supervising teacher did either. In the afternoon he had two sections of a junior English class, so I actually got a little preparation in my field.

IPS may have meant to chastise me, but it was more like throwing Bre'r Rabbit into the briar patch. The assignment to Wood was excellent because the school was even closer to my parents' house than Manual, so Daddy dropped me off in the mornings. I also identified with my marginalized young students, who, although most were white, were clearly considered disposable, just like Negroes.

The supervising teacher, Mr. Bridges, was white; a tall, thin, reticent man with dark hair. He seemed surprised at some of my ideas and was dubious at times that my plans could be carried out, but he always came around to supporting me. The few instructional materials we had for the students were boring and childish, so I spent a lot of time reading to them and learning about them. It wasn't long before I realized that about a third of the thirty-two students had no major learning problems, just physical or social limitations. Fred was a pudgy fourteen-year-old white boy with black hair, thick glasses and a withered arm. He showed me some poetry he had written. It was remarkably good. I asked to see more of his writing. Then I asked him to write essays on topics of his choice. He was delighted to do so. Fred was a very bright boy. With Mr. Bridges' help, I managed to have Fred moved to regular classes.

Sarah was blonde, shy, and had the body of a mature woman. She wasn't as bright as Fred, but she read well. It seemed that her "disability" was being poor and dressing shabbily. Sarah had no interest in class activities and spent her time looking out the window. When I spoke to her privately, she opened up. I learned that she was the oldest child in an impoverished family and was just waiting for her sixteenth birthday so she could drop out of school and get a job. When I asked where she wanted to work, she was at a loss, with no notion of what she would do. That gave me an idea. I asked the *Indianapolis Star* if they would donate a daily newspaper for each of my students. The *Star* agreed to do so.

When the daily papers came, we went through each section, paying attention to the pictures as well as the words. The students who could read, and there were several, read aloud to the others. I let them read anything they found interesting, including the comic strips. We paid particular attention to the want ads and talked about what training was needed for the jobs that were available. I got copies of job applications and we practiced filling them out. I also went to a bank to obtain information on opening accounts and brought back sample checks for them to experiment with.

The students became so interested in the newspaper that they wanted to visit the *Star* to see the paper being put together. Great idea! Mr. Bridges and school officials didn't agree. They said I could not handle the students on a field trip. School authorities apparently viewed my students as incorrigible, but I knew better. I insisted that we be allowed to take the trip, and convinced Mr. Bridges to change his mind and back me up. Of course, there was a ton of paperwork involved and permission slips to have signed. Finally, I took about twenty students on their first field trip to the offices and printing plant of the *Indianapolis Star*. There were no problems.

School officials offered nearly as much resistance and paperwork when I decided to show a film to the literature classes. I had to order the film either from the school system's film library, or the public library, I don't remember which. I do remember that everybody acted as if I had asked to have students parade naked through the halls. Then I had to coordinate use of the film projector with my class schedule. This couldn't be done until I had assured the keeper of the projector that I knew how to operate it. It was nearly enough to make me drop the whole idea. However, the class was struggling with *A Tale of Two Cities,* and I felt that seeing the Coronet Instructional film would help get them into the book.

Despite my reluctance to become an educator, I did enjoy student teaching. However, I knew I didn't have the patience to deal with the school system's dense bureaucracy and the seemingly arbitrary obstacles they erected to discourage innovation. I guess Mr. Bridges was fed up as well. At the end of the year, he resigned from teaching and became a farmer.

When I returned to campus, Dr. Olsen wanted to know how things had worked out. He was concerned about my having been assigned to Wood High School with special education students. I told him it went well, but that I didn't plan to teach. Olsen showed me Mr. Bridges's evaluation of my work, perhaps hoping to change my mind. For student teaching we received a grade of S for satisfactory or U for unsatisfactory, and a written evaluation. Mr. Bridges had told me my rating was satisfactory, but in his narrative, which I had not seen, he praised my creativity and resourcefulness, and predicted that I would be a highly successful teacher. I eventually did teach English, but in college not high school.

Back on campus on April 13, Adam Clayton Powell Jr. came to speak for the Great Issues Forum. I was excited to see him in person for the first time, and was one of the students in the crowded room who cheered and applauded his passionate and candid speech. I loved it when he said, "The question of civil rights is not the problem of Negro people—it is the problem of the United States of America. The United States is finished as a great power in the eyes of the world unless it solves this problem and solves it now. [America] cannot be a first-class power if it has second-class citizens."

The next speaker in the Great Issues Forum was George Wallace, Governor of Alabama and, at the time, running for president of the United States. In the headline announcing Powell's appearance, the student newspaper called Powell controversial, but no such term was used for Wallace. I didn't go anywhere near the Auditorium when Wallace spoke. I didn't want to hear anything he had to say, nor would I risk being in a room surrounded by his supporters. Wallace had been scheduled to speak in Ballantine 013 where Powell spoke. That room, however, had only 360 seats, hardly sufficient for the throng expected for the Wallace speech. The Ballantine space had not been large enough for Powell either. The room had been packed with people standing and sitting anywhere they could. The university permitted the Great Issues Forum to book a larger space for Wallace. They also sent an emissary to the campus NAACP to explain that Wallace was speaking in a larger, more comfortable place than Powell to preclude the safety hazard of an overcrowded room. I'll choose to believe that they had not anticipated the crowd Powell attracted, rather than that our safety was of no concern to them.

Seeing a person whom I admired as much as I did Adam Clayton Powell Jr. was the thrill of a lifetime. I had been hearing about this fiery preacher-politician all my life. Powell inherited his name, activism, and the pastorate of Harlem's Abyssinian Baptist Church from his Yale-educated father. The junior Powell was the first Negro elected to the New York City Council in 1941, and the first representative from Harlem elected to the U. S. Congress. He served from 1945 to 1970. Sometimes when you finally see a person who has been lionized the way Powell was in the black community, you're disappointed, probably because your expectations are so high. That was definitely not the case with Powell. He was engaging, sharply intelligent, and quick-witted, with plenty to say in his deep and mellifluous voice. Powell was also handsome and charismatic enough for three people. I understood why Harlemites continued to reelect him. I especially liked the fact that he was a zealous foe of *racism* and staunchly refused to accept being treated as a second-class citizen.

Chapter 18

Discarding Fantasies

If I didn't define myself for myself, I would be crunched
into other people's fantasies for me and eaten alive.

~ Audre Lorde in *Sister Outsider*

Library practice work was my next and last stop in this, my final
semester of school. I couldn't see why I needed to practice working
in a library. After all I had been employed in a library for nine years,
including sixteen months as a librarian. However, this was all that
stood between me and my degree so I did it willingly. The practice
work was at the University High School Library under the direction
of Marian Armstrong. U High was located in the Education Building
at Third and Jordan Streets and the practice work turned out to be
informative and valuable. In a high school library, the librarian does
everything—orders, processes, catalogs, and shelves books, as well as
answering questions and helping students with research. I had become
accustomed to the specialization of the State Library, where separate
departments handled each of these tasks. My experience there was
largely limited to reference situations, helping patrons with research.

Early in the spring semester of 1964, I had signed up at the
School of Ed Placement Office and told the counselor I would consider jobs anywhere in the country. I had several interviews, including
two while visiting Jessie's family in New York: one in Darien, Con-
necticut, and the other in Orange, New Jersey. I believe Orange made
an offer, but I vaguely remember being unimpressed with the town,
so I didn't consider moving there. Surprisingly, my first offer came
from the Indianapolis Public Schools. I suspect that either Olsen
went back to the Civil Rights Commission with the good report of
my student teaching assignment, or the CRC had cautioned IPS they

would monitor how I was treated. I cannot imagine IPS offering me a position in the system's prestigious brand-new school unless some kind of pressure had been applied.

Northwest High School was far away from the center of town, in the 5500 block of West Thirty-fourth Street. The school was about five miles directly west of Shortridge High School which was at the corner of Thirty-fourth and Meridian—the street that divides Indianapolis's east and west sides. Shortridge had been the city's most highly regarded secondary school, but the neighborhood around it was now predominately black and its student body was getting darker. A new school was built because the most prestigious secondary school in Indianapolis had to be white. The initial plan was to move the name Shortridge to the new site as well, but that maneuver had to be abandoned when folks in the community around Shortridge vociferously objected. IPS had successfully pulled that kind of bait and switch with Manual High School a decade earlier. After the school system was desegregated in 1949, Manual's building was declared out of date. It was necessary, officials said, to build a new school at 2405 Madison Avenue, far from the present near-downtown location. The former Manual building was not too old, however, for the students at Wood, which opened in 1953—the same year as the new Manual—and remained in use as a high school until 1978. Shortridge and Manual were the two oldest high schools in Indianapolis and their numerous and influential alumni preferred their traditions to remain untainted by the tar brush.

When the offer came from Northwest, I knew IPS must be nervous, but I discovered just how jittery they were when I went for my interview with the principal. The yet-to-be-used building smelled of fresh paint and sawdust. The principal's office was lavish for a high school. A large, gleaming wooden desk stood on a carpeted floor. The furnishings were upholstered and comfortable. Facing me as I entered the spacious office were three white men. Seated behind the desk and doing all the talking was the principal, Kenneth Smartz. To his left was Wayne Kincaid, whom I recognized; he had been my chemistry teacher at Manual. I don't recall the name of the man on Smartz's right, but he was from the IPS central office, perhaps the personnel department. I wondered why Smartz had an entourage. Was it meant to intimidate me or did he need witnesses? The tension in the room was palpable, so I squared my shoulders to keep the chip from falling. I expected Kincaid to recognize me since he had been one of my favorite teachers and I one of his better students. However, when he was introduced as Northwest's assistant principal, he greeted me as perfunctorily as the other two men, and I decided not to call him out.

This was the first of many times that I would be summoned before a gaggle of suits. When I face an array of authority figures, I assume the intent is to bully me into submission, but it has the opposite effect. My resolve is invigorated when I see a group of officials. After a few experiences with this model, I figured out that when officers gang up on a subordinate, it is a sign they feel threatened. Having their authority questioned is so rare and unsettling they feel the need to call in reinforcements.

After giving me some general information about the school, Smartz spoke slowly, enunciating carefully to emphasize every word. "We already have a Negro teacher, Mrs. Brown. She taught English at Crispus Attucks for a long time, and she has a master's degree. Mrs. Brown is a very nice woman. We all like her and we expect you to be the same kind of person she is."

I knew exactly what Smartz meant, but his patronizing tone aggravated me. "Since I don't know Mrs. Brown, you'll have to tell me what you mean by that." My civil words were bathed in sarcasm.

Then Smartz revealed how unhappy he was to have me there. He raised his voice, "What I mean is that we don't want any militant NAACP type Negroes here." Smartz must have been in debt to somebody at IPS. Not only was he getting *two* Negro teachers, but one of them was a known "militant."

"Then you certainly don't want *me* because I *am* a member of the NAACP." I stood up and calmly walked out before my chip crashed to the floor. I was seething. *THAT RACIST CRACKER! HE MUST THINK HE'S DOWN SOUTH.* (Teachers were fired in South Carolina and other southern states for belonging to the NAACP.)

IPS apparently thought I would complain to the Civil Rights Commission after the Smartz interview. They contacted me immediately about openings at other high schools. I didn't respond. I was sick of the Indianapolis Public Schools. I told the IU placement office I would only consider jobs *outside* of Indiana. I wanted a blank canvas on which to create the rest of my life. If I remained in my home state, it would definitely be painting by the numbers.

Samuel Moore traveled to Indiana University from Saginaw, Michigan to talk to prospective employees, and I was one of the people he interviewed. Moore looked more like the stereotypical absent-minded professor than a high school principal. He was about five feet nine inches, a little overweight, with brown hair, and eyeglasses. He wore a suit and tie, but looked slightly disheveled and seemed distracted. I sat across the table from him in one of the interview cubicles. He insisted that I call him Sam and he used my first name without asking permission.

"Janet, we're looking for an assistant librarian at the MacArthur High School in Saginaw."

THIS MUST BE SOME FABULOUS HIGH SCHOOL IF IT HAS TWO FULL-TIME LIBRARIANS.

"We'd like to offer you the job. I should tell you that MacArthur is an all-white suburban school. So far we have only one black person on our staff. Would you have a problem with that?"

"I'm used to that," I bragged. "I went to a white high school and was the first Negro student to work at the Indiana State Library."

"Good! The pay is the same as it is for teachers. The starting salary for a first year teacher is five thousand dollars."

"Five thousand dollars?" I was startled. IPS paid new teachers forty-eight hundred a year. As a librarian I had made slightly over four thousand dollars for twelve months.

"Okay, fifty-two hundred. We can give you credit for a year's experience as a librarian. That way you'll qualify for a second-year teacher's pay."

"I'll take it." We shook hands. Unwittingly, I had extracted an increase from a source where salaries were supposedly set in stone, constrained by board policy and union contracts. That was an important lesson that I remembered in later salary negotiations.

I had a job! And I would move to a place where I knew absolutely no one. There would be no expectations about Smith and Annie's daughter, James' little sister, Rosie and Reggie's big sister, or Holsey's ex-wife. I could be ME!

I had completed my course work in the fall semester, so once my practice work in the classroom and the library were finished, I was done. There was one more obligation before I left, however, the matter of graduation exercises. I had no interest in participating in the ritual, but Mama said she had waited all her life for this day. My parents sent money to rent the cap and gown, and they were the only members of my family present on that hot June day. We did Vesper Services, the president's reception, and Commencement. My memory of the day is a blur with the sharp exception of the conversation with my parents after the diplomas had been handed out. I returned my cap and gown and walked over to them wearing a big smile and the new dress Mama had bought for the occasion.

"I did it! I graduated from college."

"You said you'd do it even if it took ten years. You made your word good." Daddy was grinning as he reminded me of a pledge I made while I was still struggling with my studies. It was June 1964, exactly ten years since I graduated from high school.

I turned to Mama to bask in her praise. "Well, Mama, your dream has come true. One of your children graduated from college."

Mama gave me a sour look. "Yes, but it's not like it would have been if you had gone straight through."

There was that stake in my head again. I had no response for her comment. We went to eat as we had planned, but I don't remember what the rest of the day was like.

Since I no longer had a home, I kept my job at the Audio-Visual Center and stayed at IU for the summer. Jessie had gone back to New York, so I returned to my old space on Fourth Street. Helen Baker, who had been my roommate and good friend in Cedar Hall, also moved into the rooming house for the summer. She was back in school converting her liberal arts degree into an elementary education license. To make additional money for my move in the fall, I edited and typed a dissertation for a white doctoral student. His writing was so poor that for the first time it occurred to me that college degrees were not necessarily indicators of ability or intelligence. I also enrolled in two graduate courses, American Literature, 1800-1900, and a boring class called Survey of Audio-Visual Communications. I was busy, but emotionally unfettered! I had just obtained my degree, and a divorce, and I was looking forward to a new job where I would earn more than I had ever made. It was a fun, relaxing time, and that summer I partied hard with the graduate students from the South.

Janet Cheatham Hickman, age 26, a few months before I received my college degree.

I had informed the state library that I was going back to school after my summer study on their grant. They accepted the postponement, but made it clear that if I did not come back to my job after I received the degree, I would be required to refund the amount of the grant, about three hundred dollars. I promised to return, but I was itching for new experiences, and that meant a job somewhere other than the place where I had worked for more than ten years. The degree was my ticket to a completely different life. I would pay them back once I was settled and making money.

I was twenty-seven years old and for the first time in my life I felt like an adult. And it was *my life*. I was free! Free to make decisions without input from parents or husband. And not only was I a single woman, but a divorcée, meaning that I no longer needed to play the role of innocent maiden. I could identify with Malcolm X, who had split with the Nation of Islam three months earlier in March. Both of us could now do as we chose.

Mama tried to talk me out of moving away. "You can't just up and go someplace by yourself where you don't know anybody."

"Mama, people do it all the time."

"Not single women!" Mama was emphatic as if she knew something I didn't, but I wasn't falling for that anymore.

Daddy plied his network until he heard we had a distant relative living in Saginaw. He was busy tracking her down, but I wasn't concerned. If they found her, fine, but if they didn't I was moving to Saginaw anyway.

"You never did have sense enough to be afraid of anything!" Mama was beside herself because her dire warnings were having no impact on me.

She was right, I was not afraid.

Notes

Chapter 1 Rigged Outcome pages 1-15

2: "One of literary": *Thirteen Ways of Looking at a Black Man* by Henry Louis Gates Jr., Random House, 1997, p. 180.

3: "The word 'Negro'": *12 Million Black Voices*: Text by Richard Wright, Thunder's Mouth Press, 1988, p. 30. (Originally published in 1941.)

3: "As for the Negroes": *Einstein on Race and Racism* by Fred Jerome and Rodger Taylor, Rutgers University Press, 2005, p. 138.

4: "real estate": Amiri Baraka on *Race Is the Place,* Independent Lens, PBS, November 22, 2005.

5: 2005 issue of *Time*: *Time* magazine, November 14, 2005.

6: in the engraving: *Rebels and Redcoats: How Britain Lost America*, a PBS series on the founding of the country from a British point of view. Co produced by WGBH/Boston and Granada in association with BBC Wales, 2003.

6: Wynton Marsalis: in an interview on *The Charlie Rose Show*, September 6, 2005.

6: fivefold increase: Todd Clear, Distinguished Professor, John Jay College of Criminal Justice, City University of New York, toddclear.org.

7: poem: "Justice" by Langston Hughes, from *The Life of Langston Hughes: Volume I: 1902-1941, I, Too, Sing America* by Arnold Rampersad, Oxford University Press, 1986, p. 87.

7: "necessary exercise to": Truth and Reconciliation Commission, http://www.justice.gov.za/trc/.

7: President Lyndon Baines Johnson: *The Encyclopedia of the African and African American Experience* edited by Kwame Anthony Appiah and Henry Louis Gates Jr., Basic Books, 1999.

7: "Ready or not,": *All Politics* by CNN-Time web site, November 20, 1997.

8: "were embarking, with": *Mirror to America: The Autobiography of John Hope Franklin,* Farrar, Straus and Giroux, 2005, p. 344.

8: "unfortunate short-sightedness": *Ibid.,* p. 361.

8: "to help the nation": Brown University Steering Committee on Slavery and Justice, http://www.brown.edu/Research/Slavery_Justice/.

9: "Violation of the unalienable rights": Dean William Pickens as quoted in "Beneath the Surface: African American Community Life in Indianapolis, 1945-1970" Ph.D. dissertation by Richard Pierce, Indiana University, 1996, p. 26.

9: Throughout its history: *The Negro in Indiana Before 1900: A Study of a Minority* by Emma Lou Thornbrough, Indiana Historical Bureau, 1957.

10: "By what authority": "The Massacre at Deer Lick Creek, Madison County, Indiana, 1824" by Brian M. Doerr in *Indiana Magazine of History*, March 1997, vol. 93, #1. Also see the fictionalized account of this event in *The Massacre at Fall Creek* by Jessamyn West, Harvest Books, 1986.

10: national headquarters was in Indianapolis: *Indiana: An Interpretation* by John Bartlow Martin, Indiana University Press, 1947, 1992, p. 190.

10: In 1930 the Klan: *Jet*, December 5, 2005.

10: community of free: Information provided by Marie Love Johnson, a descendant of the Lost Creek settlers.

10: Black population percentages: U.S. Bureau of the Census, 2000.

11: "There is the rattle of chains": Adaptation of a passage from *Black Betty* by Walter Mosley, W.W. Norton & Company, 1994, p. 199.

12: "had the deepest necessity": *Tell Me How Long the Train's Been Gone* by James Baldwin, Dial Press, 1968, p. 189.

12: "It is impossible": *Fatheralong* by John Edgar Wideman, Pantheon Books, 1994, p. xvi.

13: twelve generations: Conservatively figuring four generations for every 100 years.

14: "A woman must be": This is an adaptation of a quotation by Howard Thurman from *Famous Black Quotations*, edited by Janet Cheatham Bell, Warner Books, 1995, p. 90.

14: "What memory repudiates controls": *The Evidence of Things Not Seen* by James Baldwin, Holt, Rinehart and Winston, 1985, p. xii.

15: "Naptown appeared": "Beneath the Surface" by Richard B. Pierce II, p. 7.

Chapter 2 My Gifts pages 16-32

17: "Jewels, Ermine and": *Indianapolis News,* May 5, 1937.

17: "Hairdresser Visits Duke": *Indianapolis Star,* May 10, 1937.

17: more malignant story: *Indianapolis Recorder,* May 1, 1937.

17: Scottsboro Boys: *Africana: The Encyclopedia of the African and African*

American Experience edited by Kwame Anthony Appiah and Henry Louis Gates Jr., Basic Books, 1999.

25: "Why should I feel": Number 33 in *Songs of Zion: Supplemental Worship Resources 12*, by The National Advisory Task Force on the Hymnbook of the United Methodist Church, Abingdon Press, 1981.

29: Between 1920 and 1930: U.S. Bureau of the Census

30: The same year: *Indiana Blacks in the Twentieth Century* by Emma Lou Thornbrough, Indiana University Press, 2000, p. 48.

30: David Curtis (D.C.) Stephenson: *Indiana, an Interpretation* by John Bartlow Martin, Knopf, 1947, 1992, p. 184+

30: Article XIII declared: *The Negro in Indiana Before 1900: A Study of a Minority* by Emma Lou Thornbrough, Indiana Historical Bureau, 1957.

30: "Nigger, Don't Let": *Indiana, an Interpretation,* p. 189.

31: twelve thousand fervent Negroes: *For Gold and Glory: Charlie Wiggins and the African-American Racing Car Circuit* by Todd Gould, Indiana University Press, 2002.

31: "the Klan dream": *The Ku Klux Klan: A Secret History*, The History Channel presentation by Bill Brummel Productions.

31: "who did not deny": *Indiana Blacks in the Twentieth Century,* p. 51.

32: "Daddy made the living": I borrowed this phrase from the late Robert Harris of Cleveland, via his daughter, Arlene Williams.

Chapter 3 Daring to Hope pages 33-48

33: or making thirty dollars a month: "African Americans and the Civilian Conservation Corps" by Barbara Quigley in *Traces of Indiana and Midwestern History,* vol. 17, #1, Winter 2005.

36: "limited housing opportunities": "Beneath the Surface" by Richard B. Pierce, *op. cit.*, p. 143.

36: "lived on the east side": *Polite Protest: The Political Economy of Race in Indianapolis, 1920-1970* by Richard B. Pierce, Indiana University Press, 2005, p. 64.

46: It was in Embree's: *13 Against the Odds* by Edwin Embree, The Viking Press, 1944, p. 97.

46: local newspaper: *Indianapolis Recorder,* January 6, 1945.

46: book written about him: *George Washington Carver: In His Own Words* by Gary R. Kremer, University of Missouri Press, 1987, p. 2.

46: John Hope Franklin: *Mirror to America: The Autobiography of John Hope Franklin,* Farrar, Straus and Giroux, 2005, p. 110.

47: Louis Harlan dubbed: *Booker T. Washington: The Wizard of Tuskegee, 1901-1915* by Louis R. Harlan, Oxford University Press, 1983, p. viii.

Chapter 4 Priceless, But Not Material pages 49-68

51: "I come to the garden": Number 44 in *Songs of Zion: Supplemental Worship Resources 12,* by The National Advisory Task Force on the Hymnbook of the United Methodist Church, Abingdon Press, 1981.

57: Father of the Year: *Indianapolis Recorder,* June 19, 1954.

62: In 1946: *Indianapolis Recorder,* January 5, 1946.

62: "On the": Emancipation Proclamation, signed September 1862 by Abraham Lincoln.

66: in the 1830s: "The Bransfords of Mammoth Cave" by Kristin Ohlson in *American Legacy,* Spring 2006.

67: Park employees: *Indianapolis Recorder,* September 8, 1945 and September 15, 1945.

67: Indiana has one: *The Indiana Way: A State History* by James Madison, Indiana University Press, Indiana Historical Society, 1986, p. 256.

Chapter 5 Warring Ideals pages 69-83

73: "indicated that at": *Polite Protest: The Political Economy of Race in Indianapolis, 1920-1970* by Richard B. Pierce, *op. cit.,* p. 98.

76: Nella Larsen: *Passing* by Nella Larsen, Knopf, 1928; Modern Library Classic, 2002.

76: Charles Chesnutt: *The Wife of His Youth, and Other Stories of the Color Line* by Charles W. Chesnutt, Houghton, 1899; Ann Arbor Paperbacks, 1968.

76: Toni Morrison: *Paradise* by Toni Morrison, Knopf, 1998.

76: "You can have your high yella": "Yellow and Brown Woman" performed by Alex (Guitar Slim) Seward and Louis (Jelly Belly) Hayes.

77: Madam C.J. Walker: *On Her Own Ground: The Life and Times of Madam C. J. Walker* by A'Lelia Bundles, Scribner, 2001.

Chapter 6 Powerful Lessons pages 84-102

85: Before 1843: *The Negro in Indiana Before 1900: A Study of a Minority* by Emma Lou Thornbrough, Indiana Historical Bureau, 1957.

85: "there were over": *Since Emancipation: A Short History of Indiana Negroes, 1863-1963* by Emma Lou Thornbrough, Indiana Division American Negro Emancipation Centennial Authority, p. 54.

86: In a move that: "Russell Adrian Lane: Biography of an Urban School Administrator" by Rosie Cheatham Mickey, a dissertation presented to the graduate faculty of the University of Akron, 1983, p. 94.

86: kindergarten was not mandatory: information provided by Kevin Mc-Dowell, Indiana Department of Education.

88: Lewis Coleman: *The Encyclopedia of Indianapolis* edited by David J. Bodenhamer and Robert G. Barrows, Indiana University Press, 1994, p. 1198.

94: wolf tickets: Negro slang for bluffing.

97: The day before: Interview with James Henry Cheatham.

98: "the 14-year-old": *Indianapolis Star,* September 25, 1947.

100: "had been after": *Ibid.*

Chapter 7 Hard Work and Talent pages 103-116

109: membership grew from: *The Indianapolis Star*, September 25,1964.

109: largest Y: *Indianapolis News*, April 14, 1948, clipping file, Indiana State Library.

109: "As long as I stay in this town": quoted in "The Monster Meetings at the Negro YMCA in Indianapolis," by Stanley Warren, *Indiana Magazine of History*, March 1995, vol. 91.

109: In a 1934 Y campaign: *The Senate Avenue YMCA: for African American men and boys, Indianapolis, Indiana 1913-1959* by Stanley Warren, Donning Company Publishers, 2005, p. 32. (Although the photo is dated 1923 in the book, the author assures me the correct date is 1934.)

112: donated $1,000: *On Her Own Ground: The Life and Times of Madam C. J. Walker* by A'Lelia Bundles, Scribner, 2001, p. 117.

113: "There is no royal flower-strewn path": madamcjwalker.com

113: Madam Walker hosted Booker T. Washington: *Ibid.*, p.147.

114: "encourage free discussion": from Indianapolis YMCA clipping file, Indiana State Library.

114: W.E.B. DuBois himself: *Indianapolis Recorder*, March 8, 1941.

114: Other Monster Meeting speakers: "The Monster Meetings at the Negro YMCA in Indianapolis," by Stanley Warren, *Indiana Magazine of History*, March 1995, vol. 91.

115: Nilkanth Chavre: *Indianapolis Recorder*, December 15, 1951.

Chapter 8 Being Invisible pages 117-131

117: The family name: *One Man's Vision: The Life of Automotive Pioneer Ralph R. Teetor* by Marjorie Teetor Meyer, Guild Press of Indiana, 1995, p. 2.

117: "the last factory door": *Ibid.*, p. 200.

117: At its peak: *Ibid.*, p. 128.

119: "In 1930 Lothair": *Charley Teetor's Hometown: The Story of an Indiana Family, Their Village, and the Industrial Revolution,* by Charles J. Teetor, Westernesse Press, Amagansett, NY, 1994, p. 243.

120: Don's living room: *Ibid.*, p. 248.

124: "It had seven bedrooms": *Ibid.*, p. 266.

125: In the summer of 1952: I've learned this memory may not be entirely accurate. I leave it here because this is how I remember what happened.

Chapter 9 Some Times Are Worse pages 132-149

133: Rosalyn Richardson's son: *When the Truth Is Told: A History of Black Women's Culture and Community in Indiana, 1875-1950* by Darlene Clark Hine, a publication of The National Council of Negro Women, Indianapolis Section, 1981, p. 76.

133: "Segregation is the established": *Indianapolis Recorder*, September 11, 1948.

133: "the Klan was merely": *Polite Protest* by Richard B. Pierce, *op. cit.*, p. 31.

134: "Schricker signs": *Indianapolis Recorder*, March 12, 1949.

134: "especially adept in": "Beneath the Surface: African American Community Life in Indianapolis, 1945-1970" by Richard B. Pierce, *op. cit.*, p.114.

134: "an unwritten law": *Indianapolis Recorder,* May 7, 1949.

134: Another example: *Indianapolis Recorder,* August 27, 1949.

135: "the sixty-two member": "Beneath the Surface" by Richard B. Pierce, *op. cit.,* p. 79.

135: Rosie, did a study of: "Russell Adrian Lane: Biography of an Urban School Administrator" by Rosie Cheatham Mickey, a dissertation presented to the graduate faculty of the University of Akron, 1983.

139: Charles doesn't remember: Interview with Charles Kenneth Barker.

144: Attucks's language offerings: "Russell Adrian Lane" by Rosie Cheatham Mickey, *op. cit.* p. 127.

149: A few years later: Interview with Mary Anna Major.

Chapter 10 Passing the Baton pages 150-164

150: "Indianapolis incorporates the": quoted in *Polite Protest: The Political Economy of Race in Indianapolis, 1920-1970* by Richard B. Pierce, Indiana University Press, 2005, p. 98.

154: The colored feature: Some details about these movies came from *Black Hollywood: The Black Performer in Motion Pictures* by Gary Null, The Citadel Press, 1975.

158: Tempé Music Club: Interview with David Hardiman.

158: Jazz Contemporaries: Interview with Larry Ridley.

Chapter 11 What a Feeling! pages 165-179

168: The Indiana High School Athletic: *Hoosier Hysteria: A History of Indiana High School Boys Single Class Basketball* by Herb Schwomeyer, Mitchell-Fleming Printing Inc., ninth edition, 1970, p. 18-19.

168: In 1927, the year: *But They Can't Beat Us: Oscar Robertson and the Crispus Attucks Tigers* by Randy Roberts, Indiana Historical Society, Sports Publishing Inc., 1999, p. 42.

168: At one time: "The Other Side of Hoosier Hysteria," by Stanley Warren in *Black History News & Notes,* #54, a publication of the Indiana Historical Society, November 1993.

169: George Crowe: *The Ray Crowe Story: A Legend in High School Basketball* by Kerry Marshall, High School Basketball Cards of America Inc.,

1992. (This book is the source of information on the Crowe family.)

169: In 1941 Senator: *Indianapolis Recorder*, February 15, 1941.

169: The black weekly: *Ibid.*, March 1, 1941.

169: the association passed: *Ibid.*, December 27, 1941.

169: "a man who had": *Hoosier Hysteria* by Herb Schwomeyer, *op. cit.*, p. 194.

170: "As nearly as I": *The Ray Crowe Story,* by Kerry Marshall, *op. cit.*, p. 102-103.

170: When it opened: Indiana Tourism Industry Media Room web site.

171: "in the days before": *The Big O: My Life, My Times, My Game* by Oscar Robertson, Rodale Press, 2003, p. 27.

172: "The Reitz team": "Reitz Stops Crowemen's IHSAA Cage Title Try" by Jim Cummings in the *Indianapolis Recorder*, March 24, 1951.

172: "doubtful": *Indianapolis Recorder,* March 8, 1952.

172: "With the score": *Indianapolis Recorder*, March 21, 1953.

173: "Stan Dubis's capricious": *Ibid.*

173: "After that Shelbyville": *The Ray Crowe Story* by Kerry Marshall, *op. cit.*, p. 93.

173: only one black referee: Interview with Reginald Cheatham.

174: "because of his color": *Indianapolis Recorder*, March 21, 1953.

175: In the next round: *Indianapolis Recorder*, March 13, 1954.

176: Attucks barely managed: *Indianapolis Recorder*, March 20, 1954.

177: Stan Dubis: *Indianapolis Recorder*, March 26, 1955.

178: At Cincinnati: *A Hard Road to Glory: A History of the African-American Athlete Since 1946, volume 3* by Arthur R. Ashe, Jr., Amistad, 1988, 1993, pp. 61-62.

178: "What Milan did": "Unlike Milan, Hall of Fame won't induct Attucks as a team" by Tracy Dodds in *The Indianapolis Star*, March 16, 2005.

178: "If it happens": *Ibid.*

179: The Indiana Basketball: Indiana Basketball Hall of Fame web site.

Chapter 12 The Cost of Ignorance pages 180-195

180: one of whom: "Memories of Emmerich Manual H.S. Class of 1954-50th Reunion," p.14

181: Houston had a strategy: *The Road to Brown*, a film from California Newsreel and the University of Virginia, 1990.

181: In 1950 only 2.5 percent: *Since Emancipation: A Short History of Indiana Negroes, 1863-1963* by Emma Lou Thornbrough, Indiana Division American Negro Emancipation Centennial Authority, p. 68.

188: The nineteen well-used: Housing files, Indiana University Archives, Bloomington, Indiana.

190: "I was reeling with": *Maggie's American Dream: The Life and Times of a Black Family* by James P. Comer, M.D., New American Library, 1988, p. 156.

194: "playing your home": *Ibid.*, p. 178.

194: Twenty-three years later: Interview with Michael James Cheatham.

Chapter 13 Evading the Dragon pages 196-215

197: Abraham Lincoln: *Forced Into Glory: Abraham Lincoln's White Dream* by Lerone Bennett Jr., Johnson Publishing Company, 1999.

197: Alan Lomax: "Book Says Alan Lomax Neglected Black Scholars," by Mark Weingarten, *New York Times,* August 29, 2005.

197: a mass meeting: *Indianapolis Recorder,* February 10, 1945.

197: taxi had run down: *The Indiana Daily Student*, January 23, 1945; *Indianapolis Recorder,* January 27, 1945.

197: "Grand Jury Fails": *The Indiana Daily Student,* January 31, 1945.

198: Elder W. Diggs: *The Story of Kappa Alpha Psi: A History of the Beginning of a College Greek Letter Organization, 1911-1999,* by Ralph J. Bryson, Kappa Alpha Psi Fraternity, 5th edition, 2003, p. 9.

198: "I had two": *Standing on Our Shoulders: The Neal-Marshall Alumni Club-History and Heritage,* DVD, Indiana University Alumni Association, 2005.

199: "the officer who": Letter from Beatrice Cooper, August 4, 1948, in President Wells' housing files, Indiana University Archives, Bloomington, Indiana.

199: "will be faced with the action": The Colored Student Situation, a report received in the president's office July 2, 1940, Indiana University Archives, Bloomington, Indiana.

199: "Circumstances have been forcing": letter from Kate Hevner Mueller, Dean of Women, to Herman B Wells, President, January 26, 1942, Indiana University Archives, Bloomington, Indiana.

200: "If the university cannot": Letter from Kate Hevner Mueller, Dean of

Women, to Herman B Wells, President, September 14, 1942, Indiana University Archives, Bloomington, Indiana.

200: join them in a petition to: Petition to Indiana University Board of Trustees, September 15, 1942, discussed at board meeting, September 25-26, 1942, Indiana University Archives, Bloomington, Indiana.

200: "There is no legal, ethical": letter from Herman B Wells in response to group that petitioned the university board of trustees, October 1, 1942, Indiana University Archives, Bloomington, Indiana.

200: Students, desperate for help: *Indianapolis Recorder,* September 9, 1944.

200: these women became the first: *Indianapolis Recorder* October 6, 1945.

201: "just as I thought": letter from Herman B Wells to Governor Ralph Gates, September 8, 1945, Indiana University Archives, Bloomington, Indiana.

201: Wells told the board: Indiana University Board of Trustees meeting minutes, September 20, 1945, Indiana University Archives, Bloomington, Indiana.

201: "I am and shall always": Letter from Ora L. Wildermuth, member of the Indiana University Board of Trustees to Ward G. Biddle, Treasurer, Indiana University, November 19, 1945, Indiana University Archives, Bloomington, Indiana.

201: "still falls short": Letter from Francis D. Wormuth, NAACP Faculty Advisor, to Herman T. Briscoe, Vice President and Dean of Faculties, January 28, 1948, Indiana University Archives, Bloomington, Indiana.

201: Wells submitted a plan: August 16, 1948 memo from Herman B Wells and Mary R. Maurer, a board member, to the Board of Trustees, Indiana University Archives, Bloomington, Indiana.

202: "a delegation of leading Negro citizens": July 12, 1948 memo from R.L. Shoemaker, Dean of Students, to President Herman B Wells, Indiana University Archives, Bloomington, Indiana.

202: Willard B. Ransom: Letter from Willard B. Ransom to Herman B Wells, August 30, 1948, Indiana University Archives, Bloomington, Indiana.

202: "until such time": Letter from Frank M. Summers, Assistant States Attorney, St. Clair County, East St. Louis, Illinois to Director, IU Halls of Residence, September 1, 1948, Indiana University Archives, Bloomington, Indiana.

202: Wells wrote the university's lawyer: letter from Herman B Wells to George W. Henley, university lawyer, May 25, 1949, Indiana University Archives, Bloomington, Indiana.

202: "In taking the steps": *Being Lucky* by Herman B Wells, Indiana University Press, 1980, p. 216.

202: "NAACP and prominent": *Ibid.*

203: "A Question of Leadership": *The Herald-Times*, (Bloomington, Indiana) August 7, 2005.

203: "The guy is": *Indiana Daily Student*, November 4, 2005.

204: "people are ignorant": *Blink: The Power of Thinking Without Thinking* by Malcolm Gladwell, Little, Brown and Company, 2005, p. 71.

204: "A large part of our": *Einstein on Race and Racism* by Fred Jerome and Rodger Taylor, Rutgers University Press, 2005, p. 141.

204: "This is the": *The Herald-Times*, November 22, 2005.

204: "Whites had a hard": *The Herald-Times*, November 24, 2005.

204: "I feel an obligation to…": http://newsinfo.iu.edu/news-archive/2799.html

205: "We'll close the": *Indianapolis Recorder,* December 24, 1955.

207: Kappa Alpha Psi: *The Story of Kappa Alpha Psi: A History of the Beginning of a College Greek Letter Organization, 1911-1999, op. cit.*

207: "Couples spent": 1955 *Arbutus,* Indiana University yearbook.

208: Indiana University had been playing: *Varsity Sports at Indiana University: A Pictorial History* by Cecil K. Byrd & Ward W. Moore, Indiana University Press, 1999.

208: George Thompson: *Glory of Old IU: 100 Years of Indiana Athletics* by Bob Hammel and Kit Klingelhoffer, Sports Publishing, Inc. 1999, p. 12.

208: Faburn DeFrantz bringing yet: "The Other Side of Hoosier Hysteria," by Stanley Warren in *Black History News & Notes*, #54, and the *Indianapolis Recorder*, October 4, 1947.

208: "The basketball coaches": Herman B Wells, *Being Lucky, op. cit.,* p. 217

209: "was astonished to": *Glory of Old IU, op. cit.,* p. 107.

209: "If there's any": Herman B Wells, *Ibid.*

209: University of Iowa reports: Memo from Bradley Cook, Photograph Curator, Indiana University Archives, Bloomington.

211: "Those who moved": "A Community Within a Community: Indianapolis's Lockefield Gardens by Rachael L. Drenovsky in *Traces of Indiana and Midwestern History*, Fall 2003.

211: "at the end of 1956": "Beneath the Surface: African American Community Life in Indianapolis, 1945-1970" by Richard B. Pierce, *op. cit.,* p.150.

212: Nancy was on: *Jet*, June 11, 1959.

213: Wells' response: letter from Herman B Wells to Iva Etta Sullivan, June 5, 1959, Indiana University Archives, Bloomington, Indiana.

Chapter 14 Walking in My Sleep pages 216-233

222: Bellamy: *A Hard Road to Glory: A History of the African-American Athlete Since 1946, volume 3* by Arthur R. Ashe, Jr., p. 302.

225: "wedding gown was": *Indianapolis Recorder,* September 10, 1960.

225: "relaxation without humiliation": "African American Resorts" by Donald Jones, the Center for Heritage Studies, the University of Maryland in College Park web site.

226: Fox Lake: "Where the Neighbors Are a Little Friendlier": The Story of Fox Lake, Indiana by Gloria-June Greiff, pamphlet sponsored by Fox Lake Property Owners Association, 2003.

231: Frost poem: "The Death of the Hired Man" in *The Poetry of Robert Frost*, edited by Edward Connery Lathem, Holt, Rinehart and Winston, p.38.

Chapter 15 Paying the Price pages 234-247

238: the per 1,000 live births: "Racial and Ethnic Disparities in Infant Mortality Rates," National Center for Health Statistics, Centers for Disease Control and Prevention.

238: By 1998: *Ibid.*

Chapter 16 Moving Forward pages 248-261

249: "mother of college presidents": *Time,* April 4, 1938.

249: first outdoor opera: *Arbutus,* Indiana University yearbook, 1963.

250: ninety-eight-page history: *Since Emancipation: A Short History of Indiana Negroes, 1863-1963* by Emma Lou Thornbrough, Indiana Division American Negro Emancipation Centennial Authority.

250: another of Thornbrough's: *The Negro in Indiana Before 1900: A Study of a Minority* by Emma Lou Thornbrough, Indiana Historical Bureau, 1957.

250: first black member: *Indiana Daily Student*, June 21, 1963.

251: "In Los Angeles alone": *The Messenger: The Rise and Fall of Elijah Muhammad* by Karl Evanzz, Pantheon, 1999, p. 200.

251: "We preach freedom": President Kennedy's televised speech to country June 11, 1963, from text in *The Indianapolis Times*, June 12, 1963.

252: Myrlie Evers: *Watch Me Fly: What I Learned on the Way to Becoming the Woman I Was Meant to Be* by Myrlie Evers-Williams, Little, Brown and Company, 1999, p. 81.

252: "look into their hearts": *Indianapolis Recorder*, June 22, 1963.

252: "most sweeping civil": *Ibid.*

252: "The [three hour] meeting ": *James Baldwin: Artist on Fire* by W. J. Weatherby, Dell, 1989, p. 251.

253: "over the sentiments": *Ibid.*, p. 255.

258: "France, England, and": *A Hard Road to Glory: A History of the African-American Athlete 1919-1945, volume 2* by Arthur R. Ashe, Jr., Amistad, 1988, 1993, p. 14.

259: "Joe, we need": *Ibid.* p.15.

Chapter 17 **Altering My Images** pages 262-276

268: "all Indianapolis high schools": *Indianapolis Recorder*, August 27, 1955.

269: In 1940: "The Colored Student Situation," a report received in the president's office July 2, 1940, Indiana University Archives, Bloomington, Indiana.

269: gave the commission: "Working Together for Equal Rights," a brochure of the Indiana Civil Rights Commission, Matthew E. Welsh, Governor.

270: In comparison: "Beneath the Surface: African American Community Life in Indianapolis, 1945-1970" by Richard B. Pierce, *op. cit.*, p. 183.

275: "The question of civil rights": *The Indiana Daily Student*, April 14, 1964.

275: called Powell controversial: *The Indiana Daily Student*, April 11, 1964.

275: Wallace had been scheduled: *The Indiana Daily Student*, April 17, 1964.

275: Powell inherited: *King of the Cats: The Life and Times of Adam Clayton Powell Jr.* by Wil Haygood, Houghton Mifflin, 1993.

Why a Memoir

I have always loved reading biographies. I am enthralled by the details of how people manage the events of their lives, especially when the person is someone I admire like Ella Baker, Zora Neale Hurston, Quincy Jones, or Nelson Mandela. When I was compiling quotation books, I found many wise and clever phrases in the autobiographies of prominent blacks, past and present. But I also enjoyed reading about the lives of people I'd never heard of—Harriet Jacobs, Nathan McCall, Ruth Reichl. For many years friends who listened to anecdotes about my adventures encouraged me to write about them, but I was hesitant. I enjoyed telling the stories, but dismissed the idea of a book because my life seemed bland. After all, I'm not famous, nor have I had to overcome child abuse or drug addiction. I've never been homeless, a battered wife, or on welfare. What was there to write about? Over the years, I observed that most people's lives are similarly "bland."

The biographies of celebrated, high-achieving black Americans, like Colin Powell, Oprah Winfrey, or Michael Jordan, are stories of exceptional people, but perhaps the best reason to write my story is precisely because, like lots of people, I think of myself as ordinary. However, the lives of ordinary people are not identical, and the details of those lives are worth sharing. I believe the widespread interest in reality television, memoirs, and film documentaries reflect a human desire to know how ordinary people cope with their lives.

I'm grateful that I finally decided to write about my life because in doing so I uncovered demons in unexpected places. I also resolved issues that had been unconscious burdens on my psyche for decades. This has been a profoundly therapeutic and spiritual experience that helped me to better understand my parents, my siblings, and myself. Every minute of the process has been valuable.

I accept that the accuracy of my memories may be disputed, but I agree with William Zinsser, a writing coach and author of *On Writing Well.* He said, "Memoir writers must manufacture a text, imposing narrative order on a jumble of half-remembered events. With that feat of manipulation they arrive at a truth that is theirs alone, not quite like that of anybody else who was present at the same events."

Acknowledgments

I could not have written this book without the input provided by my brothers, James (1932—2008) and Reginald Cheatham (1939—2010). Many times I longed to discuss what I was writing with my sister Rosie, but she died in 1996 when she was fifty-six. My brother-in-law Gordon Mickey (1939—2010), her husband of thirty-four years, filled in some of the blanks. I also had my memory jogged by my cousins, Alma Johnson Civils, Mary Ophelia Caudle Johnson and Diane Beanum Meriweather; my former husband, Holsey Hickman; and my long-time friend, Mildred Morgan Ball. Betty Bridgwaters provided a timeline for black history at Indiana University that pointed me in the right directions. David Hardiman and Larry Ridley, friends from my teen years, after decades of no contact, graciously took calls that helped me tie together a few loose ends. Another cousin, B. Denise Owens, sent important family pictures; including some I had never seen before. Marjorie Teetor Meyer, Connie Teetor Rodie, Tom Teetor, and Stanley Warren kindly offered materials and information that I could not have acquired otherwise.

I cannot fully express the immense gratitude I have for my mother, who kept scrapbooks on her children, and never threw anything away. And my brother Reggie, not only had the good sense to hang on to all that "clutter" after Mama died, but didn't seem to mind my endless calls to see more.

I remember seeing a slogan on a library promotional poster that said, "A librarian is to know." I thought of this often during the many hours I spent doing research in the Indiana Room of the Monroe County Public Library, the Indiana University Library, the Indiana University Archives, the Indiana Historical Society, and the Indiana State Library. When I got stuck, and that happened many times, the librarians and curators usually found what I needed. They seemed never to tire of my requests for assistance. A special thanks to Dina and Brad at the IU Archives who tracked down many of the obscure references I needed. I also have to give a shout out for the Internet. Without that marvel of modern technology, it would have taken much longer to write this book.

While I was writing, I received essential early feedback on the manuscript from members of the Writers Exchange in Bloomington: Kalynn Brower, Jennifer Deam, Mimi Dollinger, Antonia Matthew, and Wendy Rubin. Tonia and Jennifer read the manuscript repeatedly and made valuable suggestions for improvement. Bob Furnish, my writing partner, who, fortunately, is as well the most meticulous editor I've ever known, found and corrected tons of errors, thereby saving me some embarrassment. No doubt, despite our best efforts, some errors remain, for which I accept full responsibility.

I am fortunate to have friends who love, believe in, support, and encourage me: Madeline Scales-Taylor, Darcy and Kristala Prather, Mary Brennan Miller, Betty Rowell, Delores Logan, Cynthia Bretheim and Alvin Foster. A special thanks to the spirit of the late Sharon Sklar, for all of her help, and especially for making sure I didn't become a recluse while I was writing. Above all, unending gratitude to my son and dear friend, W. Kamau Bell, whose creative spirit inspires and feeds my own.

Index

Page numbers in italics indicate photos.

Hansberry, Lorraine, 252
Hardiman, David, 158
Hardiman, Sadie, 158
Hardrick, John Wesley, 194
Hardrick, Raphael, 194
Harlan, Louis, 47
Harlan Street, 16, 17, 38, 39, 40, 97, 153, 172
Harlem, 267, 275, 276
Harris, William H., 249
Harrison, Paul Carter, 194
Harrison, Governor William Henry, 9
Harry, Charles, 226
Harry E. Wood High School, 271-274, 278
Hate That Hate Produced, The, 251
Hatcher, Harold, 269-271
Hayes House, 201
Hayes, President Rutherford B., 7
Herbert, Adam, 203-204
Hickman, Harold Owsley "Dickie," 220
Hickman, Harry, 218
Hickman, Holsey (husband), 206, 218-233, 235-247, 253-256, 257, 280
Hickman, Paul (son), 232-239, 244, 245, 256, 270
Highbaugh, Reverend J. T., 62
Highbaugh, Richard, 95
Hill, Gladys, 150-152
Hill, William R., 150
Hispanic/Latino, 13
histoplasmosis, 236, 238
Hoggatt, Emma and Doyal, *89*
Hole, The, 205
Holiday, Billie, 140
holidays, 22, 35, 50, 55, 57- 62, 126-127, 267
Christmas, 17, 35, 36, 50, 57-62, 162, 164, 207
Holland, Fred, 197
Hong Kong, 258, 259

Hoosier Hysteria, 167
Hoosiers, 11, 209
Hoosiers, 178
Horne, Lena, 154, 252
housing, 4, 36, 56, 140, 188, 198-202, 211, 245, 256, 257
Houston, Charles Hamilton, 181
Howard University, 115, 190
Hubbard, Freddie, 158, *159*, 160
Hughes, Langston, 7, 46, 153
Hunt, Michael, 265,
Huntington, Indiana, 170
Hurricane Katrina, 6
Hurston, Zora Neale, 216 (epigraph)
Hyde, W. W., 218

IHSAA. *See* Indiana High School Athletic Association
IOA. *See* Indiana Officials Association
Idlewild, Michigan, 225-226
Illinois, 9, 10
Imitation of Life, 155
"In the Garden," 50-51
India, 13, 115, 262, 263, 264, 265
Indian/Native American, 6, 13, 67, 89-90, 104
Indiana, 5, 9, 10, 11, 14, 30, 36, 46, 62, 81, 85, 109, 116, 124, 134, 168, 169, 170, 171, 176, 177, 178, 181, 194, 202, 203, 226, 238, 250, 264, 279; Constitution, 9, 30, 116; Civil Rights Commission, 269-271, 277; Colonization Society, 9, Department of Education, 5, 147; Historical Bureau, 250; history of, 9-10, 30, 33; State Parks, 66-67, 68, 119
Indiana Avenue (Bloomington), 197
Indiana Avenue (Indianapolis), 91, 154, 158, 159
Indiana Central College/University of Indianapolis, 214, 269

About the Author

Janet Cheatham Bell is an author, an editor, a recovering academic, a mom (to comedian W. Kamau Bell) and a grateful grandmother. She grew up in Indianapolis and graduated from Indiana University. Janet was working as a Reference Librarian in the Ohio University Library in 1968 when Martin Luther King Jr. was assassinated. In response to student demands after King's murder, she was asked to teach African American literature. Two years later she accepted the position of associate editor at *The Black Scholar* in Sausalito, California. From there she was recruited as a research associate for the African and Afro-American Studies Program at **Stanford University,** where she worked with the late **St. Clair Drake.** She also enrolled in the English doctoral program at Stanford, but left when her proposed research was rejected.

Janet has also been the **Ethnic Studies Consultant** in the Curriculum Division of the **Indiana Department of Education,** and a **textbook editor** assigned to make the literature more representative in an anthology series for grades seven through twelve. That was her last full-time position. She resigned in 1984, moved to Chicago and became an entrepreneur publishing her own books, beginning with the best selling *Famous Black Quotations*, and assisting other writers to publish theirs.

In 1995 and 1996 she was named to **The Lit 50: Chicago's Book World, Who Really Counts.** In 2013 on national television, **Henry Louis Gates Jr.** referred to Janet as a "pioneer in developing books of black quotations."

For more information about the author and her work, please see
www.janetcheathambell.com

❧ ❖ ❧

Also by JANET CHEATHAM BELL

Black Family Reunion Cookbook (writer)
Famous Black Quotations®
Famous Black Quotations® on Birthdays
Famous Black Quotations® on Love
Famous Black Quotations® on Mothers
Famous Black Quotations® on Sisters
Not All Poor People Are Black and Other Things We Need to
    Think More About
The Soul of Success: Inspiring Quotations for Entrepreneurs
Stretch Your Wings: Famous Black Quotations® for Teens
Till Victory Is Won: Famous Black Quotations® from the NAACP
Victory of the Spirit: Meditations on Black Quotations
Victory of the Spirit: Reflections on My Journey

❧ ❖ ❧